Readings in World Geography, History, and Culture
with Answer Key

HOLT, RINEHART AND WINSTON

A Harcourt Classroom Education Company

Austin • New York • Orlando • Atlanta • San Francisco • Boston • Dallas • Toronto • London

Printed in the United States of America

ISBN 0-03-054911-6

1 2 3 4 5 6 7 8 9   082   04 03 02 01 00

TABLE OF CONTENTS

EXPLORING OUR WORLD

READING 1 • Ancient Geographers 1
READING 2 • Mapping Earth from Space 3
READING 3 • Preparing for the Big One 5
READING 4 • Earth's Rotation in Our Daily Lives 7
READING 5 • Protecting Our Home 9
READING 6 • The Day the Dinosaurs Died 11
READING 7 • Rain Forests at Risk 13
READING 8 • Dividing Resources 15
READING 9 • How Many Is Too Many? 17
READING 10 • People and Migration 19

THE UNITED STATES AND CANADA

READING 11 • The Expanse of Texas 21
READING 12 • Change Comes to the Hudson River Valley 23
READING 13 • Cruising to School 25
READING 14 • Nunavut: Canada's Newest Territory 27

MIDDLE AND SOUTH AMERICA

READING 15 • Mexico in Transition 29
READING 16 • No Fair Air to Spare 31
READING 17 • Village Life in Guatemala 33
READING 18 • Montserrat: Living Under the Volcano 35
READING 19 • The Land and People of Nicaragua 37
READING 20 • A Family in Rural Colombia 39
READING 21 • The Fierce People of Venezuela 41
READING 22 • River Life in Brazil 43
READING 23 • Paraguay's Bumpy Ride 45
READING 24 • Paris on La Plata 47
READING 25 • Bolivia: Land of Diversity 49
READING 26 • The Phantom Palace 51
READING 27 • Living in the Land of Fire 53

EUROPE

READING 28 • The Community of the Greeks 55
READING 29 • The Geography of Ancient Rome 57
READING 30 • A Farmer's Life in Spain 59
READING 31 • France's Unsettled Immigrants 61
READING 32 • Living Behind the Wall 63
READING 33 • Peril in the Alps 65
READING 34 • Surviving in Wartime London 67
READING 35 • A Dublin Adventure 69
READING 36 • The Sami of Scandinavia 71
READING 37 • The Estonian Way 73
READING 38 • Czechoslovakia: The Velvet Divorce 75
READING 39 • The Shepherds of Transylvania 77

RUSSIA AND NORTHERN EURASIA

READING 40 • A Russian Student Speaks 79

READING 41 • Moscow: A New Revolution 81
READING 42 • Russia in Transition 83
READING 43 • The Hutsuls of Ukraine 85
READING 44 • The Fractured Caucasus 87
READING 45 • Life in the Mahalla 89
READING 46 • Exploring Central Asia 91

SOUTHWEST ASIA

READING 47 • The People of the Empty Quarter 93
READING 48 • Change Comes to Iran 95
READING 49 • Exploring a Souk 97
READING 50 • The Islamic City 99
READING 51 • The Bedouin Way 101
READING 52 • Visit to a Kibbutz 103

AFRICA

READING 53 • Moroccans Confront Their Future 105
READING 54 • Egypt's Threatened Nile Delta 107
READING 55 • Enrolling Girls in School 109
READING 56 • Travels in the Sahara 111
READING 57 • Leo Africanus: Description of Timbuktu (1526) 113
READING 58 • Government by Magic Spell 115
READING 59 • Along the Great Rift 117
READING 60 • The Kikuyu Meet Europeans 119
READING 61 • Shopping from Salaula 121
READING 62 • The Lifeline of a Nation 123
READING 63 • Encounters with Pygmies 125
READING 64 • Namibia's Skeleton Coast 127
READING 65 • Experiencing Apartheid in South Africa 129
READING 66 • The Moors of Mozambique 131

EAST AND SOUTHEAST ASIA

READING 67 • How Dragon Pond Got Its Name 133
READING 68 • China's Coming Great Flood 135
READING 69 • Democracy Comes to Taiwan 137
READING 70 • The Talisman 139
READING 71 • North Korea on the Edge 141
READING 72 • Life in Rural Thailand 143
READING 73 • The Chicken Industry Lays an Egg 145
READING 74 • Escaping from Vietnam 147

SOUTH ASIA

READING 75 • Bombay: City of Hope 149
READING 76 • A Village Comes Into Its Own 151
READING 77 • Getting Married in Pakistan 153
READING 78 • The Water of Life 155

THE PACIFIC WORLD AND AUSTRALIA

READING 79 • Australia's Uncertain Future 157
READING 80 • The Maori People of New Zealand 159
READING 81 • Returning to the Rain Forest 161
READING 82 • Hunting Meteorites in Antarctica 163

ANSWER KEY 165

Name _____ Class _____ Date _____

 **A Geographer's World**

HISTORY

Ancient Geographers

No blank spaces exist on world maps today. This level of knowledge about our planet comes from centuries of exploring, discovering, learning, and applying ideas. This reading describes the contributions of two of the world's first geographers. Eratosthenes is commonly called the "father of geography." Ptolemy's ideas set the stage for modern mapmaking.

No one will ever know when or where or for what purpose someone got the first idea to draw a sketch to communicate a sense of place, some sense of here in relation to there. Before Europeans reached the Pacific, Marshall Islanders lashed sticks together to depict [show] prevailing winds and wave patterns. Prehistoric Europeans drew sketch maps on cave walls, and the Inca made elaborate relief maps of stone and clay. In 1805, when the explorer [of the Louisiana Purchase] Meriwether Lewis arrived at a Shoshone camp in the Rockies and inquired about the way ahead, the chief drew a wavy line on the ground to represent the river and piled mounds of sand on either side to show the mountains it ran through.

Measuring the spherical Earth ranks as the first major milestone in scientific cartography. It was the achievement of a Greek scholar, scientist, theater critic, and librarian named Eratosthenes. He lived in the third century B.C. and was a luminary [influential person] at the famous Alexandrian Library [in Ancient Egypt]. He knew of a well up the Nile [River] at Syene (the Greek name for [the town of] Aswan), where at midday on the summer solstice, June 21 [the day the sun is farthest north of the Equator], sunlight beamed straight down to the bottom. If Earth is a sphere, he reasoned, then sunlight at the same moment must strike different parts of Earth at different angles, casting measurable shadows. Since Alexandria was assumed to be due north of Syene, here were two places separated by a known distance (paced off by camel caravans), lying on the same north-south meridian of longitude.

Without leaving the library grounds, Eratosthenes examined the shadow cast by a column at noon on the solstice. Its angle measured about one-fiftieth of a circle [just over 7 degrees]. Multiply the distance between Alexandria and Syene by 50 and you get Earth's circumference—which he figured at 25,200 miles. Despite the fact that Alexandria and Syene are not exactly on the same meridian and caravan measurements could not have been precise, the librarian's calculation was remarkably accurate—the longitudinal circumference is known today to be 24,860 miles.

Even before Eratosthenes, astronomers had looked to the sun for cartography's primary lines of reference. The sun's annual movement in relation to Earth's surface yielded the Equator and the Tropics of Cancer and Capricorn, which correspond to the highest and lowest extremes of the sun's apparent seasonal migration.

. . . The astronomer and geographer Ptolemy in the second century A.D. spelled out a system for organizing maps according to grids of latitude and longitude. . . . Another legacy of Ptolemy's is his admonition [advice] to cartographers "to survey the whole in its just proportions." That is, to scale. Distance on today's maps is expressed as a fraction or ratio of the real distance. But mapmakers of Ptolemy's time lacked the geographic knowledge and measuring know-how to live up to Ptolemy's scientific principles.

From "Revolutions in Mapping" (retitled "Ancient Geographers") by John Noble Wilford from *National Geographic,* February 1998. Copyright ©1998 by **National Geographic Society**. Reprinted by permission of the publisher.

Understanding What You Read After you have finished reading the selection, answer the following questions.

1. What was the background of the world's "first geographer," Eratosthenes? What contribution did he make to geography?

_____

_____

2. What two ideas did Ptolemy introduce to mapmaking?

_____

3. What examples does the reading provide of how other early peoples communicated information about geography?

_____

4. What is "scale" in mapmaking? What would be the advantage of having a map that is to scale over one that is not?

_____

_____

_____

Activity

Make a diagram of Eratosthenes' experiment. Show the sun's rays, the Syene well, the Alexandria column and its shadow, and the measurements Eratosthenes made. Your diagram should also show how the circumference of Earth could be determined from making these measurements in this small area. Your diagram does not need to be to scale.

A Geographer's World

GEOGRAPHY

Mapping Earth from Space

Images collected by aircraft, spacecraft, and satellites provide an understanding of Earth that is not easily gained at ground level. The view from above improves our knowledge about our planet and its features. Through aerial data, geographers have been able to create more accurate and detailed maps of the world. This reading describes some of the technology that is used to gather such information.

Photographs and other images of the Earth taken from the air and from space show a great deal about the planet's landforms, vegetation, and resources. Aerial and satellite images, known as remotely sensed images, permit accurate mapping of land cover. [They] make landscape features understandable on regional, continental, and even global scales. . . . Seasonal vegetation vigor and contaminant [pollution] discharges can be studied by comparing images acquired at different times. . . .

Satellites, including manned spacecraft, usually collect images from hundreds of miles above the Earth's surface while aircraft operate at altitudes from a few thousand to more than 60,000 feet. The altitude from which an image is taken and the physical characteristics of the sensor . . . largely determine the area covered and the amount of detail shown. In general, the level of detail is greater in low-altitude photographs that cover relatively small areas, while satellite images cover much larger areas but show less detail.

Aerial photographs are produced by exposing film to solar energy reflected from the Earth. . . . Color-infrared film, which records energy from portions of the electromagnetic spectrum invisible to the human eye, was developed to detect camouflaged military objects in the 1940's. In a color-infrared (also known as a false-color) photograph, near-infrared light reflected from the scene appears as red, red appears as green, green as blue, and blue as black. Color-infrared film is useful for distinguishing between healthy and diseased vegetation, for [determining] bodies of water, and for penetrating atmospheric haze.

Black-and-white and color-infrared films are used today in both high- and low-altitude aerial photography. Natural-color film is used more rarely because it is often affected by atmospheric haze.

Cameras of various types are used to take aerial photographs. Although cameras have also been carried on spacecraft such as the Space Shuttle, satellites more frequently use electronic scanners to record ground scenes in digital form. . . . Satellite scanner data are commonly displayed as images whose colors resemble those of color-infrared aerial photographs, but the colors . . . can be manipulated by computer to enhance landscape features. . . .

Side-looking airborne radar (SLAR) instruments on aircraft or satellites generate their own energy, which is recorded on being reflected back to them from the ground. This eliminates problems associated with cloud cover and haze. The [slanted] angle of the "side-looking" instrument yields images that are especially useful in analyzing landforms. . . .

Because SLAR systems provide their own energy to illuminate the ground, the images they produce can be collected regardless of weather or time of day. So the images are valuable for mapping parts of the world that are perpetually cloud covered, such as the Amazon Basin. . . .

In 1972, the United States launched its first Earth Resources Technology Satellite, ERTS-1, later renamed Landsat 1, for experimental global coverage of the Earth's land masses. Landsats 2 through 5 were launched in 1975, 1978, 1982, and 1984. . . . Landsats 4 and 5 pass from north to south over the Equator at an altitude of 705 kilometers (438 miles) each day at about 10 A.M., and their orbits repeat coverage of the Earth, allowing the detection of change.

From *Aerial Photographs and Satellite Images* by the U.S. Geological Survey, U.S. Department of the Interior.

Understanding What You Read After you have finished reading the selection, answer the following questions.

1. Why are most aerial pictures of Earth generally taken with black-and-white or infrared film instead of with regular color film?

_____

2. Why do SLAR sensors have an advantage over cameras in gathering data about Earth's features?

_____

_____

3. How would remotely sensed images lead to a better understanding of a region's physical geography than if the geographer depended only on information collected on the ground?

_____

_____

_____

Activity

Find an aerial or satellite image of a place in a book or a magazine. Then compare the image to a map of the place. Use the map to help identify features on the image.

Planet Earth

CULTURE

Preparing for the Big One

Despite all that geographers and other scientists now know about our planet, it still surprises us. This reading describes how people in the state of Oregon are dealing with the recent discovery that they are living in a major earthquake zone.

One thing the Pacific Northwest has not been well known for is earthquakes. Ask the many Californians who moved to Oregon thinking they had left earthquake country behind.

Native Americans knew better. A spirit called Earthquake survives in stories passed on by indigenous [native] peoples throughout Cascadia [a geological region in the Pacific Northwest]. . . . "One story tells how people came [to their sacred . . . lodge] in terror when they saw the ocean standing high like hills," [says geologist Gary Carver.] "Soon waves were hitting the walls of the . . . lodge."

Since the [site of the] . . . lodge was at least 30 feet above sea level, Carter is convinced that the Yurok were describing a tsunami that struck following an earthquake along the Cascadia subduction fault. Tsunamis are sometimes . . . called tidal waves but have nothing to do with tides. . . . They are natural responses to earthquakes. . . .

Until the mid-1980s there was no evidence that a subduction quake had ever hit Cascadia. Most scientists figured the Juan de Fuca plate was diving smoothly beneath the continent. Then a geologist named Brian Atwater began publishing disquieting [disturbing] evidence [of a tsunami] he had found in the coastal marshes of Washington State. . . . Since the discovery of the tsunami in 1986 Atwater and other researchers have found similar evidence for this 300-year-old event all along the Cascadian coast, as well as evidence for many earlier subduction earthquakes. . . .

How often do the big quakes recur? Seven centuries had elapsed between the one in 1700 and the one before it. But the two before those were only three centuries apart. Using satellite positioning systems that let them measure the distances between a number of ground-based antennas to within millimeters, [scientists] can actually watch the strain build beneath Cascadia. . . . As Tony Qamar, Washington's state seismologist, puts it: "The earth here is being compressed like a big spring." . . .

"After the great earthquake, there'll be a series of large waves," says [Oregon's state geologist Don] Hull. "The first will arrive within 5 to 30 minutes, and we'd expect heights of 15 to 25 feet, but they could be much higher in places. Several more waves may strike over the next few hours."

. . . Hull explains steps that can be taken by this town [Waldport], which has an average elevation of 12 feet above sea level and two schools that sit on a floodplain. Critical facilities can be built high enough to stay dry. Tsunami warning signs can be posted along the beaches. Evacuation drills should be conducted, especially in low-lying schools. Citizens should know to head uphill as soon as they feel a strong quake. . . .

Further north along the Oregon coast, the town of Cannon Beach has already developed a tsunami awareness program. At noon on a July day . . . the air is filled by the sound of an angry cow mooing from six loudspeakers set up throughout the town. A voice explains that the bovine ruckus [noise] is simply a test of the town's tsunami warning system.

"Some people don't like the noise," says Al Aya, president of the Cannon Beach Fire District, which initiated the system in 1988. "But we've got nine miles of recreational beaches and thousands of visitors. Little kids play in the water. We can't have them swept away."

Residents might have less than half an hour to reach high ground, so powerful sirens will sound immediately after any earthquake is felt. . . .

Though such earthquake hazards have been widely publicized in the Seattle [Washington] area, many residents view the problem with detached bemusement [lack of concern]. A series of small quakes rocked the region during the summer of 1997, swaying skyscrapers and getting everyone's attention.

"We all just kind of looked at each other," reports a local friend, John Treat. "People still think earthquakes are California's problem."

From "Cascadia: Living on Fire," (retitled "Preparing for the Big One") by Rick Gore from *National Geographic,* May 1998. Copyright ©1998 by **National Geographic Society**. Reprinted by permission of the publisher.

Understanding What You Read After you have finished reading the selection, answer the following questions.

1. Why did scientists not realize before 1986 that the Pacific Northwest faced a major earthquake threat?

_____

_____

2. What other "unscientific" evidence existed to suggest that the region had a history of earthquakes?

_____

3. Why would coastal towns be at especially high risk from an earthquake?

_____

Activity

Write a letter to the editor of a Seattle newspaper explaining why people should be more concerned about the possibility of a major earthquake in the region.

READING
4

Planet Earth

Earth's Rotation in Our Daily Lives

When moving about on Earth's surface, we do not feel the rotation of our planet. But it does affect us in some very important ways. In this reading, a geographer discusses some proven effects and possible consequences of Earth's rotation.

The Earth's rapid rotation affects all moving objects on the Earth's surface and above it. It affects you when you drive your car, planes when they fly on a given course, space shuttles when they take off, winds when they blow, ocean currents as they drift, rivers where they flow.

The scientist who first analyzed the effect of the Earth's rotation on all moving things was a Frenchman, Gustave-Gaspard de Coriolis (1792–1843). . . . Ever since, it has been known as the *Coriolis* Force.

The practical effect of what Coriolis discovered is [that] . . . in the Northern Hemisphere, all moving objects are pushed to the right of their intended direction. In the Southern Hemisphere, moving things are pushed to the left. Here's one very obvious consequence: in the North Atlantic Ocean, water circulation moves in a clockwise direction, westward from Africa toward the Caribbean, northward in the Gulf Stream, southward along the northwest African coast. But in the South Atlantic Ocean, water moves counterclockwise: southward in the Brazil Current, eastward in the West Wind Drift, and northward along the African coast in the Benguela Current.

So it is in other oceans and in the atmosphere. Air circulation, too, is affected by the Coriolis Force. In the Northern Hemisphere, low-pressure systems (the kind that include fronts and storms) circulate counterclockwise. In the Southern Hemisphere, these circulate clockwise. An American weather forecaster who took a job with an Australian television station would have a tough time adjusting to this!

On September 1, 1983, a South Korean commercial airliner flying from Anchorage, Alaska, to Seoul [South Korea] strayed from its assigned course, crossed into . . . territory [of what was then the Soviet Union], and was shot down by a Soviet jet fighter, with a loss of 269 lives.

Why KL 007 should have strayed off course has remained a mystery. It was not, as the Soviets alleged [claimed], a spy plane. But if its computer program, inserted in Anchorage, failed to adjust for the Coriolis effect, the plane would have drifted to the right of its intended course, to just about the degree [of longitude and latitude] where its fatal encounter took place.

We may not notice the effect of the rotation of the Earth in our daily routines, but don't underestimate what this force is capable of. For example, if we were . . . blindfolded and asked to walk in a straight line, we would (on a perfectly flat surface) walk in a large circle, clockwise in the

Northern Hemisphere, where we'd be pushed to the right, and counter-clockwise in the Southern Hemisphere. . . .

We may be able to see the Coriolis Force at work when large crowds of people walk long distances. In Britain, where the rule is to keep left, . . . there are signposts, even lines on sidewalks, urging people to walk to the left. But people seem to move to the right anyway. I've spent quite a bit of time in Edinburgh, Scotland, on assignments. Every time I've been there, overlooking Princes Street, I've noticed that people there seem to walk on the right as they promenade by the thousands along the wide sidewalks. On the other hand, in Southern Hemisphere Buenos Aires, Argentina, the rule is to keep right, but try that on fashionable Florida Avenue. There, they seem determined to keep left.

From "Doing Something About the Weather" (retitled "Earth's Rotation in our Daily Lives") from *Harm de Blij's Geography Book: A Leading Geographer's Fresh Look at Our Changing World.* Copyright ©1995 by Harm de Blij. Reprinted by permission of **John Wiley & Sons, Inc**.

Understanding What You Read After you have finished reading the selection, answer the following questions.

1. What is the Coriolis Force and how did it get its name?

   _____

   _____

2. How does Earth's rotation affect the movement of objects on its surface in the Northern Hemisphere?

   _____

3. Why would a blindfolded person who tried to walk a long distance in a straight line, eventually make a large circle instead?

   _____

   _____

4. According to the author, how does geography influence people in Argentina to walk on the left side of paths and sidewalks, even though the rule is that they keep to their right?

   _____

   _____

Activity

On an outline map of the world, plot the effect of the Coriolis Force on ocean water that the author describes in the reading. Use library and other resources to accurately plot and label the currents the author identifies.

Wind, Climate, and Natural Environments

GEOGRAPHY

Protecting Our Home

The world's people are using ten times more air, water, and other natural resources than they did 200 years ago. This increase in consumption has affected the atmosphere, water cycle, and climate, and has altered Earth's natural systems. This reading describes some of these changes and discusses their possible impact on the future of our planet.

Earth is surrounded by a delicate envelope of air, part and product of life on the planet. Human beings have changed the composition [make up] of this atmosphere. Tons of carbon dioxide and methane, among other compounds, are added annually to the atmosphere from the burning of fossil fuels [coal, oil, and natural gas]. These and other chemical pollutants raise concerns about the effects a changing atmosphere may have on life.

Most life on Earth owes its existence, directly or indirectly, to photosynthesis, the "greening" process by which plants convert sunlight, carbon dioxide, and soil nutrients to energy. Green plants cover much of Earth's land area, and microscopic plants known as phytoplankton inhabit its waters. More than 35 percent of the planet's surface is used, at least indirectly, for harvesting food and other materials.

Grazing, agriculture, and timber harvesting disturb topsoil, increasing soil erosion. More than 75 million tons of soil are blown or washed into the oceans each year. Natural ecosystems shrink in the face of society's need to use land. Fragmentation [breaking up] of many ecosystems has created a series of ecological "islands." Some species, unable to survive in such reduced areas, become extinct.

Life requires water. On land, the amount and frequency of rainfall determine the success of crops, as well as the survival of natural ecosystems. It takes about 10 days, on average, for a drop of water that becomes airborne vapor in one place to return to Earth's surface as rain or snow in another. Precipitation varies by both season and geographic area. As one result, highly specialized ecosystems have developed, from deserts to rain forests.

In the event of global warming, regional rainfall patterns may shift. Similarly, the removal of forest cover may alter rainfall distribution because of reduced evaporation of water from plants. Changes in patterns of precipitation could have dramatic effects, positive or negative, on all life. . . .

Even moderate changes in global temperature can freeze or melt significant amounts of fresh water, building or shrinking glaciers and the polar ice caps. This affects sea levels. Inasmuch [since] as 50 percent of the world's people live within 50 kilometers [30 miles] of the sea, the effects of even a moderate rise in sea levels, on the order of a meter [about 39 inches] or less, would be significant. . . .

The environments surrounding marshes, dunes, and reefs can be unbalanced by many human activities such as fishing, building, highway construction, and the use of chemical fertilizers. Ecosystems weakened by such activity may not withstand major storms. Although occupying just 8 percent of the Earth's surface, these coastal environments produce 90 percent of the world's seafood.

Global environmental change concerns us all. Scientists are using instruments [placed] on satellites to gain new perspectives [views] on previously unknown linkages between the Earth's land, air, and water. Monitoring, however, can only show that changes are taking place. Halting or reversing changes, if necessary, will test the will and the ingenuity [resourcefulness] of humankind.

From "An Island Home" from Global Change: Earth as Home by U.S. Geological Survey, U.S. Department of the Interior.

Understanding What You Read After you have finished reading the selection, answer the following questions.

1. How does the burning of fossil fuels affect the atmosphere? How do trees and other green plants help to undo this change?

2. How does the clearing of forests to build towns or create farmland affect the soil, wildlife, and possibly precipitation?

3. Why might global warming raise the world's sea levels? Why would such a change have a major effect on human life?

Activity

Make a list of things that you could do around your home or school that would help—even in a small way—to address some of the environmental concerns discussed in the reading.

Wind, Climate, and Natural Environments

READING 6

HISTORY

The Day the Dinosaurs Died

Why did dinosaurs disappear? One popular theory is that a collision with an asteroid about 65 million years ago caused dramatic weather changes and wiped out nearly all life. This reading applies geographic evidence to imagine the death of a giant Tyrannosaurus rex *in the American West.*

Impact! A brilliant fireball flashed across the southeastern sky. . . . The T-Rex, blood dripping from his huge teeth, raised his head from the carcass [dead body] of an old Triceratops . . . and roared a challenge to the heavens.

The six-mile-wide asteroid—a rock the size of Mount Everest—slammed into the Gulf of Mexico off the coast of the Yucatan Peninsula. . . . [It] melted a huge hole through the ocean floor. . . . . As it did so, most of the asteroid vaporized. Within seconds the impact crater reached its maximum depth, likely about 30 miles. Then the center of the crater quickly began to rise—like the liquid that leaps back in the air when you splash milk into a glass. . . .

Impact Plus One Minute A monstrous earthquake rumbled over the . . . landscape. T-Rex stumbled over the Triceratops carcass, surprised but not terribly alarmed; the earth had shaken under his feet before. . . .

Current scientific thought suggests the impact of a six-mile-wide asteroid would have generated about one billion times the energy released by the atom bomb that destroyed Nagasaki [Japan] and ended World War II. . . .

Impact Plus Four Minutes T-Rex glanced towards the southeast as the ground continued to shake. Even his poor eyes could detect the huge orange flare of light along the southeastern horizon. . . . The light grew brighter and closer with amazing speed. . . .

The speed of the burning rock, minerals, and gases ejected from the impact crater . . . would have been incredible; current research suggests that the first effects of the asteroid's impact off the Yucatán coast took only ten minutes to reach present-day New Jersey. . . .

Impact Plus Six Minutes T-Rex looked up, startled, as a thunderous roar pounded his ears. Suddenly an unimaginable blast of wind knocked him down while ripping huge trees and boulders out of the ground. . . .

The shock wave created by an asteroid hitting at . . . 40,000 m.p.h. would have had a devastating impact on large plants and animals over a very great area. Indeed, pollen records in parts of western America and Japan indicate large plants were completely absent from the landscape for a long period after impact. . . .

Impact Plus Seven Minutes Battered and dying, the stricken T-Rex had one final sight—a horizon-to-horizon wall of . . . fire raging up from the southeast . . . that would consume him and almost all other life forms.

The fireball, together with burning ejecta [debris] from the impact crater, would have ignited most of the plants, animals, and surface fossil fuels in the Western Hemisphere and perhaps large parts of the rest of the world and started great wildfires. . . . The fires could have burned for weeks, filling the air with smoke and gas and temporarily blotting out the sun. . . .

Impact Plus Five Days . . . A small mouselike rodent scurried around the charred and broken landscape, stopping occasionally to nibble at the scorched meat of larger, less fortunate animals. . . . Although she was extremely uncomfortable in the mind-numbing heat, hunger forced her out of her cool burrow to hunt for food.

The fireball is thought to have raised global air temperatures by at least 50 [degrees] F. . . . This temperature increase alone probably was intolerable [unbearable] to many species. . . . Combined with changes in the food chain [it] would have led to massive death totals. The underground temperature of the Earth, however, . . . would not have changed much.

Impact Plus Two Months The small rodent-like creature stuck her head out of her underground burrow and surveyed the dismal scene. The "day" . . . was dark—dry, cold gloom untouched by precipitation. The few . . . small plants that had survived . . . now were withering [shrinking] into brown death. Each day, she was forced to roam farther . . . for food. . . .

The great quantity of dust shot into the stratosphere by the meteorite's impact soon would have circled the globe and blocked out significant sunlight over a large portion of the Earth. This brought an end to the intense heat, and began a period of bone-chilling cold. Photosynthesis would have been impossible for many plant species. . . . The global cooling . . . may have contributed to the extinction of the dinosaurs and other species. . . .

Impact Plus One Year The little rodent-like mammal had survived the shock waves, the firestorm, . . . and the icy cold. Now . . . Earth's weather shifted back towards conditions prior to impact. . . . Tiny green shoots of plants worked their way up through the burnt, crusty soil. . . . Life had survived on Planet Earth.

From "The Day the Dinosaurs Died," by Randy Cerveny from *Weatherwise*, July-August, vol. 51, no. 4, pp. 13–17. Copyright ©1998 by the **Helen Dwight Reid Educational Foundation**. Reprinted by permission of the publisher.

Understanding What You Read After you have finished reading the selection, answer the following questions.

1. List the environmental changes that followed the asteroid's impact.

_____

2. Why were small burrowing animals able to survive?

_____

Activity

Create a sketch that illustrates one of the events in the reading.

Earth's Resources

READING 7

Rain Forests at Risk

In just a few weeks in 1988, the vast rain forest around the Amazon River in South America lost one-twentieth of its area—an amount the size of Great Britain—to deforestation. The reading examines this trend, presents some consequences, and suggests ways that the problem might be challenged.

The world's forests have been steadily shrinking since antiquity [ancient times]. Cut down largely to make way for fields and settlements, the woodlands of much of . . . Europe, North America, and Asia had been reduced to fragments by the turn of the century. Today, the frontier of deforestation has shifted to the tropics, especially to the . . . evergreen rain forests once known in the West as "jungle." These forests are being cleared at a devastating rate, causing a worldwide alarm.

Loss of the forests also leads to a loss of plant and animal life. The tropical forests are home to at least two-thirds of the world's species, most of them as yet unnamed and unknown to science. According to some estimates, thousands of these are becoming extinct every year. We will never know what we have missed.

Wild plants are a vital resource. Cocoa, coffee, bananas, and sugar cane have already been improved by cross-breeding with wild species in the forest. With one in four Western medicines based on forest plants, and so much of the forest still unexplored, the potential for developing new drugs is also enormous.

Deforestation commonly results in soil deterioration and erosion. The rainforest's luxuriant [lush and dense] vegetation may suggest that the soil is very fertile. It is not. In rain forests most nutrients are embodied [kept] in the living plants and animals, rather than held in reserve in the soil.

Each of the major rainforest regions is home to indigenous [native] peoples. As the forests are cleared, their territories are diminishing [shrinking]. Some are forced into new reserves, others simply have their land appropriated [taken over] and are left to survive as best they can. Their cultures are being extinguished, and many are dying from diseases like malaria, against which they have little defense. Some 500 years ago there may have been nine million Indians living in Amazonia [the region around the Amazon River]. Today there are fewer than 200,000.

Deforestation may also be contributing to climate change. At the regional level, forest loss means less rainfall. The Panama Canal, for instance, is already forced to restrict shipping flows because there is too little water to fill its dams. At a planetary level, things may be even more serious since the burning and removal of trees contributes to the build-up of greenhouse gases. About one-fifth of the extra carbon dioxide currently being added to the atmosphere results from forest clearance.

Despite the gravity of the problems, there are many encouraging signs. Concern for the forests, and their peoples, has been raised worldwide. Pressure is mounting on governments and corporations that benefit from the products of current or former rainforests.

In northern India, women of the Chipko movement have denied loggers access to valuable timber by hugging the trees, a stratagem [plan] that is spreading to other threatened forests of the world. A planned dam on Brazil's Xingu River was scrapped, thanks to concerted [determined] action by local Kayapo Indians. National parks are being established, and reforestation projects primed [readied]. There is even a suggestion to offer debt relief to countries that undertake to protect their forests. But time is running short.

Adaptation from "The Tropical Chain-Saw Massacre: Forests at Risk," (retitled "Rain Forest at Risk") from *The Real World,* edited by Bruce Marshall. Copyright ©1991 by Marshall Editions Developments Limited. All rights reserved. Reprinted by permission of **Houghton Mifflin Company**.

Understanding What You Read After you have finished reading the selection, answer the following questions.

1. What benefits do the rain forests provide to the production of the world's foods and medicines?

_____

_____

2. Identify four problems that the author says can result from the destruction of the world's rain forests.

_____

_____

3. Describe three trends that the author identifies as providing hope for the future of the rain forests.

_____

_____

Activity

Design a poster that calls for saving the rain forests. Include an image and a slogan that will inspire others to support this cause.

Earth's Resources

Dividing Resources

In 1990 Iraq's army invaded the neighboring nation of Kuwait and attempted to annex it. This event led the United Nations peacekeeping forces to free Kuwait in the Persian Gulf War of 1991. This reading explores the geography-related causes of that conflict and discusses the problems that can arise when human-made boundaries divide Earth's resources.

International political boundaries . . . are not merely lines in the sand, on the ground, or anywhere else, for that matter. True, they appear on atlas maps as lines, but that's because . . . maps are two-dimensional. Boundaries must do much more than mark off . . . territories on the surface. Boundaries also divide what's below the surface and even what's above it. In fact, boundaries are . . . imaginary curtains that separate airspace above the ground and resources below it. . . .

It is one thing to mark a boundary on the surface, but it's quite another to locate it deep below the ground. Take a look at the Dutch province of Limburg. . . . Limburg is a narrow corridor of a province, wedged between Germany to the east and Belgium to the west. Underneath lie rich coal seams that extend from Belgium through Limburg into Germany.

The Dutch mined these coalfields vigorously. They got down to the seam, and then excavated [tunneled] it eastward. It wasn't long before they were mining coal below Germany's terrain, but of course there was nothing down there to tell the miners that they were crossing the German border. And the Germans had no way of stopping the Dutch underground; they were mining the same seams, but elsewhere. Soon there was some industrial espionage [spying], the Germans got hold of a map of the layout of the Dutch coal mines and claimed violations of their boundary. A pretty good quarrel followed, and the Dutch agreed to stop mining eastward—but only after they had secured a substantial piece of the German reserve.

Things can get even more complicated when it comes to oil and natural gas. Many oil fields and gas reserves extend from one country to another beneath their common boundary. So it was, in fact, where Iraq and Kuwait meet: the Rumailah Oil Field extends from northern Kuwait into southern Iraq. Here's the problem: when one of the neighboring countries starts to draw on such a joint reserve, oil or gas will flow from the subsurface of the [nondriller] to that of the [driller]. The Iraqis accused the Kuwaitis of drilling oblique [angled] wells, so that the pipes standing in Kuwait actually fed on oil below Iraq; the charge was never proven. But without doubt, oil flowed below the surface from Iraq toward Kuwait, which drilled much more vigorously into the Rumailah Oil Field. After the Gulf War, the United Nations redrew the boundary between Kuwait and Iraq, putting all of the Rumailah reserve within Kuwait and preventing, so it hoped, a future conflict over this resource.

The Germans and the Dutch also were at it again over natural gas. A substantial gas reserve straddles the border between the Dutch northern province of Drenthe and adjacent [neighboring] Germany. Massive Dutch exploration of this underground balloon of gas led to German complaints—but how could the loss to Germany be quantified [measured]? Contentious [quarrelsome] boundary issues, obviously, are not confined to the surface.

From "Boundaries: Neighbors Good and Bad" (retitled "Dividing Resources") from *Harm de Blij's Geography Book: A Leading Geographer's Fresh Look at Our Changing World*. Copyright ©1995 by Harm de Blij. Reprinted by permission of **John Wiley & Sons, Inc**.

Understanding What You Read After you have finished reading the selection, answer the following questions.

1. In what way did Dutch coal miners violate the national territory of Germany?

_____

2. Do you agree with the author's view that the Dutch miners had seized part of Germany? Explain why or why not.

_____

_____

3. How were Earth's resources a cause of the Persian Gulf War?

_____

_____

4. What dispute might arise between two neighboring countries over air resources?

_____

_____

Activity

Prepare a diagram showing a reason that two countries might come into conflict over water resources.

Name _____ Class _____ Date _____

READING 9

The World's People

How Many Is Too Many?

Experts, including geographers, agree that Earth's population growth is one of the most important issues for the new millennium. Here, Harm J. de Blij (pronounced "duh BLAY"), former geography expert for both the ABC and NBC television networks, presents his views.

Among the nearly 200 countries in the world, the United State's population is not growing nearly as fast as many others. . . . Still, the pressure of population is felt even here, in spacious America. Suburbanization has created vast rings of urban sprawl around original cities. . . . In parts of suburban America, the very irritations of crowding that impelled [convinced] many to move out of the city have caught up with the movers.

Sitting in a traffic jam is a small price to pay for population growth. Elsewhere in the world, people are starving or suffering from the permanent ravages [damage] of malnutrition. By the hundreds of millions, these people pay the price of being in the wrong place at the wrong time. Because the truth is that all people on Earth today *could* be fed—not well, but adequately for survival—if there were ways to distribute available supplies to all. Unfortunately, that is not happening. . . .

As recently as the 1970s, the specter of inevitable and permanent food shortages still loomed, and it was impossible to predict that the Earth's total food supply could actually catch up with the ever-increasing demand. But technological developments in farming raised production to unprecedented [never seen before] levels, and by the 1980s the fear of global hunger had receded. Today, the food problem is more geographic than anything else. Whether you'll go through life adequately nourished is a matter of location, of where you happened to be born. The powerless and influenceless peoples of the African and Asian interiors are the hungriest. But India, for example, is now able to feed itself under normal circumstances, an achievement few foresaw just a generation ago.

This does not mean that the future is risk-free. Major environmental changes over the short term could reduce the output from world breadbaskets such as the U.S. Midwest or the North China Plain. Unanticipated outbreaks of plant diseases could set back the ongoing agricultural revolution. And the inexorable [unstoppable] march of population growth could once again outstrip the Earth's productive capacity. . . .

About 180 million babies are born every year, and about 85 million people die, many of them at birth. This means that we are adding about 95 million to our number every year: nearly 8 million per month, 270,000 per day, 11,000 per hour! . . . If some killer epidemic or natural disaster or nuclear war does not slow us down, there will be 10 billion—10,000 million—people on this planet around the year 2030. Many . . . in the field of population geography see this population explosion as our greatest challenge. . . .

But not everyone agrees. There are those who argue that the world must pass through this period of explosive population growth, with all its destructive consequences, in order to reach a point where it will fizzle out—where the world's population will stabilize. The World Bank, in its annual *World Development Report,* even publishes a table giving the date when individual countries' populations are projected to cease growing. For the moment, though, world population as a whole continues to erupt, producing streams of numbers unimagined just a century ago.

From "People, People Everywhere" (retitled "How Many Is Too Many?") from *Harm de Blij's Geography Book: A Leading Geographer's Fresh Look at Our Changing World.* Copyright ©1995 by Harm de Blij. Reprinted by permission of **John Wiley & Sons, Inc**.

Understanding What You Read After you have finished reading the selection, answer the following questions.

1. According to de Blij, how has agriculture changed since the 1970s?

_____

_____

2. de Blij claims that hunger today is more a problem of geography than population growth. Explain what he means by this statement.

_____

_____

_____

3. What two possibilities does de Blij raise that could cause the prospect of worldwide food shortages to again become a concern?

_____

_____

Activity

Identify an organization in your community or region that is involved with the issue of world hunger. Prepare a report about its activities and how individuals or groups might help the organization in its efforts.

Name _____ Class _____ Date _____

The World's People

HISTORY

People and Migration

Nearly everyone comes from someplace else. Either we moved ourselves to where we now live or one of our ancestors came to this place. Most of our family trees are full of ancestors from other places. The movement of people is one of the major forces in world geography. This reading examines the reasons for and results of these population shifts.

Human migration: The term is vague. What people usually think of is the permanent movement of people from one home to another. More broadly, though, migration means all the ways—from the seasonal drift of agricultural workers within a country to the relocation of refugees from one country to another—in which people slake [satisfy] the fever or need to move.

Migration is big, dangerous, compelling. It's . . . Viking ships on the high seas bound for Iceland, slave ships and civil war, the secret movement of Jewish refugees through occupied lands during World War II. It is 60 million Europeans leaving home from the 16th to the 20th centuries. It is some 15 million Hindus, Sikhs, and Muslims swept up in a tumultuous [disorderly and confused] shuffle of citizens between India and Pakistan after the partition [dividing up] of the subcontinent in 1947. . . .

But it is much more than that. It is, as it has always been, the great adventure of human life. Migration helped create humans, drove us to conquer the planet, shaped our societies, and promises to reshape them again.

"You have a history book written in your genes," says Spencer Wells. The book . . . is a story of migration. Wells . . . spent the summer of 1998 exploring remote parts of . . . Central Asia . . . looking for drops of blood. In the blood, donated by the people he met, he will search for the story that genetic markers can tell of the long paths human life has taken across the Earth.

Genetic studies are the latest technique in a long effort of modern humans to find out where they have come from. But however the paths are traced, the basic story is simple: People have been moving since they were people. If early humans hadn't moved and intermingled [mixed] as much as they did, they probably would have continued to evolve into different species. From beginnings in Africa, most researchers agree, groups of hunter-gatherers spread out, driven to the ends of the Earth. . . . As populations grew, cultures began to differ, and inequalities developed between groups. . . .

Over the centuries, as agriculture spread across the planet, people moved toward places where metal was found and worked and to centers of commerce that then became cities. These places were, in turn, invaded and overrun by people later generations called barbarians. . . . In between these storm surges were steadier but similarly profound [important] tides in which people moved out to colonize or were captured and brought in as slaves. . . .

"What strikes me is how important migration is as a cause and effect in the great world events," Mark Miller, . . . a professor of political science . . . told me recently.

It is difficult to think of any great events that did not involve migration. Religions spawned pilgrims or settlers; wars drove refugees before them and made new land available for the conquerors; political upheavals displaced thousands or millions; economic [opportunities] drew workers and entrepreneurs like magnets; environmental disasters like famine or disease pushed their . . . survivors anywhere they could replant hope.

It's just part of our nature, this movement," Miller said. "It's just a fact of the human condition.

From "Human Migration" (retitled "People and Migration") by Michael Parfit from *National Geographic*, October 1998. Copyright ©1998 by **National Geographic Society**. Reprinted by permission of the publisher.

Understanding What You Read After you have finished reading the selection, answer the following questions.

1. What is human migration?

_____

_____

2. What six basic reasons for migration does the author identify?

_____

_____

3. How does migration affect cultures and societies?

_____

_____

4. How can genetic studies help us to learn more about migrations that occurred long ago in human history?

_____

_____

Activity

Use library and other resources to find out about a group that has migrated for a reason discussed in the reading. Write a report of your findings.

READING 11

The United States

Change Comes to the Hudson Valley

The Hudson River begins in the Adirondack Mountains of upstate New York and empties into the Upper New York Bay at New York City. Since 1960 the population of the lower half of the river valley, from New York City to the state capital at Albany, has grown by about one third. Environmental concerns in the region have gradually shifted from water quality to land use. This reading examines these changes, as well as changes in the valley itself.

The long human partnership with the Hudson has ebbed and flowed just as the tide does as far as Troy [a town near Albany]. Yet to travel this river is to discover how one-sided the partnership has been, how much a great waterway has been ignored—or abused. But a remarkable transformation is taking place. People are starting to think of the Hudson Valley as a region again. . . . They're realizing that Yonkers, Mechanicville, and Saratoga Springs have something—call it public space, call it community—in common. . . .

A few things are certain. The future won't include the passenger boats that used to ply the river up to Albany: They're all gone, and tug-and-barge traffic is a fraction of what it used to be. The old foundries and mills are gone too, leaving the river towns—lively communities in their day—suspended between decay and quixotic [unrealistic] hope. . . .

In each town I visited, the valley was on everyone's mind. The Hudson's people are a diverse assortment of farmers, merchants, factory hands, townspeople, commuters, and lingering lords of the manor. In one way or another they all ask, What shall we do with our land? How they answer that will determine within a few years whether the natural magnificence of the Hudson will survive. . . .

Thirty years ago it seemed that the river itself wouldn't survive. . . . Raw sewage, spilled oil, polychlorinated biphenyls (PCBs)—a potent mix of waste and the leavings of industry—had turned the Hudson into a virtual cesspool. General Electric's discharge of PCBs, which are used to insulate electrical equipment, prompted one of the most famous environmental battles of the 1970s. That effort and continuing vigilance [attentiveness] have rejuvenated [revived] the Hudson. Now the threats are on land. . . .

Frank Bulich knows the value of good stewardship [land management]. He benefits from centuries of it every day. On a bluff in the center of his 670-acre farm a half dozen gravestones huddle against the elements and the indifference of his grazing cattle. Here lie descendants of the Van Orden family, Dutch patroons, as the first settlers were called, who arrived in the late 1600s. Before the Van Ordens, the bluff was a hunting ground for Mahican Indians. Bulich keeps boxes full of arrowheads, axes, and simple flint tools he's found there.

. . . Bulich has been a farmer in the Hudson Valley the past 50 of his 65 years. He loves the land, but he's far from sentimental about it. . . . Out where the Van Ordens are buried is a fine place to build, and Bulich has pondered [considered] selling that patch to provide for his later years. But the town of Catskill's planning board, eager to preserve the shoreline, has blocked new building within a hundred feet of it. "We're still arguing about it," Bulich said. "The thing is, our land is our retirement. As long as I'm not hurting anybody, I shouldn't have restrictions on my property. I'm not polluting the river—that's the issue, isn't it?"

A lot of people—developers, real estate brokers, political conservatives— agree with Bulich. But a lot of others believe that farmers like him, along with developers and "wise-use" conservatives, need to rethink the idea that progress always equals growth. As the valley becomes aware of itself as a region, they say, it's time to recognize that what you do with your land affects others too.

From "Heart of the Hudson" (retitled "Change Comes to the Hudson Valley") by Patrick Smith from *National Geographic*, March 1996. Copyright ©1994 by **National Geographic Society.** Reprinted by permission of the publisher.

Understanding What You Read After you have finished reading the selection, answer the following questions.

1. What pollution problems threatened the Hudson River? How were they solved?

_____

_____

2. How have economic development problems along the Hudson River changed over the years?

_____

_____

3. How has the view that the river is a "public space" affected attitudes about land use and the rights of private property owners?

_____

_____

Activity

Write a letter to the editor stating your opinion about the contro- versy over Frank Bulich's land.

READING 12 · The United States

The Expanse of Texas

Giant, first published in 1952, is among the most widely read novels about Texas and one of the best-known works of writer Edna Ferber (1887–1968). In this excerpt, Texas cattleman Jordan "Bick" Benedict is returning to his West Texas home accompanied by his Yankee bride Leslie Lynnton Benedict, who has never before been in Texas.

"You can see miles," she said. "Miles and miles and miles!" She had her flushed face at the . . . window. . . . "I can't help it. Geography always excites me when it's new places, and I love trains and being married to you, and seeing Texas. When your grandfather came here it was wilderness really, wasn't it? Imagine! What courage!"

"They were great old boys. Tough." . . .

As far as her eyes could see she beheld the American desert land which once had waved knee-high with lush grasses. She had never seen the great open plains and the prairies. It was endless, it was another world, bare vast menacing to her Eastern eyes. Later she was to know the brilliant blurred pattern of the spring flowers, she was to look for the first yellow blossoms of the retama against the sky, the wild cherry and the heavy cream white of the Spanish dagger flower like vast camellias. . . .

It was late afternoon when their train arrived at Vientecito. "Here we are!" he said and peered out through the window to scan the platform and the vehicles beyond in the swirling dust.

"What's it mean? How do you pronounce it?"

"Vientecito? Means gentle breeze. We call it Viento for short. The wind blows all the time, nearly." . . .

He pointed at some object. "There we are. But who's that!" A huge Packard. In the driver's seat was a stocky young Mexican with powerful shoulders. About twenty, Leslie thought. . . . There was no one else in the car. There was no one to meet them. . . . "Out!" barked Bick. The boy paused, turned. Bick gave him the baggage checks. In Spanish he said, "You will wait here. The pickup will be sent." . . .

"Leslie! Get into the car, please, We're leaving." . . . She looked about her as she came—at the railway station so Spanish with its Romanesque towers, its slim pillars and useless grillwork. The sun burned like a stab-wound, the hot unceasing wind gave no relief. . . . No green anywhere other than the grey-green of the cactus, spiked and stark. Dust dust dust, stinging in the wind. Nothing followed the look or pattern of the life she had left behind her. . . .

With a neck-cracking jerk the car leaped away. Never a timorous [easily frightened] woman their speed now seemed to her to be maniacal . . . . He was silent, his face set and stern. Well, she knew that when men looked like that you pretended not to notice and pretty soon they forgot all about it.

"How flat it is! And big. And the horizon is—well, there just isn't any it's so far away. I thought there would be lots of cows. I don't see any."

"Cows!" he said in a tone of utter rage.

She was, after all, still one of the tart-tongued Lynnton girls. "I don't see why you're so put out because that boy came instead of someone else. Or the family. After all, it's so far from the railroad."

"Far!" In that same furious tone. "It's only ninety miles."

She glanced at the speedometer. It pointed to eighty-five. Well, no wonder! At this rate they'd be home in an hour or so. Home. For an engulfing [overwhelming] moment she had a monstrous feeling of being alone with a strange man in an unknown world—a world of dust and desert and heat and glare and some indefinable thing she never before had experienced. . . .

Against the brassy sky there rose like a mirage a vast edifice [structure] all towers and domes and balconies and porticoes and iron fretwork. . . .

"What's that! Is it—are we near the ranch, Jordan?"

""We've been on it the last eighty miles, practically ever since we got outside Viento. That's Reata. That's home."

Excerpt (retitled "The Expanse of Texas") from *Giant* by Edna Ferber. Copyright 1952 by Edna Ferber. Reprinted by permission of **Doubleday, a division of Random House, Inc.**

Understanding What You Read After you have finished reading the selection, answer the following questions.

1. From this passage, how would you describe the geography and economy of West Texas?

_____

_____

2. What clues does Ferber provide about Texans' understanding of distance? How do you think the state's size affects this perception?

_____

_____

Activity

The reading describes only one part of this large and geographically diverse state. Use library and other resources to identify, locate, and describe the four major geographic regions of Texas. Prepare a short report on your findings.

Canada

READING 13

Cruising to School

On the Canadian side of the Strait of Georgia that runs between British Columbia's Vancouver Island and the American state of Washington lie a group of islands known as the Gulf Islands. Life here involves some adjustments, as this reading explains.

The *Mistaya,* drenched in the golden rays of early morning, bobs gently at the wharf. The music of wind chimes carries on the salty breeze from a sailboat riding at anchor. A seal noses in and out of the barnacle-encrusted pilings. The pungent [strong] scent of low tide wafts across the quiet harbor scene. It is through this rich sensory world, in British Columbia's scenic Gulf Islands, that *Mistaya*—a water taxi that serves as a school "bus"—will soon glide: past ferries and fishing boats, instead of harried commuters; beneath flights of geese, instead of traffic lights; between craggy islets and through deep blue narrows, instead of clogged city streets.

Cruising to school by boat through an island paradise may *sound* romantic: after all, many Canadians save up for years to sail these enchanting waters. But don't try to tell that to Sarah Brooks at 7:15 a.m. When I first saw her last spring, she was trudging down the dock toward *Mistaya,* a half-awake tenth grader who has to get up at 5:30 to make the connection. First, she catches a school bus near her home at the far north end of Galiano Island. But Galiano has no high school, so the bus drops her off 45 minutes later on the island's south end, where she boards *Mistaya* for the 30-minute ride to Ganges, on larger Salt Spring Island. With an intermediate stop, the afternoon boat ride home takes almost twice as long. In mid-winter, Sarah barely gets home by dark. "Sometimes I wonder if it's worth it," she sighs. . . .

Nearly 80 teenagers from the four "outer" Gulf Islands ride the boat to school every day, and the number increases each year. . . . The daily boat ride can be exciting, especially for those, like Sara Quist of Galiano, who only have to make the 10-minute hop to Mayne Island [near Galiano Island] for junior high school. "It's fun," she says, "especially going fast over the big ferry waves in Active Pass." Her enthusiasm was not dampened by the time she missed the school bus, and then the water taxi, on the day of mid-term exams. The boat had to be called back later for a solo run, and Sara had to pay $75 out of her own pocket.

But, for high schoolers who make the much longer trip to Salt Spring Island, the novelty eventually wears thin. And there are real disadvantages. Because of the boat schedule, "you can't take part in extra-curricular activities after school," says Sarah Brooks. I'd like to be on the volleyball team and in drama, but I can't unless I board on Salt Spring Island." . . .

Around 3:30 p.m., to the accompaniment of rap music, *Mistaya* pulls in at Galiano Island, and the last students disembark. Jack Hughes [the boat's owner and captain] switches off the blaring tape deck in obvious relief, and swings his bow towards Ganges. It's been a long day for him, too, but he doesn't seem tired. "I've been doing this for years," he says, "and I still love seeing the sunrises and nature in all its glory." . . . There is always something interesting to see out on the water, and most adults think the Gulf Islands students are unusually lucky.

But back at the Galiano Island pier, the kids are just getting onto their school bus. They've been under way for almost an hour, and they're not home yet.

From "Cruising to School" by Tom Koppel from *Canadian Geographic,* September–October 1993. Copyright © 1993 by Tom Koppel. Reprinted by permission of **Tom Koppel**. Reprinted by permission of the author.

Understanding What You Read After you have finished reading the selection, answer the following questions.

1. Why do students living on the Gulf Islands have to commute to school by boat?

_____

2. Do the high school students or the junior high school students have a shorter commute time to school? Explain why.

_____

3. How does the environment of the Gulf Islands affect students' school experiences?

_____

_____

4. What choice do students have for going to school other than commuting by boat?

_____

Activity

Imagine that you are a commuter on the *Mistaya*. Write a letter to a friend in the United States describing the physical geography of your commute, including landforms, animal life, and weather.

Canada

Nunavut: Canada's Newest Territory

On April 1, 1999, after a 28-year quest, the territory of Nunavut became a reality for Canada's Inuit. The creation of Nunavut gives hope to native peoples all over the world who seek a self-governing homeland. Just before the landmark day, a Canadian journalist took a look at the territory that was about to be born.

Peter Ernerk was on the phone from Iqaluit, dealing in facts and figures about Nunavut, when he stopped and said, "Why don't I just send you an e-mail?" And then he stopped again and said, "You know, sometimes I'm amazed. Forty years ago I was living in an igloo. Now I'm sending e-mails."

Ernerk's own experiences offer a context for understanding the latest development in the lives of the Inuit of the eastern Canadian Arctic: the birth . . . of the territory of Nunavut. Changes have come dizzyingly fast to the people in this stern and lovely world. A century ago, they were living in a stone age, hunting seals and caribou with weapons of rock or bone. Four decades or so ago, they left hunting camps and semi-nomadic lives for settlements. . . . Now, with the creation of Nunavut, they will govern one-fifth of the Canadian landmass. . . .

The challenges are considerable. Nunavut will be a huge territory: 60 percent of today's Northwest Territories including most of the Canadian Arctic islands. It is a land of tundra and mountains, of tiny shoreside hamlets and extensive mineral resources. . . . The 27,219 people—85 percent Inuit and, with 56 percent under 25 years of age, the youngest population in Canada—are scattered in 28 communities, most vast distances apart.

Nunavut has two facets: the land claim settlement . . . and the creation of a new territory. . . . The land claim settlement—largest in Canada—gives the Inuit ownership of 350,000 square kilometers [135,000 square miles] of land (including subsurface minerals in a carefully selected 10 percent of that) and compensation from the federal government of $1.148 billion over 14 years (held in a trust with the interest used to finance business, student scholarships and support for hunters).

The Inuit also gain a share of resource royalties, hunting rights and a greater role in managing the land and protecting the environment. In exchange, they signed away future claims to aboriginal rights and title to all remaining lands and water in Nunavut. . . .

Canadian Inuit lived generally beyond the influence of southern society until the shift to settlement living in the 1950s and 1960s, when the Canadian government began providing health care, housing and education. Many parents' desire for their children to learn to read and write in English led to their move from the land into settlements. The launch of the Anik A-1 satellite in 1972 brought television—CBC and Hockey Night in Canada—to the Arctic and played no small role in the precipitous [sharp] decline in the use of Inuktitut [the Inuit language]. The demise [end] of the sealskin industry in the 1970s eliminated a traditional occupation. . . .

But the incursion [invasion] of southern culture brought some benefits. Aside from the practical—rifles and outboards, radios and telephones— there were new social and political concepts: almost immediately, calls for an Inuit territory in the eastern Canadian Arctic were heard. . . . The federal government agreed to an eventual [creation of an Inuit territory] on the condition that all land claims be settled. . . .

Nunavut's economic future is firmly linked to its renewable and non-renewable natural resources—mining and petroleum development, commercial fishing and hunting, and eco-tourism. The land and water that once sustained a semi-nomadic society are now expected to sustain the modern Nunavut economy: 80 percent of the territory's known mineral reserves—copper, lead, zinc, gold and silver—are on Inuit-owned land.

From: "Nunavut: Up and Running" (retitled "Nunavut: Canada's Newest Territory") by Dane Lanken and Mary Vincent from *Canadian Geographic*, January-February 1999. Copyright ©1999 by the **Royal Canadian Geographical Society.** Reprinted by permission of the publisher.

Understanding What You Read After you have finished reading the selection, answer the following questions.

1. How did Hockey Night in Canada help lead to the creation on Nunavut?

_____

_____

2. What did the Inuit have to give up to gain the government's agreement to Nunavut? Why is its creation so significant for the Inuit?

_____

_____

_____

Activity

Imagine that you have been hired by the Inuit to develop tourism. Research Nunavut and create a brochure to promote eco-tourism in the territory.

Mexico

Mexico in Transition

Mexico is a nation in transition. Its economy is struggling. The old political system is dying. Big changes seem certain. Some Mexicans fear economic collapse and civil war. This reading looks at the decline of Mexico's long-time ruling party—and ponders the country's future.

At the end of a hard century, Mexico is struggling. . . . Politics are in turmoil. . . . The gap between rich and poor is widening. The poor . . . are growing restless. Even the relatively small middle class has conducted protests and work disruptions. Everyone, it seems, wants something new. . . .

"We have everything," one Mexican told me in exasperation [frustration]. "So why are we in crisis?" The answer may lie in history. The Mexican people have survived centuries of war followed by periods of stifling [overpowering] authority. The Spaniards ruled for 300 years. After their reign the 19th century [1800s] brought a war of independence, war with the U.S., civil war, another conflict, this time with France, then three decades of dictatorship.

The dictatorship was drowned in blood in the revolution of 1910, in which more than a million people died. This led to a constitution modeled on the U.S.'s and passed in 1917. But by 1929 the party now known as the Partido Revolucionario Institucional (PRI) had shaped a system that looked like a democracy but worked like an authoritarian regime [all-powerful government]. . . . Freedoms of speech and press were curtailed [severely limited], and elections were controlled. . . . Voters at some polls were handed "ballot tacos"—several ballots stuffed into one—so they could cast multiple votes. Loyalists were bused from place to place to vote repeatedly.

But the PRI also initiated [started] some landownership reform, developed and distributed oil wealth, and provided more stability than Mexico had experienced the century before. It responded, [although] slowly, to its citizens' demands. Roads got paved; schools were built. . . . Loyalty was widespread. Today, all that has changed. . . .

The decline of the PRI began in 1968 when the army killed more than 200 students during a demonstration over social reform, shocking the nation. Then, in 1985, when an earthquake killed 10,000 people in Mexico City, the government's response was slow and inefficient; Mexican citizens, who independently rescued, housed, and fed victims, lost faith in the government's ability to take care of them. Three years later, the hotly contested national election was accompanied by fraud—computers broke down with the race undecided and were booted back up with the PRI's victory installed.

In the early 1990s the government rode high on . . . economic reforms, which encouraged the takeover of state-run industry, friendly relations with the U.S., and the signing of NAFTA [the North American Free Trade Agreement], and led to a growing middle class and hope among the poor. But catastrophe hit in 1994: Indians rebelled in Chiapas [a state in southern Mexico, on its border with Guatemala] on the day NAFTA took effect. The PRI's presidential candidate was assassinated. . . . Investors from abroad—and Mexican businessmen—lost confidence in Mexico. . . . A severe recession ensued [followed], throwing more than a million people out of work. . . . The economy is still floundering.

So is the PRI. . . . "The system is dead," [says] author Carlos Fuentes. . . . A free press is struggling to emerge in print and television. Opposition parties have won important local elections. The middle class, battered by the crisis, is restless. "People are really frustrated," says a teacher. . . .

"In Mexico," Porfirio Díaz reportedly said after he was thrown out as president and dictator in 1911, "nothing happens until it happens." He meant that Mexicans operate on both patience and inertia [inactivity], like the stone heat that brews in the depths of [a volcano]. But when the Mexicans act, they [cannot be stopped]. Such a heat is growing now. Everyone in Mexico can feel it, but no one seems able to predict its outcome. Only one thing is certain: Whatever happens to Mexico will be in character. And what is the character of today's Mexico that will shape tomorrow's? That's the intriguing [interesting] question.

From "Emerging Mexico: Bright with Promise, Tangled in the Past" (retitled "Mexico in Transition") by Michael Parfit from *National Geographic,* August 1996. Copyright ©1996 by **National Geographic Society**. Reprinted by permission of the publisher.

Understanding What You Read After you have finished reading the selection, answer the following questions.

1. In what ways have the PRI's decades of rule benefited Mexico?

_____

_____

2. How does the PRI hold on to power, according to the reading?

_____

_____

3. How did a geography event weaken the PRI's control over Mexican politics?

_____

_____

Activity

Design a protest sign about the PRI. It should either support the PRI for the benefits it has brought, or attack it for its shortcomings.

Name _____ Class _____ Date _____

Mexico

No Fair Air to Spare

Mexico City is one of the most polluted urban areas in the world. An American journalist living in Mexico City looks at the problem in detail and describes what the government of Mexico is doing to combat it.

Shortly after dawn of the new year, Mexican officials proudly announced that, in 1999, Mexico City had experienced the cleanest air in a decade. Within days, the city was . . . . again shrouded [covered] in smog that clogged nasal passages, stung eyes and made throats raw. Schools in the southeastern part of the city were ordered to keep children indoors for a few days to reduce risks to their lungs.

Prompted mostly by skyrocketing levels of suspended particles—microscopic solids in the air—the government ordered some industries to cut production by half and used emergency laws to pull more old cars off the roads. Officials shut down more than 150 brickmaking factories known to sometimes illegally use old rubber tires as fuel. People crowded into emergency rooms with respiratory illnesses. . . .

It's true that more than a decade's worth of reforms have helped reduce some air pollution, said Adrian Fernandez, the director-general of information and measurement programs for Mexico's National Ecology Institute. "But I don't like to act too triumphant," he hastened to add. "There is so much more to do."

Mexico City and the Greater Valley of Mexico are ringed by mountains that trap pollution inside a bowl teeming [crowded] with 18.5 million people, 4.5 million vehicles, and tens of thousands of factories. Residents are exposed to a sickening stew of car exhaust, industrial emissions [factory smoke], dirt blown from vast tracts of unpaved land and wind-borne fecal matter dropped by legions [thousands] of street dogs. The region's bone-dry winter air makes pollution even worse. Relief usually comes only with spring rains. . . .

When air pollution here began approaching alarming levels in the late 1980s, Mexico established one of the world's most sophisticated pollution-monitoring systems and began to enact a series of reforms. [In 1999], measurements showed that action had indeed paid off. . . . Major contaminants such as carbon monoxide, lead and sulfur dioxide fell within normal levels with only a exceptions during 1999. The city had only five air contamination emergency days . . . compared with 37 in 1998. . . .

What helped Mexico City . . . was the phasing out of leaded gasoline in Mexico. It was eliminated in 1997. . . . All cars made in Mexico since 1991 have catalytic converters. Because many Mexicans can't afford new cars, however, only about 40 percent of vehicles are equipped with the pollution-reducing devices. Mexico's . . . "Today You Can't Drive" law pulls about 20 percent of the city's older cars off the streets every day. . . . The bad news is that ozone is still an alarming health hazard, and it hovered well above healthy levels for several hours almost every day [in 1999]. . . .

The other contaminants still plaguing Mexico City's air at dangerously high levels are suspended particles, the product of vehicle and industrial fuel emissions, dog droppings and soil erosion. The particles lodge in the lungs and cause acute [sudden] or chronic [long-term] respiratory problems.

Reforestation projects have helped reduce suspended particles caused by soil erosion, but the city still needs to do more work to fill in bare patches of land. . . . Mexico City, with more than a million stray dogs roaming the city, [also] started a crackdown on pet waste, but disregard for the law is common.

. . . Ozone and suspended particles should decline as more industries and vehicles in Mexico City run on natural gas. Two large natural-gas underground distribution centers are under construction. . . . More enforcement of Mexico City's existing environmental laws is also a must. At least half a million of the 4.5 million vehicles in the city haven't undergone mandatory [required] smog-control testing. . . . Mexico recently gave regular police, rather than special environmental officers, the power to crack down on the law.

From "Mexico City's pollution getting better, but slowly," (retitled "No Fair Air to Spare") by Susan Ferriss in the *Austin American-Statesman*, March 17, 2000. Copyright ©2000 by **Austin American-Statesman**. Reprinted by permission of the publisher.

Understanding What You Read After you have finished reading the selection, answer the following questions.

1. How do technology and physical geography combine to create air quality problems for Mexico City?

_____

_____

2. How have Mexico City's dogs contributed to its air pollution problem?

_____

3. What reforms have been put into place to deal with Mexico City's air pollution? What remains to be done?

_____

_____

Activity

Find out how many air contamination emergency days were declared in Mexico City last year. Create a graph to show trends in the city's air contamination emergency days since 1997.

Central America and the Caribbean Islands

CULTURE

Village Life in Guatemala

This reading focuses on two villages in western Guatemala. Like the majority of people in this region, most of the villagers and residents of the surrounding countryside are Maya.

As early as 600 B.C. the Maya lived throughout Central America. Around A.D. 300, they began to build cities with magnificent palaces and temples. Then the Spanish arrive in the 1500s and ruled for three centuries. They enslaved the Maya, took away most of their land, and even tried to force them to give up their beliefs and traditions. . . . But the Maya resisted, passing down many parts of their heritage through the generations. . . .

[Today] most Spanish Guatemalans live in the larger cities and follow the latest trends in music, entertainment, and fashions. In contrast, most Maya live in the highland villages, follow their centuries-old customs, and speak their native languages. The Maya also tend to wear colorful handwoven *traje,* or traditional clothing. Each village has its own colors and patterns of cloth that the women and young girls weave by hand.

. . . Todos los Santos Cuchumatán [is a] little hamlet . . . nestled among the Cuchumatanes Mountains, over ten thousand feet above sea level. Little has changed in Todos los Santos over the last hundred years. It takes three hours by bus or car to reach Todos los Santos from the nearest city. Steep, twisting dirt roads make travel in and out of the village very difficult, especially during the wind-whipped, chilly winters. Some people living in the mountains around the village must walk up to twelve miles on weekly market days to buy and sell their wares and produce.

In preparation for this week's market, twelve-year-old Joel drains the blood from a slaughtered sheep his family will sell. With the blood drained, the animal weighs less and is easier to carry. . . . Joel and his family are among the very few Ladinos living in Todos los Santos. Ladinos are Guatemalans of mixed Mayan and European heritage. Most Ladinos live in Guatemala City or the coastal and eastern lowlands. However, Joel and his family choose to remain in the highland, because they believe this is the best region for raising animals. . . .

Sara also lives in the western highlands. The closest town to her home is San Francisco el Alto, meaning "the high one." Like Todos los Santos, San Francisco hosts a huge weekly market. Thousands of people gather to buy and sell livestock. On Fridays before dawn, Sara and her mother set out with their sheep for the market. Crouched in the back of a small, covered pickup [truck], Sara and her mother and several sheep ride two hours through the cold morning. The truck stops twice to pick up more villagers who wait by burning fires along the roadside with their livestock. They reach the market at 6:00 A.M., and one by one the villagers and animals climb out, stretching their cramped muscles.

The market in San Francisco is well underway by 7:00 A.M. Villagers warm themselves with coffee and hot tortillas. Thirteen-year-old Manuela and her mother run a food stall where they sell fresh bread, coffee, corn tortillas, and *chuchitos*—small dumplings made of corn flower and lard, and filled with a meat and tomato sauce. One of these . . . breakfasts sells for three *quetzales*, or about fifty cents. . . .

After the flurry of activity on market days, things quiet down in the highland villages—until Mass on Sunday morning. Most Guatemalans are Roman Catholic, though many practice a mix of Christianity and their ancient religion. The Mayan gods guide them in farming and other work, while the Christian saints guide them in family life. Every Guatemalan town has a patron saint with a special *fiesta*, or celebration, to honor it. . . . Many Maya [accept] the cross as a Mayan symbol as well as a Christian symbol. It represents the four directions: north, south, east, and west.

Excerpt (retitled "Village Life in Guatemala") from *Children of Guatemala* by Jules Hermes. Copyright ©1997 by Jules Hermes. Reprinted by permission of **Carolrhoda Books, Inc**.

Understanding What You Read After you have finished reading the selection, answer the following questions.

1. How do the Maya of Guatemala indicate which village they are from?

_____

2. In what ways do the Maya differ from Guatemalans of Spanish descent?

_____

_____

3. How do you think that Joel will get his sheep to the market in Todos los Santos? What clues make you think so? What is the farthest distance that Joel will likely have to travel?

_____

_____

4. What roles do Christianity and traditional religions play in Mayan life?

_____

_____

Activity

Write the copy for a travel brochure describing a village market in Guatemala.

Central America and the Caribbean Islands

GEOGRAPHY

Montserrat: Living Under the Volcano

Soufriere Hills, a volcano in the south of Montserrat, ended almost four centuries of inactivity in July 1995, when it began a series of eruptions that turned life on this small Caribbean island upside down. Events on Montserrat show how human experience, which is measured in decades, can be shaped by forces of nature that occur over centuries, or even millennia. A journalist who visited Montserrat in 1997, during the second year of the ordeal, filed this report.

Gerard Dyer was harvesting his crops, a normal enough pursuit on a cloudless April morning on Montserrat. Half a mile above him, however, at the top of a peak . . . steam curled from fissures in a dome of gray rock. . . . Moving from patch to patch on ten sloping acres, he hoed sweet potatoes from long mounds of earth, pulled up carrots, picked parsley and tarragon. Satisfied that he'd taken enough, he loaded the produce into a battered pickup truck parked by the dirt track that led to the main road—our only escape from Soufriere Hills Volcano.

On Montserrat these days there's no telling when a quick exit might be needed. . . . Eruptions . . . have forced . . . evacuations of thousands of people from the south to community centers, churches, and schools in the sparsely populated northern hills. Families there have taken in relatives and friends, filling bedrooms to overflowing; foreign property owners have rented their vacation villas to locals who can afford the double burden of rent and mortgage payments on their [abandoned] houses. . . .

Evacuees are prohibited from occupying their homes and businesses in the south, designated as an unsafe zone. Some 4,000 Montserratians—one-third of the population—have abandoned their erstwhile [one-time] paradise, most emigrating to other Caribbean islands. Others have gone to Great Britain, which still holds the 39-square-mile island as a dependent territory.

Who can blame them? . . . Hotels and restaurants closed down. Cruise ships skirted the island. . . . Unemployment rose from 7 to 50 percent. . . . Plymouth, the capital and only place of any size, with a pre-eruption population of 4,000, became a ghost town; it lies well within the unsafe zone, three miles west of the volcano. "The lifeblood of the country was there," said Midge Kocen, who helps run Montserrat's media center. "All the government offices and utilities, most of the shops and petrol [gas] stations, the post office, the cinema, the public market. . . ."

When the mountain [is] judged quiet enough, people [can] get passes to visit the unsafe zone, which is how Gerard came to be working on the flanks [sides] of Soufriere Hills that bright morning. "If you have animals and crops, you can't just leave them," said Gerard. . . . "You have to come look after them and hope nothing happens." As he spoke, the volcano made a crackling sound like distant thunder—blocks of solid lava rolling down the side of the dome. . . . As long as Gerard can plant and harvest his crops, the Dyers will get by. But there's always worry. "We're afraid they'll stop giving passes for us to get to our fields. I don't know what we'll do then." . . .

Minutes before midnight on September 17, 1996, the volcano ratcheted up [increased] the action. Part of the dome collapsed, and rock shot sideways out of the crater. Charged ash particles sparked lightning, thunder boomed, and for the first time pebbles pounded the southern end of the safe zone. Terrified, people in villages in the line of fire . . . ran barefoot from their beds to their cars to escape the volcanic hail. . . . "It sounded like a war," recalled a man whose car windshield was smashed by the debris. "It could have been artillery shells falling around the house." . . .

"I'm never turning my back on that volcano again," said Gertrude Shotte, a teacher. . . . "I was one of the ones who spent the night in a car by the side of the road after those stones started to fall. We're getting the idea that this thing really can blow and affect us all." . . .

Most likely the volcano will go on throwing out ash and stones for years without making the island uninhabitable. Acting on this expectation, the government began the task of shifting human activity out of danger. Public services, roads, and utilities, all centered around Plymouth, are being reestablished in the north. . . . "The north of the island has not been affected by a volcano in two million years, so we've based all our contingency [back up] plans on that," Frank Savage, Britain's governor on Montserrat, told me. . . . "We have to have faith in the scientific advice and hope to God they've got it right."

From: "Montserrat: Under the Volcano," (retitled "Montserrat: Living Under the Volcano") by A.R. Williams from *National Geographic*, July 1997. Copyright ©1997 by **National Geographic Society**. Reprinted by permission of the publisher.

Understanding What You Read After you have finished reading the selection, answer the following questions.

1. How has the Soufriere Hills volcano affected population distribution and settlement patterns on the island of Montserrat?

_____

_____

2. In what ways has the volcano's eruption affected the daily lives of Montserratians?

_____

_____

Activity

Check on the status of Montserrat's volcano and people today. Summarize your findings in a short report.

Central America and the Caribbean Islands

The Land and People of Nicaragua

Many Americans know of Nicaragua because of the civil war that raged there from the 1960s into the early 1990s. When the communist Sandinistas rebels took over in 1979, the U.S. government backed anti-communist Nicaraguans, called "Contras." The Contras forced the Sandinistas to hold elections in 1990. Nicaraguans then voted the Sandinistas out of power. This reading looks at the land and people on which Nicaragua hopes to build its future.

Picture an area about the size of the state of New York, covered with forests, lakes, and mountains. Imagine long western and eastern coasts looking out on the Pacific and Atlantic Oceans. . . . In all, Nicaragua has about 560 miles of coastline. At 50,193 square miles, Nicaragua is a little bigger than Louisiana and a little smaller than North Carolina. Large areas of the country are uninhabited; most of its people are concentrated in the western region and in a few cities. The country's population per square mile is relatively thin compared to other Central American countries.

Nicaragua is divided into three geographic regions: the western Pacific lowlands, the eastern Caribbean lowlands (also called the Mosquito Coast), and the central highlands. Each region has features and weather characteristics that differentiate it [make it different] from other parts of the country.

Three out of four Nicaraguans live in the western part of the country, between the Pacific coast and Lake Managua. Here the land is good . . . because it has been naturally fertilized over the years by ashes discharged from the area's many volcanoes. Many of the people who live here work on farms, but Nicaragua's three biggest cities are also in this region. The largest is Managua, the nation's capital.

East of Managua lies the area known as the central highlands. This mountainous area is covered with dense rain forest and receives an annual rainfall of between 70 and 100 inches. The region is nearly uninhabitable, but in the mountains is a rich mining district called Nueva Segovia. For many decades, a few people have been willing to live in this humid place in order to mine the silver and gold found here.

Even wetter than the central highlands is the Mosquito Coast, which runs along the eastern third of the country. . . . This region is the wettest in Central America, with average rainfall ranging from 100 to 250 inches per year. Much of the area's soil is gravel and sandy clay, with the only variation being a treeless, grassy plain called the savanna. Four main groups live here: the Miskito, Rama, and Sumo Indians are native to Nicaragua, and the Garífunas are blacks who originated [came from] from Africa. These groups have lived in this swamp-like region for many generations. . . .

Few Nicaraguans travel between the Pacific coast and the Mosquito Coast. Only a few roads link the two sides of the country. . . . The two coasts . . . are like two different countries. . . . The main natural resources of the two areas are quite different, and the lifestyles are different. Farmers in the western Pacific lowlands know a lot about corn, cotton, and coffee, while farmers in the east are used to growing coconuts and bananas. The main industries along the Atlantic coast are fishing and catching lobsters. On the Pacific coast there are many more schools, colleges, and businesses. In the east, many Indians follow the traditions and customs of their ancestors. On the whole, the people of western Nicaragua think the Atlantic coast people are rather backward. . . .

Ethnic identity became an important issue only recently. Past governments mostly ignored the Atlantic coast, but when the Sandinistas came to power, they guaranteed civil rights for blacks and Indians and made ethnic identity a political issue. They promoted respect for traditional Indian religions, languages, and celebrations, but sometimes offended the Indians by trying to integrate [mix] them with the rest of Nicaragua. What the Indians really wanted was independence and control of the abundant natural resources in the region. Peace between the government and the Indians came when the Sandinistas helped organize an autonomous [independent] local government on the Atlantic coast.

From "Geography" and "Nicaraguans" (retitled "The Land and People of Nicaragua") from *Nicaragua* by Jennifer Kott. Copyright ©1995 by **Times Editions Pte Ltd**. Reprinted by permission of the publisher.

Understanding What You Read After you have finished reading the selection, answer the following questions.

1. In what ways does the geography of Nicaragua's coasts differ?

_____

_____

2. Why do you think the people of the Pacific coast have a low opinion of those on the Atlantic coast? How does Nicaragua's geography contribute to this situation?

_____

_____

_____

Activity

Create a poster for a campaign to promote national unity by improving western Nicaraguans' opinion of the people who live on the Atlantic coast.

Name _____ Class _____ Date _____

Caribbean South America

CULTURE

A Family in Rural Colombia

The nine-member Urrego family lives in Colombia's mountainous Tolima region, southwest of the city of Bogotá. This reading describes their work and their lives.

We have to drive for several hours through the Andes mountains along snow-covered roads. . . . The lower slopes of the mountains and the valleys are green with lush foliage and dotted with farms. . . .

As we approach our destination we can see the plantation's production plant and the coffee-bushes clustered together. There are 50,000 coffee plants growing on this plantation. In one year, some 12,000 sacks of beans can be picked, each sack weighing 12.5 kilograms (27 lb). Most of the picking is done by hand, by the families that live nearby. . . .

We meet four members of the Urrego family at the coffee plantation where they work as pickers. Celmira Urrego, who is 36, works there with three of her daughters—Elvira, aged 18, Cecilia, who is 16, and Janeth, who is 13. It's noon, so their working day is nearly over. . . . Celmira and her husband, Guillermo, have four other children. There are two little boys, Mario, who is 7, and Pablo, the youngest, who is only 2. The younger girls are Carmen, who is 9 and Juanita, who is 6.

The Urregos live near the coffee plantation. The potholed track that leads to their house passes a small supermarket. Here they buy all the essential goods they need. . . . The Urrego's house is made of bricks, planks of wood, and branches. The roof leaks when it rains, but since the weather in this region is never extreme, the family doesn't seem to mind too much. There are only three rooms in the house—a kitchen, a washroom, and one bedroom, where the whole family sleeps together. . . .

"I get up at about five o'clock every morning," Celmira tells us. "The first thing I do is make breakfast for the whole family. Usually, we have bread with a little butter and jam, and some coffee." By eight o'clock, she, Elvira, Cecilia and Janeth are already at work.

"All four of us work on one bush at a time," says Elvira. "And as the plants are sometimes as high as two meters (6 feet) we often have to stretch to reach the highest branches. It's hard work when it's hot."

The small, round fruits of the coffee plant are green or red in color and soft, like cherries. Inside the fruits there are two coffee beans. . . . "We have to work as fast as we can," says Cecilia. "The more we pick, the more we earn.". . . Celmira usually manages to pick about 50 kilograms (110 lb) a day. For this she is paid about 300 pesos ($2.40). . . . Elvira, Cecilia and Janeth are not yet as fast at picking as their mother. They are usually allowed to keep all the money they earn. But if the family is hard-up, then they have to contribute to the household budget.

. . . Guillermo . . . . is 42 years old and has been a painter and bricklayer for twenty years. At the moment he is working nearby, but often he has to look for work far away from home. . . . "There have been times," he tells us, "when I have been away from home for four months. . . . It is usually worth it, though, because I can earn up to 9,000 pesos [$72] a month. . . .

"When Guillermo is away from home and I'm out working, the older children look after the younger ones," [Celmira tells us]. . . . "They go to school from the age of seven until they are thirteen," says Guillermo. "But from the age of about ten they have to help out by earning money in their spare time."

. . . "All we want for our children is for them to have enough clothes and an education," [says Celmira]. "For ourselves," says Guillermo, "I suppose we would like a better home, or maybe even a farm. But we are content to remain as we are for a while yet."

Excerpt (retitled "A Family in Rural Colombia") from *A Family in Colombia* by Peter Otto Jacobsen and Preben Sejer Kristensen from Families Around the World series. Copyright ©1986 by Peter Otto Jacobsen and Preben Sejer Kristensen. Copyright ©1986 by **Wayland Publishers Ltd**. Reprinted by permission of the publisher.

Understanding What You Read After you have finished reading the selection, answer the following questions.

1. How many members of this Colombian family work? What type of work do they do and what are their earnings?

2. Describe the Urrego family's house and the area in which they live.

3. What information does the reading provide about education and other opportunities for children in rural Colombia?

Activity

Imagine that you are a teenage worker on a coffee plantation in Colombia. Write a letter to a student in the United States describing your life, your hopes, and your expectations for the future.

READING 21

Caribbean South America

The Fierce People of Venezuela

Venezuela's Orinoco River begins in the country's southernmost state of Amazonas—a dense rain forest the size of Oklahoma. This remote region is home to some 16,000 Yanomami. These Indians are also known as the "Fierce People" because of their behavior. Here is a report of a meeting with the Fierce People of Venezuela.

Jesús Cardozo, a Venezuelan anthropologist, and I are . . . surrounded by a friendly group of Yanomami. After a sweaty, six-hour hike through the rain forest, we are at Hasupiwei-teri, Village of the Bullfrogs, where roughly 40 Yanomami from six families live communally [together] in a *shabono*, a circular, 25-foot-high lean-to of woven palm fronds and logs. . . . Despite their off-putting reputation, my visit with the Fierce People has been nothing but neighborly. When we arrived in Hasupiwei-teri, for example, they greeted us with hoots and screams, their headman slapping us repeatedly on our chests and backs as a sign of welcome.

Our Yanomami guides from other villages didn't receive the same friendly displays. Instead, they had to hang their hammocks inside the shabono and lie there until they were approached and menaced [threatened] by a village member. As the threats came . . . our guides could not flinch or blink. . . . The Yanomami believe that men descended from drops of blood spilled on the dirt in a struggle between mythical beings after Earth's formation. Because of this legend, violent confrontation between individuals and neighboring villages is a part of Yanomami life and heritage.

"It is the traditional style," Cardozo says. "The visitors know they can be killed. The village also learns that the visitor is fierce, so they respect him. . . . The ritual ends when they bring the visitor a sort of milk shake of crushed plantains [a fruit similar to a banana] mixed with water. Then the visitor is welcome to partake [participate] in the life of the shabono."

Cardozo and I are free of such rigid manners. We are called *nape* (NAH-peh), which means "outsiders," less than human. Like all the Yanomami I meet, those of Hasupiwei-teri are curious. . . . While the Yanomami don't understand the concept of clocks, they love my watch's hourly chime and anticipate its arrival. . . . [They] also took an instant shine to my . . . nylon hammock, which I'd hastily strung to reserve my sleeping spot in the shabono. . . . Around us life as it has probably been lived for thousands of years goes on in the shabono's open interior. Children chase each other with toy bows and arrows, honing [practicing] hunting techniques. In the shadows families are cooking and eating plantains and the day's collection of game—a few turkey-size birds called guans. . . .

Isolation from the rest of the world is nothing new for the Orinoco's tribes. . . . While the Yanomami have adopted some modern technologies from visitors, they live as they always have, a source of some impatience in shabonos that now catch glimpses of what they're missing. Though they may fish with steel hooks given to them by missionaries and the few anthropologists who are allowed [by Venezuela's government] into these forests, the tribe is thirsting for more from the outside world.

. . . Discussions about the fate of the Yanomami occupy the conversation of many Venezuelans from Caracas [the nation's capital] to Amazonas. "What will the future hold for the Yanomami?" Cardozo asks one night in Hasupiwei-teri. "They desire so many things that we take for granted. Who can blame them? We can't keep them like a human museum."

. . . I ask the village headman, who is cooking nearby: What does he want for the people of Hasupiweiteri? The headman's face is painted an oily crimson from a healing ceremony performed this afternoon. He thinks about my question. Finally he says, "The nape and the Yanomami were once the same tribe—all Yanomami. Then a great flood came and washed some of the people down the river, where they learned new things. They became subhuman, nape. But some of what they learned I would like to know. Their medicine. The material from which they make hammocks. Their steel. But I would have to give up my life here. And why? To have what the nape have? . . ." He stirs his fire with a stick. Sparks fly. "I am like all men," the headman says. "I want to know my future—then I want to control it. It is not possible."

From "The Orinoco: Into the Heart of Venezuela," (retitled "The Fierce People of Venezuela") by Donovan Webster from *National Geographic*, April 1998. Copyright ©1998 by **National Geographic Society**. Reprinted by permission of the publisher.

Understanding What You Read
After you have finished reading the selection, answer the following questions.

1. What behavior has earned the Yanomami the name "Fierce People"?

_____

2. For what reasons is Yanomami life largely unchanged from what it was thousands of years ago?

_____

_____

Activity
Write a letter to the president of Venezuela stating whether the government's policies toward the Yanomami should be changed or should stay the same. Explain your reasons for your position.

Atlantic South America

River Life in Brazil

Brazil's rivers play a major role in the lives of many rural Brazilians. Here, an American outdoorsman, on a fishing trip to Brazil, describes the scene along the Rio Negro, in northern Brazil near its border with Venezuela.

Life on the river, in the equatorial jungle, isn't exactly unchanged and timeless, but it's close. Planes do occasionally fly over on their way to [the cities of] Manaus or Rio de Janeiro. Diesel generators provide power that lights some of the houses dotting the higher reaches of the river bank. Some of the native canoes are pushed by gasoline engines.

Still, some of these 20th century intrusions are somehow softened by the fact that the planes are the only way other than the river to travel across this immense country. The few isolated houses are on stilts to escape the inevitable [expected] rainy-season floods and the canoes are dugouts, made by hand to fit a fishing lifestyle.

"I've had a house on the river for 26 years and it hasn't changed much," said Gilberto Castro [a fishing-trip guide]. . . . "Life moves back and forth. When times get hard, people move back to the jungle." Times do occasionally get hard. There are no welfare programs in Brazil, and many of the millions who have sought a different life in Manaus or Brasilia often don't find the things they seek.

"People go to the cities because they want to find hospitals or better schools for their children. But in town, everything you have to pay for," Castro said. "On the river, you don't pay for the land. You don't pay for the water and you don't pay for the food."

Anyone who wishes can find a small spot on a river—the Negro or Solimões or dozens of others—and erect a small house. They can clear a little land to grow potatoes and manioc—a root vegetable that is used to make flour, a staple in their diet—and they can fish for food. They fish as families have for centuries and send their kids to small schools in the larger villages. Most of the guides who work the . . . [fishing] boats on the rivers go back to their villages and fish during the off-season.

Everyone is taught in Portuguese, Castro said, a unification movement dating to Brazil's decision to join the Allied forces in World War II. City folk can talk to country folk and that gives them a head start if they do go back to the land, Castro said. "Brazil is still very family oriented," he said. "If you move to the city, you have family there to help you. It's the same on the river."

The lone exception . . . are the country's small tribes of primitive Indians. "Nobody is allowed to go near them," Castro said. "They are living far up the rivers. It's more the fear of disease they are not equipped to handle than anything else."

But even those Indians share the river with the rest of Brazil and the river, by any name, still is life in Brazil. At the peak of the rainy season, the waters of the Amazon can be more than 100 miles wide. At the peak of the rainy season, about one-fifth of all fresh water on earth can be found in the Amazon Basin. Half the freshwater fish in the world—2,500 to 3,000 species—are found here.

There are more species of animals and plants than anywhere else on earth. Where else can one see on a single day giant river otters, alligators, pink dolphins, tree sloths, and pythons? There are howler monkeys, macaws, parrots and parakeets squawking and fighting for territory in the jungle canopy. . . . The size and diversity [variety] are beyond any real comprehension for anyone who hasn't pushed a boat out into the black waters of the Rio Negro or stood on the north shore in [the city of] Manaus and tried to see across [the Rio Negro's] confluence [meeting point] with the Amazon.

"The river is still the road in Brazil," said Castro. . . . In five days traveling the Rio Negro . . . we passed communities that comprise a few small houses and usually a school and a church or two, Catholic and sometimes Baptist. Residents farm and fish and watch the river flow by.

From "Brazilian life flows on river currents, even in the 21st century," (retitled "River Life in Brazil") by Mike Leggett in the *Austin American-Statesman*, March 12, 2000. Copyright ©2000 by **Austin American-Statesman**. Reprinted by permission of the publisher.

Understanding What You Read After you have finished reading the selection, answer the following questions.

1. According to the reading, why do many people who have gone to live in Brazil's cities return to its rivers during hard times?

_____

_____

2. How do most of the people who live along Brazil's rivers survive?

_____

3. What evidence does the reading cite to show the tremendous amount of natural resources that are present in the Amazon Basin?

_____

_____

Activity

Create a poster for a government campaign to convince the poor people of Brazil's overcrowded cities to relocate along a river in the Amazon Basin.

Atlantic South America

Paraguay's Bumpy Ride

In February 1989 the overthrow of General Alfredo Stroessner ended 35 years of dictatorship in Paraguay. Throughout the 1990s the nation struggled to establish democracy. The decade ended in the same uncertainty it began. Paraguay's vice president was assassinated, and its elected president resigned and fled the country. This reading looks at how Paraguay's past has shaped the nation's problems.

In Paraguay it's sometimes unclear who's giving the orders these days. The country's transition [change] from the longest dictatorship in 20th-century Latin America seems like a roller-coaster ride, with the passengers uncertain of the ups and downs ahead. . . .

"An island surrounded by land" is how the Paraguayan novelist Augusto Roa Bastos described this California-size country. Landlocked and dwarfed by larger, more populous neighbors, Paraguay has been a backwater since colonial days. There was no gold to attract conquistadores, just thick forests, rolling hills, and friendly Guaraní Indians.

Politics reinforced the country's natural isolation. Between 1811 and 1840 the first dictator all but sealed its borders, and later, the War of the Triple Alliance against Argentina, Brazil, and Uruguay claimed the lives of nine-tenths of its adult male population. Then as now Paraguay's salvation lay in its fertile soil, and today it remains South America's most rural nation. . . .

Asunción seems like a small town when compared with most of the other great Latin American capitals, yet in Paraguay it dominates, with 1.2 million people in its metropolitan area. . . . The country's isolation under Stroessner was so long and so complete that even old ideas find new life in this slow-paced city. As communism crumbled around the world, members of Paraguay's tiny Communist Party convened openly for the first time. . . .

Three-quarters of Paraguayans live outside the capital. Twelve hours and worlds away from Asunción . . . . we reached Arroyito. Lost in the wilds of central Paraguay, this small community was started by squatters and embodies [is an example of] the country's most sensitive political issue: the struggle for land by destitute [poverty-stricken] peasants. . . .

"Paraguay," the saying goes, "is a nation of men without land and land without men." There is plenty of land in Paraguay: With 29 people per square mile, it is one of the world's most sparsely populated countries. . . . Most of the property is controlled by only a few landowners. . . . The problem dates back to the War of the Triple Alliance from 1865 to 1870, which left Paraguay financially ruined. To raise money, the government sold off public lands to foreigners. For decades there was so much land and so few people that the question of property ownership [was not an issue]. But in the 1950s and '60s, with population growing and demand for cotton, soybeans, and other crops rising, the struggle for land began.

Dejesús Sosa . . . set out to address this problem [in the early 1980s] when he . . . had nine acres and ten children. . . . Sosa's promised land lay across the highway: 34 square miles of forests and prairies owned by the Unión Paraguaya livestock company. When he and his fellow farmers . . . asked for government help in obtaining the property, they saw no results.

On April 12, 1989, more than 1,200 people took over the land, joining thousands of frustrated peasants across the country who conducted similar peaceful invasions following the . . . coup [that overthrew Stroessner]. Though soldiers evicted Sosa's group within five days, Unión Paraguaya was eventually forced to sell the land to the government. The farmers were allowed back, with promises that they would be able to buy the property.

Obtaining land was just the first step for Sosa and the others. . . . Despite the difficulties, the people of Arroyito seem hopeful. . . .

From "Paraguay: Plotting a New Course" (retitled "Paraguay's Bumpy Ride") by Sandra Dibble from *National Geographic*, August 1992. Copyright ©1992 by **National Geographic Society**. Reprinted by permission of the publisher.

Understanding What You Read After you have finished reading the selection, answer the following questions.

1. What factors in Paraguay's geography and history have made it "an island surrounded by land"?

_____

_____

2. How did its history make Paraguay both a nation of "men without land and land without men"?

_____

_____

3. How did the change of government in 1989 change life for the landless people of rural Paraguay?

_____

_____

Activity

Use library and other resources to research and report on the political situation in Paraguay today.

Atlantic South America

CULTURE

Paris on La Plata

The people who live in Buenos Aires are known as porteños, or port dwellers. Located at the mouth of the Río de la Plata, the city was built on trade. Porteños used the profits to turn Buenos Aires into what many consider to be the Paris of South America.

The first Spanish settlement here was attempted in 1536; besieged [surrounded] by Indians, the settlers were reduced to eating snakes, rats, their shoes, even the flesh of dead companions, before abandoning the place. In 1580 the Spanish tried again; this time the port of Nuestra Señora Santa María del Buen Aire—Our Lady Holy Mary of the Good Air—was firmly rooted, the Indians subjugated [conquered]. . . .

In time, with independence and commercial links with Britain, Buenos Aires flourished. From 1880 to the 1930s the port sent out the bounty of the vast Pampas that stretch to the west: hides, beef, wool, wheat, corn, grains.

The money flowed in. "Rich as an Argentine" became a saying. *Porteños* visiting Europe brought back architects to create for them great houses and streets as in Paris, an opera house like Vienna's; they ordered English tweeds and French silks. At the same time, hundreds of thousands of Spanish and Italian immigrants poured in seeking their fortunes. The great city swelled and swelled. . . .

The metropolitan area now sprawls over 1,500 square miles and holds 11 million people—a third of the country's population. The central city bespeaks [shows] the golden age: Paris-like streets, sidewalk cafés, thousands of shops—simple and elegant. . . . "We are a surrealistic [multicolored] society," Jorge [a Buenos Aires art dealer] said. "People don't know what we are or what we are about. If you look for local color, for sombreros or Indians, you will not find it. This is a European city transplanted to Latin America—but we are not totally European, we are Latin American. This leads to confusion. . . ."

It *is* a society of immigrants. Along with the floods of Spaniards and Italians had come Irish, Swiss, French, Arab, and Armenian immigrants. . . . Argentina's well-established Jewish community numbers 300,000. . . . Ninety percent of them now live in Buenos Aires.

Larger currents of immigrants have come more recently from Korea and . . . from the neighboring countries of Paraguay, Bolivia, Uruguay, Peru, and Brazil. I discovered the reason one day in the dirt lanes of a slum named Villa 21–24. . . . Porteños call slums *villas miserias*, villages of misery; the military, with its taste for order, assigned them numbers. . . .

We stopped at the house of an illegal immigrant. . . . The man of the house introduced us to a new arrival. "He came only yesterday, looking for work. They're paying only five dollars a day in Paraguay." The newcomer shook our hands vigorously, his eyes shining with anticipation of a better life. He might not find it. The slum holds 20,000 squatters. Most are from the Argentine provinces; some represent the second or third generation in the slum. Others arrived more recently, having slid downward from the lower middle class. . . .

I met Emilio Alzaga, 84, at the Jockey Club, which is housed in two fine old mansions. . . . [Here] it seems the golden age persists [continues]. But Emilio, whose family is among the oldest in Buenos Aires, insisted that change has come even for the oligarchs—the great and fabulously wealthy landowners who controlled Argentina's destiny for decades.

"I am not a rich man," Emilio said. "The cattle industry is bad; I make only enough to pay taxes." And there is the long-term problem. "Unlike in England, where the eldest son inherits, in Argentina you must divide the inheritance equally among the children, so the land is broken up each generation. My father's land was divided between me and my brothers. I have 1,200 hectares (3,000 acres), my father had 10,000. Once my family had 200,000. Now the strategy [plan] has to be for the children to come together in a corporation, holding the land together. . . . And they will need to go into new crops: raspberries, asparagus, high-value things. Which is to say, in the future, one has to change absolutely."

From "Buenos Aires: Making Up for Lost Time," (retitled "Paris on La Plata") by John J. Putnam from *National Geographic*, December 1994. Copyright ©1994 by **National Geographic Society**. Reprinted by permission of the publisher.

Understanding What You Read After you have finished reading the selection, answer the following questions.

1. In what ways does the reading suggest that Buenos Aires is like Paris, France?

_____

2. Why do many porteños consider Buenos Aires to be a European city transplanted in Latin America?

_____

_____

_____

Activity

Imagine that you work for the Buenos Aires chamber of commerce. Create a travel brochure with text and images about your city that promotes its growth and multicultural heritage.

Atlantic South America

Bolivia: Land of Diversity

The only country in South America with no access to the sea, Bolivia is the continent's poorest and most isolated nation. This reading provides an overview of the people and most heavily populated regions in this land-locked country.

Bolivia is a land of amazing diversity [variety]. A traveler can go from the snowy peaks of the Andes Mountains in the west to steamy rain forests in the north, and then find low, open grasslands in the east. Situated in the heart of South America, Bolivia covers an area about twice the size of Texas.

The Andes Mountains spread into two major ranges in Bolivia. Between them lies the Altiplano, or high plateau, which holds about half the country's eight million people. This vast, desolate [empty] region once cradled an ancient civilization known as the Tiahuanaco, which reached its peak around A.D. 900. In the1400s and 1500s, the Altiplano became part of the great Inca Empire. . . .

Two main groups of native peoples account for about 60 percent of Bolivia's population. One group, the Aymara, are probably descendants of the Tiahuanacans. The other group, the Quechua, are descended from the Incas. In Bolivia, native people are called *campesinos*, which means "country people." *Mestizos*—people of mixed Spanish and native ancestry—make up about 30 percent of the population. The remaining 10 percent are people of European heritage. Most of them are descended from Spanish colonists.

. . . Like an inland sea, Lake Titicaca [on Bolivia's western border with Peru] covers 3,200 square miles and has dozens of tiny islands scattered throughout its waters. . . . East of Lake Titicaca, the Altiplano suddenly drops into a 1,000-foot-deep basin. Sprawling in this basin is La Paz— Bolivia's largest city and one of its two capitals. Life in La Paz seems to be layered. *Campesinos* live at higher altitudes near the rim [of the basin]. Wealthy people live more comfortably at the city's lower altitudes. . . .

Campesinos in La Paz make an average wage of 200 bolivianos (about 50 dollars) per month. . . . A social revolution in 1952 brought about great improvements in the lives of Bolivia's *campesinos*. For the first time, all adult Bolivians were allowed to vote. Some of the land that had been taken by the Spaniards was returned to *campesinos*. Since the revolution, however, frequent changes in government leadership have taken away many of the reforms. Bolivian *campesinos* still struggle to keep their rights and to improve their standard of living.

While La Paz is Bolivia's actual capital, the city of Sucre is its official capital. . . . Founded by the Spaniards in 1538, Sucre has glorious churches and Spanish colonial architecture. By city law, most buildings must be kept whitewashed, as they have been for centuries. . . . [Southeast of Sucre] the Andes drop off gradually into sloping hills and wide fertile valleys. Known as the Valles, this area is the heart of Bolivian agriculture. Most Quechua in Bolivia live on the southern rim of the Altiplano and in the Valles. . . .

Rivers and narrow waterways were once the only way to travel in the Oriente—Bolivia's vast eastern lowlands. Few people lived in the resource-rich region, and trade was difficult. But in the 1950s, the government built a road connecting Santa Cruz, the Oriente's major city, with La Paz. Workers came to drill newly discovered oil deposits, and new farmlands were opened up. Santa Cruz ballooned to a population of nearly one million people by 1990, making it Bolivia's second largest city. . . .

The people of Bolivia have overcome many obstacles. Since gaining independence from Spain [in 1825], Bolivians have endured unending problems building a stable economy and government. Bolivia lost more than half its territory in wars with its neighbors. Despite the discovery of oil and natural gas deposits and improvements in transportation, Bolivia remains South America's poorest country.

Excerpt (retitled "Bolivia: Land of Diversity") from *The Children of Bolivia* by Jules Hermes. Copyright ©1996 by Jules Hermes. Reprinted by permission of **Carolrhoda Books, Inc**.

Understanding What You Read After you have finished reading the selection, answer the following questions.

1. Who are the *campesinos*? What is their ethnic make-up?

_____

2. Where are Bolivia's Valles and Oriente regions located? How does the economy of these two regions differ?

_____

_____

_____

3. How have the *compesinos* benefited from changes in Bolivia? What challenges are they still struggling to overcome?

_____

_____

_____

Activity

Consult an atlas to draw an outline map of Brazil. Then locate on your map the geographic features, cities, and regions noted in the reading. Also include Bolivia's rain forest region, called the Yungas, on your map.

Pacific South America

GOVERNMENT

The Phantom Palace

Isabel Allende is one of Chile's most famous authors. A writer of fiction that is highly critical of Latin American politics, she left Chile in 1973, following the military coup there. In this reading from a short story, she tells of a poor South American country whose leader has decided to build a splendid palace as a summer home away from the capital.

Europe consumed more coffee, cocoa, and bananas than we as a nation could produce, but all that demand was no bonanza for us; we continued to be as poor as ever. . . . The fact was that the gold flowed only into the coffers of El Benefactor . . . but there was hope that someday a little would spill over for the people. Two decades passed under this democratic totalitarianism, as the President for Life called his government. . . .

The idea of the Palace had originated [begun] with some Italian builders who had called on His Excellency bearing plans for a . . . villa . . . [with] more than thirty baths decorated with gold and silver faucets. . . .

El Benefactor was a crude man with the comportment [conduct] of a peon [peasant]; he bathed in cold water and slept on a mat on the floor with his boots on and his pistol within arm's reach; he lived on roast meat and maize [Indian corn], and drank nothing but water and coffee. . . . Nevertheless, he was forced to accept a few refinements, because he understood the need to impress diplomats and other eminent [important] visitors if they were not to carry the report abroad that he was a barbarian. He did not have a wife to mend his Spartan [plain] ways. He believed that love was a dangerous weakness. . . .

The celebration for the inauguration [grand opening] of the Summer Palace was a stellar event in the [history] of El Benefactor's government. For two days and two nights alternating orchestras played the most current dance tunes and an army of chefs prepared an unending banquet. The most beautiful mulatto women in the Caribbean, dressed in sumptuous [elegant] gowns created for the occasion, whirled through salons with officers who had never fought in a battle but whose chests were covered with medals. There was every sort of diversion [entertainment]. . . . El Benefactor did not want to know the details. After greeting his guests with a brief speech, and beginning the dancing with the most aristocratic lady present, he had returned to the capital without a farewell. Parties put him in a bad humor. . . .

The Palace was never again the scene of a bacchanal [gala celebration]. Occasionally El Benefactor went there to get away from the pressures of his duties, but his repose [rest] lasted no more than three or four days, for fear that a conspiracy might be launched in his absence. . . . The only people left . . . [there] . . . were the personnel entrusted with its maintenance. . . .

A few years later the nation was jolted by the news that the dictatorship had come to an end for a most surprising reason: El Benefactor had died. He was a . . . sack of skin and bones that for months had been decaying in life, and yet very few people imagined that he was mortal [would die]. No one remembered a time before him; he had been in power so many decades that people had become accustomed to thinking of him as an inescapable evil, like the climate. The echoes of the funeral were slow to reach the Summer Palace. By then most of the guards and servants, bored with waiting for replacements that never came, had deserted their posts. . . .

A generation later, when democracy had been established in the nation and nothing remained of the long history of dictatorship but a few pages in scholarly books, someone remembered the marble villa and proposed that they restore it and found an Academy of Art. The Congress of the Republic sent a commission to draft a report, but . . . no one could tell them where the Summer Palace was. . . . The jungle had erased all traces. . . .

Now a highway has been constructed that links [the region] to the rest of the country. Travelers say that sometimes after a storm, when the air is damp and charged with electricity, a white marble palace suddenly rises up beside the road, hovers for a few brief moments in the air, like a mirage, and then noiselessly disappears.

From "Phantom Palace" from *The Stories of Eva Luna* by Isabel Allende translated by Margaret Sayers Peden. Copyright ©1989 by Isabel Allende; English translation copyright ©1991 by **Macmillan, a division of Simon and Schuster**. Reprinted by permission of the publisher.

Understanding What You Read After you have finished reading the selection, answer the following questions.

1. Why are the people of the country in this story so poor? What form of government does this country have during most of this story?

_____

_____

2. Why has El Benefactor decided to build a luxurious Summer Palace?

_____

3. Why did Allende nickname her character "El Benefactor" (the helper)? What point is she making about South American dictators in this story?

_____

_____

_____

Activity

Imagine you are a citizen of the country in this story. Write a letter to the editor of U.S. newspaper expressing your opinion of your president and his palace. Explain why you hold this opinion.

Pacific South America

ECONOMY

Living in the Land of Fire

Sergio Santelices is a rancher in the rugged Magallanes, a region in southern Chile. The region is named after the Strait of Magellan. This narrow body of water at the tip of South America passes between the island of Tierra del Fuego and the mainland, linking the Atlantic and Pacific oceans. Across the strait from Tierra del Fuego is the port town of Punta Arenas. Santelices' ranch is nearby. Here he describes the ranch, the region's development, and his life in this isolated part of his country.

Punta Arenas was founded in 1848, by a Chilean army officer. The first Europeans arrived twenty years later. They decided to try stock farming, and the first three hundred sheep were brought from the Falkland Islands. The area had previously been inhabited only by nomadic Indians, who lived by fishing and hunting guanacos, animals related to the llama.

By the beginning of this century [1900s], the wool industry was well developed. Huge *estancias* (ranches) were established and leased by the State [Chile's government] to private farmers. These have since been divided into smaller *estancias*, which are much easier to maintain.

I came to own my *estancia* after the last big distribution of land, in 1978. *Estancias* of 5,000 hectares (12,355 acres), with 5,000 sheep, were offered for sale. Applicants were required to be from the region and to have cattle-ranching experience. I was able to meet these requirements, and so bought my farm.

In Magallanes, it is commonly accepted that 5,000 is a sufficient number of animals to provide a farmer with a living. The sale of the meat pays for the running of the farm, and the wool pays for living expenses.

The climate in this part of the world is very harsh. Winters are cold and summers are very windy. I prefer the winter, when the cold is easier to cope with—the constant sound of wind in summer drives me crazy! But although the climate is harsh for humans, it isn't for sheep. Good quality grass which is resistant to cold and wind allows our animals to produce very high quality wool. Our main buyers come from England, France, and Italy.

Traditionally, we have always bred sheep in Magallanes, but during the sixties, people started breeding cattle. I have 630 head of cattle, which I sell at Santiago [Chile's capital city]. The 3,000 kilometer (1,800 mile) journey by truck through Argentina takes between seven and ten days. But a transport ship now operates from Punta Arenas to Puerto Montt, taking only two days. From there to Santiago, the journey is only 1,000 kilometers (621 miles) on good roads.

The sheep-shearing season is from December to February, when farmers contract [hire] shearers to do the work. They are skilled and do their job very fast. A good shearer takes two minutes to shear a sheep. Groups of twenty-six men will shear 1,200 to 1,300 animals in a day. At my *estancia,* the work takes five or six days. The rest of the year I work the *estancia* with only two workers. The wool is usually sold unwashed in bales to independent buyers who travel around the region buying wool.

Soon we will have to move to the city so that our children can go to secondary school [high school]. Although I love living in the country, I suppose that I will soon get used to traveling to my *estancia* from Punta Arenas, two or three times a week.

From "'The Wind Drives Me Crazy'" (retitled "Living in the Land of Fire") from *We Live in Chile* by Alex Huber from *Living Here* series. Copyright © 1985 by **Wayland Publishers Ltd**. Reprinted by permission of the publisher.

Understanding What You Read
After you have finished reading the selection, answer the following questions.

1. What is the main economic activity in extreme southern Chile?

_____

2. What natural resource is present in the Magallanes that allows sheep to be raised profitably there? Explain why this is so.

_____

_____

3. Identify four pieces of information that suggest Magallanes is a remote area and that life there is an isolated existence?

_____

_____

Activity
Imagine that you are one of Santelices' children. Write a entry for your diary describing the typical day on your estancia.

READING 28

Southern Europe

The Community of the Greeks

Nearly all the people who live in Greece are ethnic Greeks and are of the Greek Orthodox faith. Their common religion, language, and cultural heritage tend to make Greeks feel as one people. This unity can be seen in Greeks' relationships with others, both within and outside of their families.

The basic household in Greece consists of the husband, wife, unmarried children and, quite often, the grandparents. In the cities it is also common to have other relatives living in the same household. Unmarried adult children rarely live outside their parents' home and, in some regions, it is customary for married children to reside with parents until they have established their own households.

Traditionally, a rural newlywed couple will return to the home of the groom's parents or to a residence provided for them in the village. This extended family living arrangement may continue indefinitely, especially when labor is needed for the family farm. On some of the islands, it is the custom for the married couple to live in the wife's village and often, it is her family that will provide the home as part of the dowry [the gift from the bride's family that is traditional in some cultures].

Family members in Greek homes have established roles; all work together to preserve the family property. In poorer families which have no property, the sons contribute their wages. The child's duty is to share his or her home with the parents for as long as they live. As a result, few senior citizens live alone in Greece and fewer reside in old folks' homes.

Relationships between families that are not related are often created by the selection of a *koumbaros* ("koom-BAH-ros"). This individual is the godparent at a baptism or a sponsor at a wedding. The *koumbaros* is like a member of the family in this spiritual kinship. Often the sponsor of the wedding couple will be the godparent of the couple's first child. Though it is an artificially created kinship, religious law prohibits marriage between godchildren and children of a *koumbaros* because the relationship between the family and the godparent represents such an important family linkage.

Greeks not only maintain close times with an extended family of parents, godparents, uncles and aunts, but they also feel a strong obligation to their native village, district or province. When meeting fellow Greeks, people will try to determine whether they come from the same region or if they have any relatives that stay in that region. This way, Greeks will create a type of kinship with non-relatives when they are away from home. This devotion to one's home is called *patrida*.

Because Greeks are intensely loyal to their family, they often feel that the world of non-relatives is a hostile place, and that they will not get fair treatment from non-family members, especially government officials. This widespread belief has created a heavy reliance on patrons. A network of patrons bypasses "red tape" and allows the client to achieve his goals. It is a clear give-and-take relationship which serves both the patron and the client equally. For example, in addition to pledging loyalty and political support, a fisherman can offer a weekly fresh catch to the patron in return for a favor such as obtaining a passport. An artificial kinship is created via this process, and a lifetime relationship is established.

Greek hospitality, or *philoxenia*, is part of a long tradition. Some say it began in [ancient] times as a sacred duty; others feel that the cruelty of the land itself caused Greeks to accept with open arms any soul that has been at the mercy of the terrain [land]. Whatever its origin, it is clear that the stranger benefits from the respect the Greeks have for the wants and needs of others. The Greeks judge themselves by the extent of their hospitality. Should they fail in their duty to put their guests' needs before their own, it is considered a black mark against their ancestors and community as a whole.

From "Lifestyle" (retitled "The Community of the Greeks") from *Greece* by Jill DuBois from *Cultures of the World* series. Copyright ©1992 by **Times Editions Pte Ltd**. Reprinted by permission of the publisher.

Understanding What You Read After you have finished reading the selection, answer the following questions.

1. What responsibility do adult Greek children have to their parents?

_____

2. What is the difference in the roles a *koumbaros* and a patron play in Greek families?

_____

_____

3. How do *patrida* and *philoxenia* maintain the closeness and unity of Greek society?

_____

_____

Activity

Write a letter to a Greek teen explaining how ideas about family and community in American society differ from those in Greece.

READING 29

Southern Europe

The Geography of Ancient Rome

According to ancient legend, Italy's capital city of Rome was founded by the mythical figure Romulus—half human and half god—in 753 B.C. The early city occupied several hills along the Tiber River about 15 miles from the Mediterranean coast. From this modest beginning, Rome eventually became the center of one of the world's greatest empires. One of the most famous Romans during that time was the statesman and philosopher Marcus Tullius Cicero, who lived in the first century B.C. In this reading, Cicero explains the importance of ancient Rome's geography to the city's success.

The location [Romulus] chose for the city . . . was unbelievably favorable. For he did not move his city down the coast . . . or [found] a city at the mouth of the Tiber. . . . But with singular foresight Romulus saw and divined [realized] that a location upon the seaboard was not the most advantageous for cities intended to enjoy permanence and imperial sway [influence over the region], chiefly because maritime [coastal] cities are exposed to dangers both numerous and impossible to foresee. A city surrounded on all sides by land receives many warnings of an enemy's approach . . . such as the crashing [of the forest] and even the noise [of marching troops]. No enemy, if fact, can arrive by land without enabling us to know both his hostile intent and who he is and whence he comes. On the contrary, an enemy who comes by ships over the sea may arrive before anyone can suspect his coming; and indeed, when he appears, he does not show by any signs who he is, whence [from where] he comes, or even what he wants. . . .

In addition, cities located on the sea are subject to certain corrupting influences and to moral decline, for they are affected by alien [foreign] forms of speech and by alien standards of conduct. Not only foreign merchandise is imported but also foreign codes of morals, with the result that nothing in the ancestral customs of a maritime people can remain unchanged. The inhabitants of the seaboard do not remain at home but are tempted far from their cities by the hope and dream of swiftly gained wealth. . . .

How, then, could Romulus with a more divine insight have made use of the advantages of a situation on the sea, while avoiding its disadvantages, than by placing his city on the banks of a river that flows throughout the year with an even current and empties into the sea through a wide mouth? Thus, the city could receive by sea the products it needed and also dispose of its superfluous [unneeded] commodities [goods]. By the river the city could bring up from the sea the necessaries of a civilized life as well as bring them down from the interior. Accordingly, it seems to me that even then Romulus foresaw that this city would sometime be the seat and home of supreme dominion [government]. For practically no other city situated in any other part of Italy could have been better able to command such economic advantages.

Is there, moreover, any one so unobservant as not to have marked and clearly appraised [evaluated] the natural defenses of our city? Romulus and the other kings planned the extent and location of the city's wall with such wisdom that it followed everywhere the brink of the high steep hills; that the only access. . . was blocked by a great rampart [fortification] and girt [encircled] with a deep ditch; and that the citadel, thus fortified, rose from an ascent steep on every side and above a precipitous [steep] cliff. As a result, even at the terrible time when the Gauls [a people of ancient France] attacked us, the citadel remained safe and uncaptured. In addition, the location which he chose is plentifully watered with streams; and although in an unhealthful region, the site is healthful because of the hills, which are themselves cooled by the breezes and which also give shade to the valleys.

From *On the Commonwealth: Marcus Tullius Cicero*, translated by George Holland Sabine and Stanley Barney Smith. Ohio State University Press, 1929.

Understanding What You Read After you have finished reading the selection, answer the following questions.

1. For what reasons did Cicero think Romulus wise for locating Rome on the Tiber River instead of the Mediterranean coast?

_____

_____

2. Why did Rome's location give it an advantage over potential enemies?

_____

_____

Activity

Using the reading as a guide, create a sketch of the early city, showing its natural and man-made defenses.

Southern Europe

ECONOMY

A Farmer's Life in Spain

Joseph Solé owns a farm in far northeastern Spain, near the French border and about twenty miles from the Mediterranean Coast. Here he tells about the agricultural economy of the region, and how farming has changed over the years.

My farm is in Cataluña [Catalonia] in the northeast of Spain. Farms are very much affected by their location. Spain is a big country and the geographical, climatic and cultural conditions vary enormously from one region to another. In provinces such as Galicia, which is very poor, you have *minifundios*, tiny landholdings, which are really too small to make a profit. In provinces such as Andalucia and Castilla, there are huge estates called *latifundios*, where half the land is owned by a tiny minority of the farmers. These *latifundios* mean that the vast majority of farmers are, in fact, farm laborers. They don't own the land and only work in the olive-picking and harvesting season. So, although there are a very few rich landowners, the region is poor and underdeveloped. Both the *minifundios* and the *latifundios* have brought unemployment, and many people have moved to the richer provinces of Spain and to Europe.

I'm perhaps a typical Catalan farmer, with a medium-size farm of 100 hectares (250 acres). Up until a few years ago, my farm was worked in the traditional Catalan way. It was divided into *masoverias* (tenant farms), each of about 15 hectares (37 acres). The rent for these farms is normally paid in kind—that is to say the crop is divided so one third goes to the owner and the tenant keeps the rest. The decision on what crop to sow is usually taken jointly, because both want a profitable harvest.

My main crop is wheat, which is the main [grain] crop in Spain as a whole. Small crops of barley, oats and maize [corn] are grown, and we have to import these cereals [grains] to cover our needs. The central region of Spain—*la Mancha*—is the biggest producer of cereals. Like most farmers, I sell my cereals through the state [government] organization, which offers a guaranteed price. It is not obligatory [required], but it is easier to use this system. The guaranteed price is, in my opinion, very low, and as we hardly receive any subsidies [government financial aid], it is very difficult to make ends meet. This has hit the small *masover* [tenant farmer] the hardest. Of the five *masovers* I had a few years ago, I have only one left and he will be leaving shortly. The land is not profitable any more and everyone is leaving to work in industry.

. . . I have had to reorganize my farm in view of these changes. I decided to specialize in cereals rather than cattle, which require more manpower. I sow these crops on half my land, and turn the remaining half over to forestry. I plant fast-growing trees such as the plane, which takes about twenty years to grow, rather than the pine, which takes between eighty and a hundred years to grow. Pine is used for making furniture and you can get a good price for it, but it doesn't compensate [make up] for having to wait eighty years to receive your money! I sell timber direct to the sawmills, and from there it goes to make paper, laminates for furniture, or wooden boxes for use in industry. I've also invested in modern machinery, which means that the farm can basically be worked by one man—except when I rent a combine harvester for three days at harvest time.

As is the tradition, my eldest son will inherit the farm and work it by himself. In fact . . . most of the work is done by him already. My two other children have received a university education to give them a good start in other careers.

From "It's difficult to make ends meet" (retitled "A Farmer's Life in Spain") from *We Live in Spain* by Richard Bristow from *Living Here* series. Copyright ©1982 by **Wayland Publishers Ltd**. Reprinted by permission of the publisher.

Understanding What You Read After you have finished reading the selection, answer the following questions

1. In what way does landholding vary from region to region in rural Spain?

_____

2. How do the *minifundio* and *latifundio* systems each help keep rural Spaniards poor?

_____

_____

3. What was the traditional way a Catalan farmer worked his land? How and why has that system changed in recent years?

_____

_____

Activity

Imagine that you are living in rural Spain. Write a letter to a relative explaining why you are leaving home to live in the city.

West-Central Europe

READING 31

France's Unsettled Immigrants

Like the United States, France has attracted millions of immigrants to its shores in recent years. In France for Bastille Day—the French equivalent of the Fourth of July—an U.S. journalist examines French multiculturalism.

Pick any dozen Frenchmen and one will be a foreigner. Pick any twenty and one will be a Muslim. Go to the great Mediterranean port of Marseille and pick any six. One will be *Arabe*.

These numbers . . . have in recent years tested France's long tradition of accommodating foreigners. Marseille, after all, was settled by foreigners: Anatolian Greeks some 25 centuries ago settled there and called it Massilia. They may have chosen a site occupied earlier by Phoenicians. . . .

After the 1789 Revolution the young French republic became known as a "land of asylum [refuge]." Today it shelters 140,000 political refugees: Vietnamese, Chileans, Iranians, Poles, Palestinians. After both World Wars, workers flowed in from Italy and Spain and Portugal to help rebuild, and share in, France's prosperity. They blended in; perhaps 750,000 Portuguese remain.

Then came the revolts in [Vietnam] and Algeria and the ending of France's empire. French colonials came home, many of them bitter. After them came thousands upon thousands of former colonial subjects in search of work—perhaps a million and a half from Algeria, Morocco, and Tunisia alone. They were welcomed at first, since France had a labor shortage. The labor shortage evaporated, but the population of Muslims in France continued to grow.

Marseille is the clank and drone of cranes and conveyors, the hum of pipelines, and the curses of longshoremen in a dozen languages along 40 miles of modern docks and yards that dominate commercial shipping in the Mediterranean. . . . Marseille is [also] the gateway for the Arab influx. Some of the immigrants entered illegally. Many more were legal but have remained strangers to almost all aspects of French society. Yet others have become fully acclimated and find themselves strangers to their North African or Islamic heritages. Who is then a foreigner and who French?

. . . She wore her hood of bouncing curls over a chic leather jacket, designer jeans, and red heels. And when Malika Chafi spoke, her dark Arab eyes danced to the beat of her rapid-fire French. "My father has lived here 50 years," Malika said. "He fought in the French army against the Germans, then he spent all of his working life here in the dockyards. . . . I was born here. I can have French nationality. But still I keep my Algerian passport. Sometimes I feel like that white ferryboat, sailing the blue sea in between."

"Each of those ferryboats brings another 800 problems into the country," complained a journalist acquaintance when we talked about France's immigrants. The conversation was disquieting [disturbing]. Jean-Paul was an educated man, well traveled, articulate [fluent] in French and English. Yet he was convinced the "foreigners" were a menace. . . .

France's ringing national anthem, "La Marseillaise," immortalizes the people of this city, and it is so named because Marseille's regiments sang it so enthusiastically during the Revolution. And on Bastille Day its people still do. Close by the reviewing stand I squeezed in among some of the darker faces that peppered the crowd. . . . Squads of young soldiers and sailors passed in smart revue followed by blue helmeted gendarmes [police officers] on motorbikes, lumbering tanks, and a convoy of polished red fire trucks. . . .

Through it all a young Algerian father next to me watched passively [without expression]. His thoughts were easy enough to divine [determine]. These proud regiments once occupied his country; one man's patriotism is often another man's tyranny. Hospitality here has done little to thaw his soul. But the toddler aloft on his shoulder enjoyed a different perspective. He wiggled his toes, chewed a croissant [a French pastry], and in his brown fist fluttered a tiny French flag.

From "Unsettled Immigrants," (retitled "France's Unsettled Immigrants") by Thomas J. Abercrombe from *National Geographic*, July 1989. Copyright ©1989 by **National Geographic Society**. Reprinted by permission of the publisher.

Understanding What You Read After you have finished reading the selection, answer the following questions.

1. In what ways did World War I and II contribute to population changes in France?

_____

_____

2. Why are many Algerians and Vietnamese living in France? For what reasons might some of them not feel strong patriotism for that nation?

_____

_____

Activity

Use the Internet and other resources to research recent developments in the immigration issue in France. Prepare a short report of your findings.

West-Central Europe

Living Behind the Wall

On November 9, 1989, the communist government of East Germany began allowing the citizens of East Berlin to travel into the free, western half of the city. For decades East Germans who tried to cross the border into West Germany or West Berlin without government permission risked being arrested or even shot. In Berlin, a high wall kept East Berliners in their part of the city. By 1989, however, communism was collapsing in Europe, and the Berlin Wall was soon torn down. In this reading, East Berliner Helga Schültz remembers the night the wall tumbled down.

It was clear to me that the Wall had to come down. . . . I knew that it wouldn't be possible to open the Wall only a little bit, for only a few people to be allowed to travel, or for only a certain number of people to be able to have a look at the other side. . . . Even so, November 9 was a tremendous surprise for me. I thought the announcement meant an easing of travel restrictions, but I expected that people would still have to apply for permission to travel and that only a small number would be granted that permission. I knew that our people would simply not be satisfied with that. The Wall had to go. But I imagined it would happen differently. I thought the Wall would disappear overnight, that they would come with hammers and wheelbarrows and take it away. It didn't happen like that of course, but the whole thing . . . . was very hard to comprehend.

I lived for eighteen years with the wall in my backyard in Großglienicke, on the border to West Berlin, and we talked about the Wall every single day of the year, how inane [stupid] it was. You could hear people on the other side talking but you would have been shot if you had tried to talk to them. When the wall was finally down, we rode our bikes over every evening with hammers and chopped away at it, trying to get it out of our sight. We would ride along the Wall, looking for a hole that was big enough to slip through. It was completely crazy. Suddenly you could walk where only weeks or days before you would have been shot.

On November 9 I came home at around midnight. . . . On the bus I heard some people saying that now everyone would be allowed to travel; they had heard it on the radio. When I got to my stop, there was a group of young people who said that they wanted to take the bus . . . to West Berlin. The driver told them to get on if they thought it would work. Then we saw the first Trabis [a type of car manufactured in East Germany] driving in the direction of the border. When I got home my son and I sat and watched TV, intoxicated with joy. We watched the entire night. The next day he told me that they were going to open the Glienicke Bridge at 6:00 P.M., so we all marched over the bridge. . . . I was with friends of my son's, and we simply floated over the bridge. It was pure joy. . . .

It was wonderful for me that it was no longer a privilege to cross the border—now everyone could cross. I had always had the feeling that our people here were being deceived; they didn't know what was really going on over there because they couldn't see it. . . . When I was in the West I felt I could do without many things that were available there: I didn't need that pair of shoes, that book. Then I got home and realized that I really did need those things. My son wanted a certain record, for example. They were little things, but because you couldn't get them they represented paradise. Now everyone could finally see this paradise themselves. . . .

I see unification as positive because I don't think there was any other way. . . . I wasn't a supporter of the so-called Third Way, the establishment of a democratic but separate East German state. . . . I didn't feel like a citizen of the German Democratic Republic [East Germany]; I felt a part of something bigger. . . . I never had the feeling that the common cultural heritage between West and East had been broken off.

From "The Wall in My Backyard" (retitled "Living Behind the Wall") by Helga Schütz from *East German Women in Transition*, translated by Dinah Dodds. Copyright ©1994 by the **University of Massachusetts Press**. Reprinted by permission of the publisher. Previously appeared as "Die Mauer stand bei mir im Garten" in *Women in German Yearbook 7: Feminist Studies in German Literature and Culture*, edited by Jeanette Clausen and Sara Friedrichsmeyer. Copyright ©1991 by the University of Nebraska Press.

Understanding What You Read After you have finished reading the selection, answer the following questions.

1. What was the announcement to which Schültz refers in the first paragraph of the reading? How did East Berliners react to the announcement?

_____

_____

2. Besides preventing escapes to West Berlin, how else does Schültz think the Berlin Wall helped the communist government keep the people of east Berlin under control?

_____

_____

Activity

Imagine that you are a young East Berliner on November 10, 1989. Write a journal entry describing your feelings and activities on the previous night.

West-Central Europe

Peril in the Alps

The Swiss Alps are among the world's most popular skiing destinations. In recent years, however, concern has arisen among government officials and environmental groups about just how much tourism the region can sustain. This reading examines the problem, its causes, and its consequences.

The people of the Alps have always reshaped their breathtaking and dangerous landscapes. But in recent years they have become more than ever the masters of the mountains, . . . razing forests for roads and ski runs and covering slopes with tourist resorts. Yet in the scramble to accommodate 100 million visitors a year in a region that ranges from southern France to Slovenia, a debate is raging over how much further man can go in extracting pleasure and profit before nature strikes back. Some say nature is already doing so. . . .

Not that life was ever without danger among these stunning peaks, which range across France, Germany, Italy, Switzerland, Liechtenstein, Austria and Slovenia. Yet since the skiing boom of the seventies, things have changed: Alpine villages, once protected by thick forests, have become more exposed. Mountain roads have changed watercourses and destabilized the slopes. The sick and diminished [smaller] forests and erosion have in turn brought more mudslides, floods and avalanches. Experts warn that such disasters are likely to increase. . . .

In every Alpine nation, environmentalists are pressing for a slowdown in the conquest of the mountains. They argue that the 40,000 ski runs, with their 12,000 lifts and cable cars, are enough, that there is no need for more revolving restaurants on mountaintops. Dozens of groups are demanding a ban on new resorts, on helicopters dropping skiers on untouched glaciers, on bulldozers. . . .

George Roth, a farmer who looks out on three stunning Swiss valleys on the heights above Leysin, says he does not mind skiers. Even in winter, Mr. Roth and his wife Josianne, get up early and milk the cows. Then they take the cable car up to 6,000 feet, where they have converted a summer stable into a skiers' cafe. They like the extra income and mingling with the visitors. But they hate "all those machines."

"Everyone wants bigger and better ski runs," said Mr. Roth, so machines flatten the runs and harden the snow, which turns to ice. The ice melts later than the snow, "so we get less grass." Mrs. Roth added, "There must be a way to ski and not destroy so much." As they spoke, two helicopters broke the . . . stillness. . . .

The Roth family owns one of the last four farms around Leysin. Twenty years ago there were 25. The story of the vanishing farmers is repeated throughout the Alps, although many governments subsidize [give assistance to] farmers to keep them on the land, to take care of trees, and guard the landscape. "If you take away the farmers, the landscape degrades even faster," said Mr. Berghold, [an environmental] advisor in Zurich. "Many chalet owners are outsiders and they don't know or care."

Furthermore, Government officials and environmentalists worry about the dwindling number of cows, seeing cattle as useful, rather than the environmental burden they are viewed as elsewhere: The cows crop grass and short grass holds snow, while long grass bends and lets the snow slide off, leading to snowslides in these steep slopes. . . .

In all Alpine countries citizens' groups have banded together to protect the mountains. Some belong to national Green [political] Parties, while others work locally, lobbying against garbage dumps or ski lifts. . . . What amazes Alpinists is how much people are willing to soil the beauty they have come to admire. The head of Alp Action, Prince Sadruddin Aga Khan, warns that tourism may yet kill tourism unless the precarious [uncertain to continue] beauty of the Alps is protected. . . .

From "Alps Caught in Vice Between Tourism and Trucks" (retitled "Peril in the Alps") by Marlise Simons from *The New York Times*, April 6, 1992. Copyright ©1992 by **The New York Times Company**. Reprinted by permission of the publisher.

Understanding What You Read After you have finished reading the selection, answer the following questions.

1. What have the people of the Alps gained from the skiing industry?

_____

2. How has skiing affected the land and environment of the Alps?

_____

_____

3. How has the decline of farming in the skiing regions increased the danger there?

_____

_____

Activity

Create a poster that the Swiss government could use in a campaign to protect the Alpine environment.

Northern Europe

Surviving in Wartime London

After the German army conquered France early in World War II, Hitler turned his attention to Great Britain. From September 1940 to June 1941, the German air force conducted a massive bombing campaign against England. About 30,000 people were killed and 120,000 injured in the nightly air raids on London alone. A U.S. diplomat in England wrote this report on life in London during what was called the Battle of Britain.

Somehow, under the stress of war, we are inclined [seem] to forget that the ordinary pursuits of life continue and, what is more, continue pretty much as in time of peace. This is especially true in England today. . . . Thousands have been killed and wounded; hundreds of millions of dollars worth of property has been destroyed; the country is bombed almost nightly, and it is faced with the ever-present threat of invasion. Yet the people manage to keep going. Government and industry continue to function. Life goes on. . . .

I remember vividly the first terrible night (September 7, 1940). More than 300 persons were killed and some 1,400 seriously wounded. The East End of London was one vast inferno. Surely, we thought, human beings cannot stand such punishment. Another night went by. Five hundred more were killed. The people stood fast. A week passed . . . . two weeks. . . . The people adjusted themselves to the nightly attacks from the skies. They resisted the impulse to flee. They obeyed the Government's injunction [order] to "stay put." . . .

Millions of them nightly go underground to seek such safety as there is from flying splinters. . . . In the daytime, however, life goes on more or less as usual. We had an extremely heavy raid one night . . . in January, 1941. . . . Bombs came shrieking down at the rate of one a minute. A number of fires were started, and a good share of the City—London's financial district—was wiped out. . . .

It was almost with dread that I opened my curtains in the morning. But there was no reason for dread, then. The sun was shining brightly. Traffic moved in Berkeley Square as usual. . . . Models and seamstresses tripped [walked] into the gown shop up the street. Large posters in a travel agency window advertised cruises to Australia. . . . The difference between that morning and the experiences of the night before is symbolic . . . of the two kinds of life that now exist in England.

One of the biggest surprises . . . has been the ability of the public utilities to take the punishment and still keep going. When I left London, late in January, every railway station was functioning more or less as in time of peace. The 20-odd bridges over the Thames were all open. Thousands of double-deck buses wound through the twisted streets just as they have done for the past thirty years. Although 150,000 people nightly crowded into the tubes [subways] to sleep, service was being maintained on all lines. The . . . taxicabs of London . . . continue to operate. They remain in the streets throughout the heaviest raids. . . .

The war has brought many changes to the social life of England. Dining out, that great ceremony of English life, has almost disappeared. People do not go out in the evening any more than they have to. It is too hard to get around in the dark streets. Besides, there is always the danger of bombs and that equally great danger—the possibility of being hit by splinters from antiaircraft shells. . . .

Many forms of evening entertainment have been pushed back into the day. Theaters and most of the cinemas close at 7 p.m. . . . Thousands of people still congregate at greyhound tracks and at soccer and rugby matches. Some of them have been machine-gunned [by German fighter planes], and some of them have been bombed, but the sporting instinct . . . has proved stronger than the menace of the Luftwaffe [German air force].

From "Everyday Life in Wartime England," (retitled "Surviving in Wartime London") by Harvey Klemmer from *National Geographic,* April 1941. Copyright ©1941 by **National Geographic Society**. Reprinted by permission of the publisher.

Understanding What You Read After you have finished reading the selection, answer the following questions.

1. How did daytime London differ from London at night during the German bombing campaign of World War II?

_____

_____

2. Identify three ways in which the lifestyle of Londoners changed due to the bombing.

_____

_____

Activity

Create a poster to boost Londoners' morale during the bombing campaign.

Northern Europe

A Dublin Adventure

Ireland is known for its writers, and one of its greatest is James Joyce (1882–1941). In this excerpt from one of his short stories, Joyce gives us a view of Ireland's largest city, Dublin, in the early 1900s. The story is about two well-to-do Irish boys who skip school for an adventure in the working-class part of town.

We walked along the North Strand Road til we came to the Vitriol Works [factory] and then turned to the right along the Wharf Road. Mahoney began to play the Indian as soon as we were out of public sight. He chased a crowd of ragged girls, brandishing his unloaded catapult [slingshot] and, when two ragged boys began, out of chivalry [protection of the girls], to fling stones at us, he proposed that we should charge them. I objected that the boys were too small, and so we walked on, the ragged troop screaming after us *"Swaddlers! Swaddlers!"* thinking that we were Protestants because Mahoney, who was dark-complexioned wore the silver badge of a cricket club in his cap. . . .

We came then near the river. We spent a long time walking about the noisy streets flanked by high stone walls, watching the workings of cranes and engines and often being shouted at for our immobility [lack of movement] by the drivers of groaning carts. It was noon when we reached the quays [docks] and, as all the labourers seemed to be eating their lunches, we bought two big currant buns and sat down to eat them on some metal piping beside the river. We pleased ourselves with the spectacle of Dublin's commerce—the barges signalled from far away by their curls of woolly smoke, the brown fishing fleet beyond Ringsend, the big white sailing vessel which was being discharged on the opposite quay. Mahoney said it would be right skit [fun] to run away to sea on one of those big ships, and even I, looking at the high masts, saw, or imagined, the geography which had been scantily dosed [taught] to me at school gradually taking substance under my eyes. School and home seemed to recede from us and their influences upon us seemed to wane [become less].

We crossed the Liffey [a river that empties into Dublin Bay] in the ferryboat. . . . When we landed we watched the discharging [leaving] of the graceful three-master which we had observed from the other quay. Some bystander said that she was a Norwegian vessel. I went to the stern and tried to decipher the legend [name] upon it but, failing to do so, I came back and examined the foreign sailors to see had any of them green eyes, for I had some confused notion . . . The sailors' eyes were blue, and grey, and even black. The only sailor whose eyes could have been called green was a tall man who amused the crowd on the quay by calling out cheerfully every time the planks fell: "All right! All right!"

When we were tired of this sight we wandered slowly into Ringsend. The day had grown sultry [hot], and in the windows of the grocers' shops musty biscuits lay bleaching. We bought some biscuits and chocolate, which we ate sedulously [eagerly] as we wandered through the squalid [run down] streets where the families of the fishermen live. We could find no dairy and so we went into a huckster's shop [retail store] and bought a bottle of raspberry lemonade each. Refreshed by this, Mahoney chased a cat down a lane, but the cat escaped into a wide field. We both felt rather tired, and when we reached the field we made at once for a sloping bank. . . .

Excerpt (retitled "A Dublin Adventure") from *Dubliners* by James Joyce. Copyright ©1914 by James Joyce. Reprinted by permission of the **Estate of James Joyce**.

Understanding What You Read After you have finished reading the selection, answer the following questions.

1. From this description of Dublin, what kinds of activities were important to the city's economy in the early 1900s?

_____

2. What evidence from the reading suggests that the two main characters in the story were in the working-class part of town?

_____

_____

3. Think about Ireland's history in the early 1900s. Why would Mahoney's cricket club badge have caused the children to think he was Protestant? What clues does this incident provide about the dominant religion in Ireland?

_____

_____

_____

Activity

Using the descriptions in the reading, create a pencil sketch of a typical street scene in Dublin in the early 1900s.

Northern Europe

The Sami of Scandinavia

Scholars disagree about the origins of the Sami people. Some believe that they migrated to Scandinavia from the Siberian region of Russia. Others theorize that they were originally an Alpine people of Central Europe. In either case, they are believed to have occupied most of Scandinavia in early times. Gradually Finnish, Norwegian, and Swedish settlement pushed the Sami north into the region they live in today.

The Samis . . . have been in Sweden since the pre-Christian age. It is believed that they came in nomadic groups from the east at various periods of time and traveled through southern Finland to eventually settle in the interior of the Finnish-Scandinavian land mass.

Today, some 40,000–50,000 Samis are found all over the entire Finnish-Scandinavian arctic region and along the mountains on both sides of the Swedish-Norwegian border. About 15,000–17,000 live in Sweden and vary in their commitment to their culture. Some identify strongly with being a separate ethnic group while others have been assimilated [mixed] into Swedish culture.

Sami children can go to a regular state-supported school or a state-run nomad school. Both types have the same aims, except the nomad schools include teaching the Sami language and culture. Those who choose to go to a regular school can still learn their language and culture at home through a special home language project. Efforts are being made to preserve and renew the language of this minority group, especially since it does not have a strong written tradition. The culture has been passed down orally, and it takes the form of *yoiking*, a kind of singing.

Reindeer breeding, once dominant, no longer holds the same significance. Only some 2,500 people are engaged in the breeding of the animals for their meat. Previously, they were bred for milk and used as beasts of burden. The importance of reindeer breeding can be seen in the way breeders are still organized, They belong to a village which is an administrative and economic unit as well as a geographic grazing area. Common facilities are planned, constructed and maintained by the village and the costs shared among its inhabitants.

Over the years, nomadism has ceased as the breeders and their families have established permanent settlements in the low fell region, where the mountain reindeer mate and have their calves. Today, only the herders follow the animals, and in keeping with modern times, they use aircraft, motor vehicles and snow scooters [snowmobiles] to do their job.

Reindeer breeding, however, is not very profitable as it requires at least a herd of 500 to earn enough to support a family. Also, the 1986 nuclear accident at Chernobyl in the USSR has had a lasting impact on the reindeer, and it will be many years before the meat will be free of cae-sium [a chemical element] and fit for consumption.

Thus, many families supplement their income through other means such as hunting, fishing, handicrafts and tourism. The last two are most evident at the winter market fairs at Jokkmokk [a Swedish city just north of the Arctic Circle]. Genuine Sami handicraft made from traditional mate-rials are found here, as well as delicacies like *lappkok*, a broth of reindeer marrow bones and shredded liver. . . .

The music of the Samis, believed to the oldest form of music in Europe, reflects their nomadic history and way of life. It is very different from Swedish and other European music. For example, the *jojk* is a sponta-neous, improvised song which recalls people or places and evokes [arous-es] emotions linked to that memory. It is intensely personal and sung with-out accompanying instruments. Musical instruments are rarely used in Sami music.

Excerpt (retitled "The Sami of Scandinavia") from *Sweden* by Delice Gan from *Cultures of the World* series. Copyright ©1992 by **Times Editions Pte Ltd**. Reprinted by permission of the publisher.

Understanding What You Read After you have finished read-ing the selection, answer the following questions.

1. In what parts of Scandinavia are the Sami people mainly found?

_____

_____

2. How have the Sami organized reindeer breeding in the regions where they live? Why has this activity become less important in recent years?

_____

_____

3. In what ways have the Sami adapted their lifestyle and culture to mod-ern Scandinavian society?

_____

_____

Activity

Imagine that you work for a Swedish government agency whose goal it is to promote tourism. Create an brochure about the Sami that will help attract tourists to Sweden.

Eastern Europe

GEOGRAPHY

The Estonian Way

Long dominated by Russia and a part of the former Soviet Union, Estonia became an independent nation in 1991. This reading describes the Estonian culture and the challenges this small nation faces in reestablishing it.

Estonia is a multicultural country. . . . The ethnic mixture of people in Estonia has changed drastically over the last 50 years, as a result of the Baltic country's incorporation into the Soviet Union and consequent Soviet migration policies. In the last five decades, Estonia has become the home of more than 100 different ethnic groups, mainly from other parts of the Soviet Union. In 1934 a census showed that 88% of the people in Estonia were ethnic Estonians. In the 1990s that figure had fallen by a quarter, while the number of Russians dramatically increased. . . . Between 1945 and 1990, approximately 1.4 million mostly Russian-speaking peoples passed through Estonia. Such a dense flow of people has had a corrosive [wearing down] effect on traditional Estonian society and has led to domestic tensions. Today, it has been estimated that a quarter of the country's residents were born outside of the country.

The population of Estonia has dropped through the 1990s. . . . This decrease is mainly the result of a halt in migration from the former Soviet Union and a drop in the birth rate. . . . Estonia has a low population density. Despite being a bigger country than, for example, Switzerland, Estonia has only one quarter of the population.

Estonians are a Finno-Ugric people, one among an ethno-linguistic group that includes the Finns, Lapps, and Hungarians. They first arrived in Estonia around 6000 B.C., having journeyed across the Asian landmass from the marshes of Siberia. Estonians are not related to their Baltic neighbors, the Latvians and Lithuanians, who are Indo-European peoples. Ethnically and culturally, Estonians are close cousins to Finns and have more in common with them than with the other Baltic peoples. Estonians feel themselves to be Scandinavian and not at all linked to Slavic peoples.

Estonians are traditionally a rural people. In Estonia today, the rural areas are totally dominated by native Estonians, many of whom still pursue the traditional vocations of farming, forestry, and fishing. . . . The ethnic minorities tend to predominate in the industrial towns and cities. . . .

Estonians are typical northern Europeans in that they are extremely individualistic and love solitude. . . . This explains the popularity of country homes: in the summer, most Estonians like to retreat to their country homes for as long as possible. . . . Visitors find Estonians cool and reserved . . . and say they have mastered the art of being polite without being friendly. The Slavic peoples, especially the Russians, tend to be more expansive and openly affectionate, offering hugs to each other when meeting.

Estonians shy away from open displays of affection. . . . Friendship is highly prized and not easily proffered [extended].

. . . For Estonians, ethnic identity is the essence of their nationhood. Domination by foreign powers is most apparent in the architecture of the country, which is mainly German, Swedish, and Russian in character. Many Estonian institutions were also introduced by these conquerors. Consequently, Estonians have retained a sense of themselves through their traditions, language, and lifestyle. As a part of the Soviet Union, Estonians were not allowed to express their separateness or celebrate their culture and were instead encouraged to adhere [follow] to the Communist Party ideal of the Soviet citizen. . . . As a result of nationalistic feeling, Estonians have turned resolutely toward the West to find a new lifestyle and sense of purpose; one not dominated by Russia and communist ideology [beliefs].

Excerpt (retitled "The Estonian Way") from *Estonia* by Michael Spilling from *Cultures of the World* series. Copyright ©1999 by **Times Editions Pte Ltd**. Reprinted by permission of the publisher.

Understanding What You Read After you have finished reading the selection, answer the following questions.

1. How are Estonians different from their Baltic neighbors, the Latvians and Lithuanians?

_____

_____

2. What factors in its history have made Estonia a multicultural nation? What effect do you think this might have on Estonian nationalism?

_____

_____

3. How does nationality and ethnicity affect settlement patterns in Estonia? What Estonian character traits contribute to this division?

_____

_____

Activity

Create a poster that celebrates either Estonia's multiculturalism or Estonian nationalism.

READING 38 — Eastern Europe

Czechoslovakia: The Velvet Divorce

On January 1, 1993, Czechoslovakia formally divided into two nations—the Czech Republic and the Republic of Slovakia. A journalist present for the event describes how Czechs and Slovaks feel about the split.

In the chill waning hour of 1992, the winding back streets of Bratislava were dim and strangely quiet on this momentous evening. At midnight Bratislava would become the capital of Europe's newest small nation, the Slovak Republic. . . . I drifted with the gathering crowd toward Slovak National Uprising Square. . . .

Shortly before midnight the crowds parted for a platoon of goose-stepping Slovak soldiers bearing the new white-blue-and-red striped flag emblazoned with the Slovak cross. Fireworks banged and skyrockets swooshed to light the sky with bursts of color.

Then church bells and the boom of a distant cannon marked the birth of a new year—and a new country. The republic's prime minister, Vladimír Mečiar, mounted a small stage. "Skovakia is yours!" he shouted, as the jubilant crowd of some 50,000 cheered approval. . . .

Not all Czechs and Slovaks reacted so enthusiastically to the dissolution [break up] of their country, I learned during my visits there before and after the split. "We're a sovereign nation now—for better of worse," a Slovak friend said, with a shrug. "At least the parting was peaceful; that's something."

Czechs and Slovaks are products of the same central European geography and similar in language and culture. "The nation was cobbled together after World War I from provinces of the defeated Austro-Hungarian Empire," explained Martin Bútora, a Slovak sociologist who teaches in the Czech capital, Prague. "Slovakia had been occupied by Hungarians for a thousand years. The Czechs were influenced more by Austria and the West."

Recently they rejoiced in the same victory over 41 years of communist rule, a nonviolent triumph led by intellectuals from both lands: the 1989 Velvet Revolution. Barely two years later, they had sued for a "velvet divorce."

"The split is mad," an economist told me in Prague. "All of Europe is straining for unity, and we're dividing ourselves in two. Slovakia, smaller, less developed, will suffer the most."

A Bratislava psychologist disagreed. "The Czech population is ten million, twice that of Slovakia; the Czechs are richer, more industrialized— and they have always lorded this over us. It is time to step out of Prague's shadow," he insisted. "Let them go," said a Czech bookseller. "It will avoid bloodshed. Look what happened to our neighbors in Yugoslavia."

Many in both regions of Czechoslovakia prepared for the split in advance. A young Slovak I met at Charles University had already applied for her Czech passport—one of some 40,000 to do so before the separation. "Prague is where the future will happen," she said. . . .

And what of the future? Taking the long view, some political leaders are not surprised by the split-up of Czechoslovakia; look at the once united Sweden and Norway, they say. Like them, the new republics share many common interests and a powerful ancient kinship that augers [promises] close alliance even under separate flags.

In any event, other fracturing nations can only envy the ease of the Czechs and Slovaks in coping with history's caprice [unpredictable turns]. "Look, I was born in Austria-Hungary," said . . . a man in his 80s. "I grew up in Czechoslovakia, suffered from Germans, spent 40 years in a colony of Russia—without ever leaving Prague. Now we're Czechs again, like we've been for a thousand years. What's so bad about that?"

From "The Velvet Divorce," (retitled "Czechoslovakia: The Velvet Divorce") by Thomas J. Abercrombie from *National Geographic*, September 1993. Copyright ©1993 by **National Geographic Society**. Reprinted by permission of the publisher.

Understanding What You Read After you have finished reading the selection, answer the following questions.

1. Why is Czechoslovakia's overthrow of communism known as the Velvet Revolution? Why was its division called the "velvet divorce"?

_____

_____

2. To what situation was the Czech bookseller referring in his remarks to the author?

_____

3. What is the likelihood that the Czech Republic and Slovakia will exist as peaceful and friendly neighbors? Explain why.

_____

_____

Activity

Imagine that you work for a Slovak newspaper. Write an editorial or create an editorial cartoon expressing your position on dividing Czechoslovakia.

Eastern Europe

The Shepherds of Transylvania

The plains of Transylvania, a region of central Romania are dotted with rural villages. More isolated communities, concealed by pine and oak forests, are scattered in the foothills of the nearby Transylvanian Alps. One of these villages is Poiana Sibiului, elevation 2,850 feet, whose only approach is a long, steep climb through hilly terrain. Here the villagers pursue the same lifestyle and occupations that their ancestors have for centuries.

Of the 800 families in Poiana Sibiului, four-fifths own sheep herds, ranging from 200 to more than 3,000 animals. Some of the smaller herds (200 to 400 sheep) move about on the nearby plains all year round. . . . The larger herds must travel farther. Many Poianar shepherds travel three to four hundred miles each year. In the summertime they go to specific mountain ranges in northern and western Transylvania, while to pass the winter months they move long distances, westward . . . and eastward as far as . . . the meadows of the Danube [River] flood plain east of Bucharest [the capital of Romania]. Like other shepherds in Transylvania, the Poianars reach these pastures along a series of "sheep roads," many of which have been in use since at least the eighteenth century. . . .

A shepherd starts his journey to his winter grazing area toward the end of September, when the mountain pastures are depleted [used up]. Traveling on foot, shepherds go across mountains and through valleys, following water courses to the warmer plains. Aaron Banu and his uncle have traveled the same route for the past ten years. They walk 250 miles, passing through forty-seven villages.

Shepherds with small herds often travel together. Donkeys and horses transport their blankets, food, and other necessities. While the trip can take anywhere from three weeks to two months, the shepherds are never in a hurry, as long as they are able to feed the herd en route. The winter shelters are, at best, makeshift lean-tos of wood and tar paper. The shepherds build them themselves and return to them each year. Life is generally lived outdoors; at night, near a roaring fire, the shepherds enjoy a few moments of refreshment with a pot of soup and *mamaliga* (cornmeal mush).

In the winter months, finding sufficient food for the herds becomes difficult. . . . In February and March, as the ewes' five-month gestation period [pregnancy] nears its end, they need more than the stubs of old grass that stick through the snow and must be fed an extra ration [serving] of [purchased] corn. . . . As soon as the lambs are strong enough to walk long distances, which may be within a month of birth, they are started on their journey to the summer sheepfolds, where milking and cheesemaking take place. . . .

Sometimes there is a stopover at the village, for shearing, if it is on the way to the summer pastures; otherwise shearing takes place at the summer sheepfold. At Poiana Sibiului, local gypsies are hired to do the shearing. . . . The piles of wool are set aside until the heat of the summer for washing in the rushing streams above the village. Much of the spinning is done at the village mill . . . run by the grandson of a wealthy shepherd.

Spring and summer are the busiest seasons for the whole family, both at the sheepfolds and at the village. . . . By mid-May the women—and a month later the children, when school is out—travel 150 to 200 miles to the sheepfold in a jeep or truck. There they help the men with the milking and cheese making, which go on about four and one-half months while back at the village the grandparents care for the hay and the small potato patches that many families own. Hired shepherds and cheese makers are sometimes employed, especially while the shepherds are busy in the village, processing and marketing the wool. . . . People who are too old to withstand the hardships [of herding] and who have no sons or close male relatives rely on hired shepherds throughout the year.

From "Shepherds of Transylvania," (retitled "The Shepherds of Transylvania") by Ayse Gürsan-Salzmann from *Natural History*, July 1984. Copyright ©1984 by **American Museum of Natural History**. Reprinted by permission of the publisher.

Understanding What You Read After you have finished reading the selection, answer the following questions.

1. What types of products do Poiana Sibiului's sheep provide in the village's economy?

_____

2. Why must the Poianar shepherds spend so much time away from home?

_____

_____

3. What contribution do the women and children make in its economy?

_____

_____

Activity

Create a diagram that illustrates the yearly cycle of the Poianar shepherds. Indicate the activities that take place and fill in the months where possible.

READING 40

Russia

A Russian Student Speaks

Nineteen-year-old Ilya is a student at Moscow State University. In this interview he recalls the 1991 coup in which communist conservatives, backed by elements of the army, tried to overthrow Communist Party leader Mikhail Gorbachev in order to stop his reforms of communism. Ilya also describes Russian life and government in the 1990s, after the collapse of communism and the Soviet Union.

During the coup in August we were at the dacha [summer house]. The night before the coup. . . . I was in bad spirits. All of my optimism had left me, and . . . I was saying how terrible things were, how awful it all was. In the morning our friend had to leave early to get to work, and he woke us up. So I said, "Seryozha, really, why are you doing this? Why did you have to wake us up so early?" And he said, "Listen, do you remember what we were talking about last night? Well, they've gotten rid of Gorbachev!" And I said, "Stop joking, it's not April Fool's Day!" But then we turned on the television and saw that it was true. . . . At the same time I had the feeling that none of it was very serious. During the first hours of the coup I thought, "This can't last for long."

So . . . I went into Moscow from the dacha and in the subway I saw leaflets with [Boris] Yeltsin's [president of the Soviet Union] call to resist— they were stuck on the walls with wheat paste. . . . But people weren't really all that upset. In the bus I even heard some people saying, well, that's what they needed to do with Gorbachev! . . . They were saying that some soldiers were on Yeltsin's side, but it was hard to figure out what was going on.

About the Soviet Union breaking up, I suppose that on the one hand it sounds bad—after all, Europe is uniting and here we are, splitting up. . . . Well I think the breakup is natural. The hope that something would change had already passed. . . .

It seems to me that the best thing a person who supports this government can do at the moment is simply to endure a while longer. . . . to just wait it out, have faith that something better will come. There are times, of course, situations, in which one wants to get out there and take a stand to support this government. . . . But even that's gotten more difficult now, because the reforms are not really popular at the moment. It's not so much that people are against the reforms as they are simply against the high prices! . . . All the effort it takes to feed yourself, well, everybody has really grown tired. It's true that people are eating less than before. I can say that from my own experience. Little by little you get used to less. Somewhere along the way the standard became a different one. But all these things will pass.

As far as freedom is concerned, at least I can say that I am not limited in any way by anything. And as far as political parties, please! There are about eight hundred of them now in Russia. And some are important. I think our political life is going well enough. There are lots of newspapers, things like that. But of course there are economic problems, and full political freedom has an effect on the economic situation. Now there's been a wave of strikes—miners, doctors, teachers, and so on. . . .

Three years ago I was full of hope. I think I didn't understand the difference between glasnost—freedom of speech—and freedom in general. Freedom in general happened after the coup, without a doubt. Up to that moment things were still very much under the control of the Communist Party, which was preventing the reforms from being carried out. I started saying that things were fine here too early, before they really were. But I'm not a pessimist now.

From The *"Children of Perestroika" Come of Age*, by Deborah Adelman (M.E. Sharpe, 1994).

Understanding What You Read After you have finished reading the selection, answer the following questions.

1. What evidence does Ilya present to suggest that not all Russians go along with that nation's move away from a communist economic system?

_____

_____

2. What does Ilya mean when he states that he did not understand the difference between *glasnost* and "freedom."

_____

3. Do you agree with Ilya's optimism about the future of Russia? Explain why or why not.

_____

_____

Activity

Use library and other resources to learn more about the 1991 coup and its aftermath. Then write a news story about the event.

READING 41

Russia

ECONOMY

Moscow: A New Revolution

The collapse of communism in Russia in the early 1990s has brought great change to that nation. Perhaps the greatest change has been to Moscow, its capital and once the capital of the former Soviet Union. Here, a frequent visitor to Moscow describes some of the ways in which the city has changed.

To visit Moscow . . . since the collapse of communism and the Soviet state is to be thunderstruck on a daily basis. . . . Youth gangs form, recapitulating [repeating] . . . the history of young people in the West— Hippies, Punks, Grungers, Skinheads, Metal Heads, Tolkienites; . . . a 19th-century downtown apartment building is cleaned out [of its residents] by mafiosi [mobsters] who have decided "to privatize" the place. . . . The changes reach to the most basic stuff of everyday life. Lines are rare now, but there are more homeless living in underpasses, train stations, city parks. . . .

Not long ago, on one of many trips to Moscow since the Soviet collapse, I met a woman named Larissa Pavlova. She was a teacher who now sold old clothes evenings and weekends to supplement her family's income. Countless thousands of Muscovites work second and third jobs to get by in a world of higher prices, greater appetites, and disappearing social guarantees. "Moscow is filled with what our good Comrade Lenin called contradictions," she said. "The rich get richer and the rest of us tread water or drown. I work much harder than I did in the old days, and sometimes that makes it hard to remember what we've gained. Freedom is sweet, but it's also a heavy, heavy load."

The rules of class and privilege in Moscow are approaching the draconian [extremely harsh] code of the industrialized West. Money talks. . . . If you have cash (or a credit card) in Moscow, you can taste it all: lobsters flown in from Maine, salmon from Scotland, caviar from Azerbaijan, lamb from Auckland, pineapple from Hawaii. Visitors to Moscow in the seventies remember well the dreary ritual of eating at restaurants offering shoelike "cutlets" and bonelike "chicken tabaca." Now there is every cuisine imaginable. . . .

There are other cities in Russia that have, each in its own way, joined this process of transformation . . . but the center of it all is still Moscow. There really is no second place. Even St. Petersburg, with its historical role as [Russia's] window on the West, cannot compare. More than 60 percent of foreign investment in Russia is in Moscow. The banks, the businesses, the political actors, the cultural and intellectual institutions, the information and communications nexus [connections], the trends in fashion, language, and culture—all of it is centered in the capital. . . . "You cannot understand Russia just by understanding Moscow," the reform politician Grigory Yavlinsky told me, "but without understanding Moscow you can't understand the future." . . .

If you have money in Moscow, you might live in a gated mansion outside town and send your kids to boarding school in the Alps; you also might meet your end in a contract hit, blown to smithereens by a bomb ignited by state-of -the-art remote control. . . . If you have money in Moscow, you might slap down several thousand dollars to join a private club; the highlight of the evening at one now defunct [no longer open] establishment was a rat race, featuring real rats sprinting though a neon-lit maze. (The race did not begin until a dwarf dressed as an 18th-century page rang the bell.) The owner of a nightclub called the Silver Century is planning to open a new club near Lubyanka Square within firing distance of the old KGB (former Soviet secret police) headquarters. He has announced a . . . desire to have party games. He said he would like to hold mock arrests and serve dishes like "Brains of the enemy of the people." Outside one club I talked to a guard named Vasha, a wiry and ancient man, who told me, "When I was a boy, we used to hunt down rich people and jail them. Now we guard them. For money."

From "Moscow: The New Revolution," by David Remnick from *National Geographic,* April 1997. Copyright ©1997 by National Geographic Society. Reprinted by permission of National Geographic Society.

Understanding What You Read
After you have finished reading the selection, answer the following questions.

1. According to the reading, how are most Muscovites adjusting to the change from a communist economic system to a capitalist one?

_____

_____

2. The author writes of "rules of class and privilege" that are developing in Moscow. What does he mean by this, and how are these "rules" affecting the city and its people?

_____

_____

Activity
Imagine that you are a citizen of Moscow. Write a letter to the editor of a local newspaper expressing your feelings about how Moscow is changing.

READING 42 Russia

Russia in Transition

To investigate how the change from communism to capitalism is affecting Russians' everyday lives, a journalist traveled the Trans-Siberian Railroad. As the world's longest railroad line, it is a nearly 6,000 mile journey across the vast interior of Russia. Here is part of what he found.

Traveling across Russia on the Trans-Siberian Railroad is a journey of epic proportions. It is also a good way to judge the mood of the people. . . . While some Russians, particularly in the cities, are adjusting to the new capitalist order, many more, stripped of the security that was a hallmark [characteristic] of the Soviet system, are angry and bewildered.

Experts say at least 6.4 million people are out of work; millions more don't receive salaries for months at a time. Nothing symbolizes the present reality—the need for self-reliance—more than the vegetable gardens I saw from my [railroad car] window. Especially now, a thriving garden often means the difference between a full stomach and a growling one. . . .

Some 2,000 miles out of Moscow. . . . I decided to make Novosibirsk my first stop because it is Siberia's largest city, with 1.4 million people, and the hub of commerce throughout the region. Even a brief visit made it plain that . . . economic reforms have left this city reeling. State orders for military goods and farm machinery have plummeted [fallen], and new production is stymied [prevented] because factories across the nation confront a tangle of unpaid debts.

The giants of the city's military-industrial complex—including the Chkalov Industrial Aviation Factory, which made fighter planes, and SibSelMash, which once produced military vehicles and now turns out farm equipment—have laid off . . . more than half their workforce. Tens of thousands of people have lost their jobs. . . .

One afternoon I struck up a conversation with Yuri M. Maksimov. Now 51, he had put in 13 years as a metal-worker at the nearby Chkalov factory, but he left two years ago after not having been paid for six months. Today he earns 500 rubles a month—about $85—sweeping up around a cluster of kiosks that sell food and alcohol. "I never used to really think about tomorrow," Maksimov said. "But if they had told me back then that I, with my good hands and experience, would be sweeping courtyards in the future, I never would have believed them. I felt I was necessary to the government. Now, no one needs me." . . .

Tossed out of their jobs, or only occasionally receiving salaries, many Siberians have become street—or "shuttle"—traders, buying cheap Chinese, Turkish, and Polish goods in big cities and selling them in their hometowns. . . . [At the train station] I approached three middle-aged women resting on multicolored sacks the size of steamer trunks. Shuttle traders from Irkutsk, they come to Novosibirsk once a month to buy Chinese goods at the *barakholka*, a bustling dirty wholesale market on the edge of town. There they load up with $7.50 blouses, 70-cent socks, $12 jogging shoes, and $4 rip-off Fila and Reebock shirts, which they haul to Irkutsk to sell for a small profit. On each trip they spend a total of 72 hours in third-class train compartments and about 12 hours in Novosibirsk, returning to Irkutsk like exhausted pack animals.

"I am forced to do this," said Nina Pushkareva, who quit her low-paying teaching job and began shuttle trading a year and a half ago. Her husband, a factory worker, is paid irregularly, and with prices for food, gasoline, and consumer goods approaching U.S. levels but salaries lagging ten times behind, this seemed the only way to help her family of four get by.

"At first it was embarrassing and unpleasant," Pushkareva said of the transition [change]. "Now everyone accepts it. . . . I really can't say I live better or worse than before—I just have to work a lot more." Then, reflecting a common belief that people's attitudes have changed too much to return to communism, she added, "One thing I do know: Whether we like it or not, we can never go back to the old system."

From "Russia's Iron Road," by Fen Montaigne from *National Geographic*, June 1998. Copyright ©1998 by National Geographic Society. Reprinted by permission of National Geographic Society.

Understanding What You Read After you have finished reading the selection, answer the following questions.

1. Why is unemployment so high in Novosibirsk? For what two reasons are even people who still have jobs not necessarily well off?

_____

_____

2. What about communism might now seem attractive to the Russian people? According to the reading, is it likely that Russia will return to communism? Explain why or why not.

_____

_____

Activity

Create a poem or a rap about life in Russia, based on the title "The Price of Freedom."

Ukraine, Belarus, and the Caucasus

CULTURE

The Hutsuls of Ukraine

The Hutsul people live in a remote part of the Carpathian Mountains in Ukraine, where they practice the customs they have for centuries. They are the subject of Shadows of Forgotten Ancestors, *a novel by Mykhailo Kotsiubynsky. Considered a masterpiece of Ukrainian literature, it reveals Hutsul culture through the life of the novel's central character, Ivan. In this selection, several years have passed since the tragic death of his sweetheart, Marichka. Ivan has finally come to terms with his grief, married another woman, and moved on with his life.*

When the songs and pistol shots of the wedding had died down and his wife had driven her livestock into his pens, Ivan was satisfied. His Palahna came from a rich family. She was a haughty [proud] and robust girl with a coarse voice and a thick neck. It was true that she liked fine clothes and would spend much money on silken kerchiefs [scarves] and coin necklaces, but Ivan did not worry as he looked at the sheep bleating in the folds and the cows grazing in the forest.

Now he had something to tend. He was not greedy for riches—that is not a Hutsul's purpose in life—simply tending to the livestock filled his heart with joy. The animals were for him what a child is for its mother. All his thoughts revolved around the hay, the comfort of the livestock, and concern that it did not grow weak or have a spell cast on it. . . . Danger lurked everywhere, and he had to guard his livestock against snakes, beasts, and witches, who did everything they could to harm the cows and deprive them of their manna [nourishment]. He had to know a great deal and had to . . . cast spells, and gather useful herbs. Palahna helped him. . . .

"What neighbors the Lord has given us!" she complained to her husband. . . . Khyma was the worst nuisance. An ingratiating [charming] old woman, she was always friendly, but at night she would turn herself into a white dog and wander about the neighbors' enclosures [barnyards]. Ivan often had to throw a pitchfork or an ax to drive her away. . . .

How many cares Ivan had! He had no time to stop and think. The farm required ceaseless work, and the life of the livestock was so closely linked with his own that it pushed aside all other thoughts. But sometimes, when he raised his eyes to the green meadows, where the hay was resting in stacks, or to the deep, pensive forest, a long forgotten voice would waft [come] to him: "Think of me, my sweetheart, twice a day, and I will think of you seven times an hour."

Then he would drop his chores and disappear. Haughty Palahna, who was accustomed to working six days a week and resting only on Sundays, when she showed off her fine clothes, scolded him for his whims. . . .

He was vexed with himself, too. Why do I do it? he would wonder and then return to his cattle with a guilty feeling. . . . The glossy humid eyes would look at him kindly, and the fresh scent of milk and dung would restore his peace and balance. In the sheepfold he would be surrounded by a sea of small round sheep. . . . He would sink his fingers into their fluffy wool . . . and then the spirit of the upland pastures would waft over him and call him to the mountains. Such was Ivan's joy.

Did he love Palahna? The thought had never entered his head. He was the master and she the mistress, and although they had no children, they did have the livestock. What more could they want? The good life had made Palahna plump and pink. She smoked a pipe, like Ivan's mother; she wore . . . silken kerchiefs, and the necklaces sparkling around her thick neck made the womenfolk green with envy. Ivan and Palahna would go together to the town or to parish fairs. . . . At the parish fairs beer would foam, whiskey would flow, and news from distant mountains would fly back and forth. Ivan would embrace other men's wives, and Palahna would be kissed by strange men. What a strange marvel it all was! Satisfied at having spent the time so well, they would go home to their daily concerns. . . .

Thus life passed: weekdays for work and holidays for magic.

From *Shadows of Forgotten Ancestors* by Mykhailo Kotsiubynsky, translated by Marco Carynnyk (Ukrainian Academic Press, 1981).

Understanding What You Read After you have finished reading the selection, answer the following questions.

1. What part of his life provided Ivan with the greatest peace, satisfaction and joy? What part of his life was most troubling and upsetting to him?

_____

_____

2. What information does this reading provide about the lifestyle, values, and beliefs of the Hutsuls?

_____

_____

Activity

Using the reading as a guide, prepare a journal entry for a typical day in your life as a Hutsul.

Ukraine, Belarus, and the Caucasus

READING 44

The Fractured Caucasus

Three major powers, three small nations, and more than 50 ethnic groups compete for space, influence, and independence in the mountainous neck of land that separates the Black and Caspian Seas. Once the southern-most part of the Soviet Union, the Caucasus is today one of the world's most diverse—and turbulent—regions.

Territorial disputes, a thirst for independence, and exploding nationalism afflict the Caucasus' new nations, would-be nations, and ethnic enclaves [areas]. The Chechen war that began at the end of 1994, when Russia sent an army to quell [stop] that region's secessionist [separatist] government, was the latest of numerous conflicts that erupted after the Soviet Union collapsed in 1991. Tens of thousands of people have died, perhaps 45,000 in Chechnya alone, and almost two million have fled as refugees.

Caucasia (as it is also known) is volatile [unstable] in part because it is dauntingly [frustratingly] complex, with at least 50 ethnic groups and nationalities spread like a crazy quilt across a California-size territory. These peoples range from the six million Turkic Azerbaijanis, the predominant inhabitants of Azerbaijan . . . down to groups like the Ginukh, numbering 200. The Ginukh are members of a complex family of indigenous [native] Caucasians—some 40 groups, including other little-known peoples such as the Akhwakh and Lak, many of them crowded into the mountainous Russian republic of Dagestan. They evolved a babel [mixture] of languages in their isolated valleys and cling to these tongues today. Many, like the Chechens, are Muslim and, worrisome to Moscow, look favorably toward the Middle East.

Ivan the Terrible started Russia's southeastward expansion in the 1500s. Over time Russia gained warmwater ports on the Black Sea and farmlands yielding great bounty; Caucasia's cherries and apricots gladdened the citizens of Moscow and St. Petersburg at the end of the long northern winter. There was oil too from Azerbaijan and the Caspian Sea. But the price was steep: multiple wars with Persia and the Ottoman Empire, which claimed parts of the Caucasus region, as well as the determined resistance of many Caucasian peoples.

Resistance was particularly stubborn in the 19th century among the mountaineers—the Chechens, Circassians, Avars, and others. For a quarter of that century a Muslim imam, Shamil, led a holy war against the Russian "infidels." . . . Even after Shamil surrendered in 1859, the Chechens often rebelled. They were, and are, Caucasia's most obstinate [stubborn] freedom seekers.

Besides fighting the Russians, the inhabitants of Caucasia war among themselves. Though they have often lived in peace, the end of ironfisted Soviet control unleashed old grievances.

Armenia and Azerbaijan have battled for the region of Nagorno-Karabakh—within Azerbaijan but populated by Armenians. . . . In another conflict, Georgia tried to suppress the Ossetians, a people descended from nomads from north of the Black Sea; their territory arcs across the Caucasus Mountains into central Georgia. . . .

Russia clearly intends to keep a grip on its turbulent southern border, especially to shore [protect] this flank against regionally powerful Turkey and Iran. Also, Russia wants a slice of the profits from the oil and gas of the Caspian Sea basin. But to control the Caucasus . . . will not be easy.

From "The Fractured Caucasus," by Mike Edwards from *National Geographic*, February 1996. Copyright © 1996 by **National Geographic Society.** Reprinted by permission of the publisher.

Understanding What You Read After you have finished reading the selection, answer the following questions.

1. Why is Russia concerned about its Caucasian citizens and other events in the Caucasus nations to its south?

_____

_____

2. What are the basic causes of the conflict that exists in the Caucasus?

_____

_____

3. How did the Soviet Union's collapse in 1991 affect the stability of the Caucasus region? Explain why.

_____

_____

Activity

Use library and Internet resources to learn about one of the many small ethnic minority groups that live in the Caucasus. Create an illustrated booklet of information about the group.

Central Asia

Life in the Mahalla

Writer Scott Malcomson journeyed to Uzbekistan in the 1990s, after that nation gained its independence from the Soviet Union. He lived among the Uzbeks, learned their language, and immersed himself in their culture. Here, he describes his neighborhood in Tashkent, the capital of Uzbekistan.

Mahalla: from Arabic, it can mean "street, corner, district," or "ward in a city or town." . . . In Uzbek, *mahalla* means everything. You will probably be born, live, and die in the same *mahalla.* You'll play with the other kids in your *mahalla.* Later, they'll form the core of your circle of friends. People do marry across *mahallalar,* though usually they don't wander too far. The woman comes to live in the man's *mahalla.* A new couple will parade through the district, preceded by musicians. . . . The wife will regularly return to visit her own *mahalla,* where her husband will always be something of a stranger.

Each *mahalla* is its own world, a refuge, and a place with its own rules. "If your daughter marries a man from another city, that is a tragedy," a man on your street explains. "If a man comes to the *mahalla* from Samarkand, for example, no matter if he spends his whole life here, he will still be called 'the man from Samarkand'.". . .

In the *mahalla* you feel safe. The street is narrow: a connected row of brown-rose, two-storey houses with small gardens between the facade [front of the house] and the street. Before each door is a bench, where you while away the day and the evening. Across the street are larger gardens. Ideally, as at your home, the garden will be filled with fruit trees. . . . Some people keep sheep in their gardens, even a cow.

The street where you live in Tashkent is populated entirely by Uzbeks. Historically, Russians have not wanted to live with Uzbeks and vice versa. Tashkent has an "Asian side" and an "European side." Russians in Tashkent tend to live in apartment blocks and are far less likely to have gardens; thus, now, they have less food than do Uzbeks. They also have fewer friends. Though only about eight percent of Uzbekistan's population . . . , Russians rarely know Uzbek. Until 1989, they were the occupiers, usually better educated and wealthier than Uzbeks. Since 1989 or 1990, they have been the unloved detritus [debris] of colonial rule. . . .

The best times on your street are early morning and night. In the morning, the young wives of each household emerge to hose down the street. The youngest wife occupies the bottom of the household hierarchy [order]. On the female side, above her are the less-young wives, with the mother-in-law above them and, possibly, a grandmother-in-law. One way for her to demonstrate her rectitude [character] as the youngest wife is to hose down the street around sunup. The earlier the better. The first to water her patch of street wins. You can tell a lot from when households have their piece of street watered. . . .

During the day, the young wives control the *mahalla*. Their children play in the street, which resembles nothing so much as a chaotic play-ground. Kids come by with wheelbarrows to collect food scraps with which to feed their animals. Bad kids come by and shake the fruit trees, grabbing their booty and running away. During infrequent rests, the young wives visit with each other, slumping a bit on the benches because of the heat and constant work.

At night, you sit on the benches or in the garden under the fruit trees, eating whatever's ripe, drinking tea from shallow bowls, talking with your *mahalla* friends. Eventually, the children go to bed and you can hear the leaves flutter and shake; you drink your tea and talk and life is sweet.

From *Borderlands: Nation and Empire.* by Scott L Malcomson. Copyright ©1994 by Scott L. Malcomson. Reprinted by permission of **Faber and Faber Ltd.**

Understanding What You Read After you have finished reading the selection, answer the following questions.

1. What is a *mahalla* and what role does it play in everyday Uzbek life?

_____

_____

2. Describe the relationship between Uzbeks and Russians in Tashkent. Explain the reasons for this relationship.

_____

_____

3. What evidence exists in the reading of the Uzbeks' love of the outdoors?

_____

4. How might the *mahalla*'s influence affect Uzbek unity and nationalism?

_____

Activity

Compose a poem or rap that reflects Uzbek life and feelings in the mahalla.

Central Asia

Exploring Central Asia

In 1898 army officer O. Olufsen was commissioned by Denmark's parliament to explore areas of Central Asia that were largely unknown to Europeans. One of the places Olufsen visited is now the nation of Tajikistan. Here he describes child raising and other customs of the Tajiks.

The natives are very fond of children, who are much spoiled, especially by the father, and are considered as a gift from God—the more children they get the greater their bliss. A childless marriage is looked upon as a punishment from God. Boys are especially desired; and when a boy is born in the kislak [village] all the neighbours rush to the house to congratulate the parents; there is feasting, with music or guitar and tambourine, whilst volleys [gunshots into the air] are fired outside the house. . . . But if the child is a girl there is no banquet, nor are volleys fired. . . .

The little children are the only members of the family who sleep in a kind of bed ("gahvarra"); all the others sleep in their clothes on skins, rugs, straw, or hay. The children's bed is . . . a small wooden box on four legs. A kind of awning is made with some wooden hoops, covered with cloth, to keep the sun and wind off the child when it stands outside the house. . . . The bedclothes are rags and pieces of cloth and skin. . . .

During their youth the children do odd jobs of a small kind about the house—tend to the cattle and so on; and, if possible, they attend a kind of school, which is generally only temporary, kept by a wandering Mullah [a teacher]. In the larger kislaks there are also professional teachers who can read and write. . . . In these schools the children learn to read the language of the country, sometimes also a little writing and arithmetic, and the recital of some Mahometan [Islamic] prayers by rote [memorization through repetition]. The language the children learn to read is Shugnan (the Tadjik). Many children, however, get no other instruction than what their parents can give them. . . . In some houses little wooden slates hang on the walls with the Persian alphabet for the instruction of the children, and as a useful memorandum for the adults. If there be a school in the kislak or in its neighbourhood, both girls and boys are sent there at the age of seven or eight. If a man does not send his children to school or the wandering Mullah, the elders of the town remonstrate with [scold] him in the matter; but he is quite independent, and can do as he likes in this respect. The poor people often send their boys into the service of the rich, but never the girls. . . .

The children and young people are remarkable for the great modesty of their conduct towards their parents and elders . . . . and when the grown up people go to their meals the children always keep at a respectful distance. When a son receives an order from his father he always bows to him. It may be said that implicit [unspoken] obedience and respect is common in both the family and the community. Great respect is always paid to old people, and each old white-beard is called Bâbâ (grandfather).

The ordinary salutation [greeting] of the natives to their superiors consists in crossing the hands over the breast and bowing, after which both hands are drawn down past the face, one after the other. If they want to show an exceptional respect they kneel down on the ground. [They] salute their superiors by placing both hands on the forehead and bowing.

They salute their equals by pressing both hands together, and kissing their fingers to them; and when saluting a very dear friend they touch him under his chin with one hand and then kiss the hand that has touched him—sometimes they kiss both his hands.

If a man of quality comes to a kislak, whether he be a foreigner or a native, he is always received outside the kislak by a deputation [committee] of the men of the town . . . who welcome him with a Salam Aleikum. They also bring him gifts consisting of bread, and fruit, and eggs, and the like. Whether he be foreigner or Mussulman [Muslim], he is entertained free for three or four days, but if he remains longer he has to pay or work for his food.

From *Through the Unknown Pamirs* by O. Olufsen, originally published in 1904 by William Heinemann; reprinted by Greenwood Press, 1969.

Understanding What You Read After you have finished reading the selection, answer the following questions.

1. What similarities and differences existed in the Tajiks' attitudes and practices regarding sons and daughters?

_____

_____

2. In what ways do Tajik children show respect for adults?

_____

_____

Activity

With a partner, use the descriptions provided in the reading to carry out one of the traditional Tajik greetings.

The Arabian Peninsula, Iraq, Iran, and Afghanistan

GEOGRAPHY

The People of the Empty Quarter

Saudi Arabia's Empty Quarter is one of the world's most forbidding deserts. Even many Saudi Arabians believe this vast region of their country is uninhabited. However, a hardy Bedouin people known as the Āl Murrah call the Empty Quarter home. Here an American professor living in Egypt describes the Empty Quarter and its people.

The Āl Murrah provide for most . . . of their subsistence [basic needs] through the herding of camels, sheep, and goats in the deserts of eastern and southeastern Arabia. Camels are the most important species of animals to the Āl Murrah. . . . These animals provide them with the staples of their diet, and the Āl Murrah work hard to search out the best pastures and to obtain and keep control of sure sources of water. . . . Both the humans and the camels are necessary for each other's survival. Neither species could live alone in the desert environment they inhabit without the contributions of the other. . . .

The most prominent [important] element in the diet of the Āl Murrah is milk. The camels they herd are special breeds famous for their milk. . . . Sheep, purchased from urban markets or from other Bedouins, are the major source of meat; but meat is not a regular part of their diet. Milk is the basic element, and they continuously talk about how . . . it gives strength and power. . . .

Since before they can remember, the Āl Murrah have [inhabited] a vast area of southeastern and eastern Arabia . . . known as *dirat-Āl Murrah*. . . . [It] covers approximately 250,000 square miles and is by far the largest and least densely populated territory of any Arabian tribe. . . . The Āl Murrah have an area about as large as France exclusively to themselves. . . .

To outsiders, what is most striking about the Āl Murrah is their inhabitation of the vast and mysterious region of southeastern Arabia known as the Rub' al-Khali, the Empty Quarter. This 200,000-square mile area, one of the last regions to experience European exploration, has only gradually begun to divulge [reveal] its curious mysteries to Westerners. . . . All these travelers have experienced the Rub' al-Khali as a wild and harsh land where the edge of survival is very thin. . . . All have used Bedouin guides, but they have traveled separately from the herds and the herders. To go there without the herds is, as the Āl Murrah say, to court death. With the herds, it can be a land of plenty. . . .

The Rub' al-Khali is separated from the more populated areas of the northeastern Arabia by wide gravel plains that are devoid [empty] of vegetation. . . . These plains extend for as much as 50 miles. . . . Once across the gravel plains, the Āl Murrah are in the land they say has everything: clean sand, fresh air, the best plants for camels, good hunting, and only one's brothers. Not all the Āl Murrah regularly utilize this area, but their really fine herds of milk camels, probably the best in all Arabia, are based here. Their owners and herders, about one-third of the tribe, are known proudly as *bedu al-bedu*, nomads of the nomads. . . .

Vegetation in the Rub' al-Khali . . . is associated directly with sand. . . . The Āl Murrah recognize three major types of sand formation, the *jazirah* [island], the *goz* [sand hill] and the *'erg* [sand dune]. The *jazirahs* are small patches of sand that [are] scattered across the barren gravel plains and support a few desert grasses. . . . The *goz* are gently rolling sand hills that reach thirty to forty feet above the floor of the plain and support both bushes and grass.

The *'erg* is the . . . most spectacular feature of the Rub' al-Khali. . . . Dunes vary between twenty-five and one hundred miles in length and from several hundred yards to two miles in width. They are parallel to each other, running always in a southwest-northeast direction. The sharp crests of the dunes reach a height of 100 to 200 feet. Bushes and various types of desert grasses grow at the foot of the *'erg* and in sandy areas that sometimes stretch for miles behind them. The most important single plant here and in the *goz* is a bush called *abal*. According to the Āl Murrah, this bush stays green for at least four years after a single rain and maintains its moisture for several seasons.

From "The Environment: Land, Animals, and Special Skills" (retitled "The People of the Empty Quarter") from *Nomads of the Nomads: The Al Murrah Bedouin of the Empty Quarter*, by Donald Powell Cole. Copyright ©1975 by Donald Powell Cole. Reprinted by permission of **Aldine Publishing Company, a division of Aldine de Gruyter.**

Understanding What You Read   After you have finished reading the selection, answer the following questions.

1. What is the main economic activity of the Āl Murrah?

_____

2. How do their camels help the Āl Murrah survive in the Empty Quarter?

_____

3. Where do the Āl Murrah find food for their camel herds?

_____

_____

4. Why would the properties of the *abal* bush be valuable to the Āl Murrah?

_____

_____

Activity

Imagine that you are a member of the Āl Murrah tribe who has taken a job in the capital of Saudi Arabia. Write a poem or song lyric that expresses your homesickness for the Empty Quarter and why you prefer your way of life there to your new life in the city.

READING 48

The Arabian Peninsula, Iraq, Iran, and Afghanistan

Change Comes to Iran

Since the revolution in 1979, Iran has been ruled by conservative Islamic clergymen. However, in recent years some Islamic leaders, with the support of many Iranians, have begun to call for change. This reading looks at this second, much slower and quieter revolution and how it is affecting young people in Iran.

On a sparkling afternoon in April, three young couples climbed the steep hiking trail that follows the Darakeh River in northern Tehran. . . . At nearly 5,000 feet the area along the Darakeh is one of the few refuges from the dirty air and clamor [noise] of Tehran, and on this Friday, an Islamic day of rest, the couples were chatting easily as they strolled under willows and plane trees loaded with brilliant green buds. . . .

Suddenly a stranger . . . approached one of the young men, . . . barking, "What are you doing, Why are you holding that woman's hand. Are you afraid someone will steal her?" In Iran, displays of affection between the sexes, however innocuous [innocent], are frowned on. . . . The young people were indignant [offended] at the intrusion but held their tongues. . . .

Twenty years after Ayatollah Ruhollah Khomeini and his devoted followers overthrew Shah Mohammad Reza Pahlavi . . . and installed a religious government, many of Iran's 64 million people are fed up. . . . Iran has been undergoing . . . a second revolution . . . one that seeks to soften the overbearing rule of the theocracy [religion-based government].

. . . Under the Islamic revolution many Iranians had seen basic improvements in their lives: Paved roads, water, and electricity in most rural areas; access to higher education for the masses, especially women; and a greater sense of unity in this richly multiethnic nation. . . .

[Yet,] the yearning for change cuts across Iranian society: women, resentful of inequities [unequal treatment] and restrictions; journalists, intellectuals, and artists, chafing [restless] under government censorship; workers and businessmen, weary of the economic stagnation [decline] brought on by the government's handling of the economy; and most of all, the young. In Iran 40 million people are younger than 25 years old. Comprising two-thirds of the population, they are the baby boom that followed the 1979 Islamic revolution. Many of them have no memory of either Ayatollah Khomeini or the birth of the Islamic republic.

. . . A fisherman in his early 30s, Abadin Salimi, invited half a dozen teenage girls to chat with me one evening. Sitting on the floor of Salimi's home, the young women said they wanted to retain [keep] Iranian and Islamic traditions, such as tightly knit families and respect for elders, but the theocracy's steady drumbeat of anti-American propaganda had done little to blunt their keen interest in the West.

When I asked one of them . . . what appealed to her about life in America, she talked of the freedom to enjoy simple pleasures in mixed company. "Things like riding a bicycle or swimming," she said. "We have wishes for enjoyment and a different lifestyle, but with this government we can't achieve them." . . .

In the hinterland [isolated rural regions], where the roots of Islam go deepest, women are emerging more slowly. . . . I visited Khvor [a village], tucked into the folds of the barren, dusty brown mountains [of central Iran]. . . . In one house I watched as Tahereh Salmani, 20, and her two sisters, ages 16 and 17, wove a carpet. . . . Tahereh—who has been weaving since she was 11—deftly threaded wool through the string guides. . . . In nearly every household in Khvor young women like Tahereh make carpets to sell to dealers in nearby Tabas. The carpets usually bring from $300 to $1,000, a handsome sum in a place where the average monthly income is less than $150. The village school ends at fifth grade, which is when most girls drop out to begin weaving. While some families send their sons to middle school in Tabas, they prefer to keep their daughters at home under sheltering parental wings.

Standing beside the girls was their father, Mohammad Salmani. . . . he has 10 children, so the extra money his daughters make is important. . . . "They are the hardest working girls in the village," he said proudly.

From "Iran: Testing the Waters of Reform" (retitled "Change Comes to Iran") by Fen Montaigne from *National Geographic*, July 1999 by **National Geographic Society**. Reprinted by permission of the publisher.

Understanding What You Read After you have finished reading the selection, answer the following questions.

1. How have young women benefited from the Islamic revolution? What changes do they seem to want? Why are young people's attitudes so important to the future of Iran?

_____

_____

2. What other benefits has the Islamic revolution brought to Iran? What complaints do other groups of Iranians have about it?

_____

_____

Activity

Imagine that you own a newspaper in Khvor. Write an editorial for your newspaper. Your editorial should either defend the culture and values of your village or call for specific changes and explain why they are needed.

The Arabian Peninsula, Iraq, Iran, and Afghanistan

CULTURE

Exploring a Souk

Many early cities in Southwest Asia were built on trade. At the heart of every city was its souk, or marketplace. This remains true today. In this reading, a traveler describes two souks. The first is in Manama, the capital of Bahrain. The second passage describes the souk in Abu Dhabi, capital city of the kingdom of Abu Dhabi in the United Arab Emirates.

I drifted into a maze of streets on which mine was the only Western face in sight. One narrow alley was full of carpenters and the smell of freshly sawn pine; another was a dazzling canal of brilliant Hong Kong cottons; another, the car-repair zone, was loud with lines of men banging shapeless bits of metal with hammers. . . . Things are kept separate—gold and meat, vegetables and clothing . . . every category has at least one street to itself. . . . You cannot go more than a hundred yards without trespassing across a clearly defined boundary. A blind man could find his way through the labyrinth [maze] by smell alone: machine oil gives way to turmeric and coriander [spices], sweet sawdust to the acrid [sharp] barnyard odor of live chickens, roast coffee to the oddly musky scent of cheap plastic. . . . Unposted, unmapped, without names on its streets, it is open only to those who are prepared to take pleasure in getting lost. . . .

I wanted to get really lost. I found my way back to the street full of mechanics by listening for the sound of hammering, and hired a very old, very thoroughly hammered Toyota from an Indian who demonstrated what a thoroughly excellent car it was by walking around it and kicking its fenders. I pointed out that two of the tires had large triangles of torn rubber projecting from them . . . so he took a couple of flying kicks at the tires as well. ". . . good tires, Not to worry."

[Later] I found my way back to the [souk]. . . . In the gold market, I watched a beggar counting his day's takings. He wrapped up his bowl in an old cloth, hoisted himself onto his crutch, and went swinging up the street. At the corner, fifty yards from his own post, he reached another beggar who was missing both legs; without slowing his pace by a fraction, the first beggar flipped a pair of coins into the second beggar's plate. Almsgiving is one of the most strictly enjoined [commanded] duties of the Muslim. . . .

I walked around the [Abu Dhabi] *souk*. The old market had been torn down long ago, and in its place there was a shopping precinct [district] of purple concrete. . . . Its pedestrian streets were too wide and windy. It had lost all the labyrinthine intricacy of a real souk, although its architect had clearly had some hazy idea in his head that a *souk* ought to be a complicated place with a lot of alleys and turnings. . . . The only good thing one could say for it as a piece of construction was that the concrete was riddled with cracks and it looked as if a few more years of use would turn the place into a cheerful purple ruin.

Instinctive habits are, mercifully, much more powerful than bad architecture; and the residents of the *souk* were simply ignoring all the architect's designs on them. They had set up stalls in the walkways and constructed their own labyrinth in spaces which had been meant as routes of access. There were no straight lines to walk down; one had to zigzag through a maze of one-man businesses which were conducted from upturned packing cases under torn umbrellas. There were repairers of sandals and transistor radios, tailors sitting cross-legged in front of ancient Singer sewing machines, hawkers of plastic junk and plastic carpets. Men on prayer mats were bent due west to Mecca; . . . under one umbrella an old man with a mouthful of gold teeth was crouched over the Koran [Qur'an]. The book, which looked older than he was, was coming apart in his hands. Its pages were brittle and gray: the oldest, grimiest, most battered object in the whole of Abu Dhabi.

From "The Island Labyrinth" and "Temporary People" (retitled "Exploring a Souk") from *Arabia: A Journey Through the Labyrinth* by Jonathan Raban. Copyright ©1979 by Jonathan Raban. Reprinted by permission of **Simon & Schuster**.

Understanding What You Read After you have finished reading the selection, answer the following questions.

1. According to the reading, how are the shops in the Manama souk organized?

_____

_____

2. How has the culture of the souk overcome modern architecture in Abu Dhabi?

_____

_____

3. Why does the author use the term "labyrinth" to describe a souk? Does the description seem to be accurate? Explain why or why not.

_____

_____

Activity

Write an article for your school newspaper describing your imaginary shopping trip in a souk.

READING 50 The Eastern Mediterranean

The Islamic City

From Southwest Asia, Islam spread west into North Africa and east into India from the 600s through the 900s. Throughout this region, Muslims applied the principles of their faith to the cities they built. More than a thousand years later, the results of this practice can still be seen in the cities of the Eastern Mediterranean.

Despite the chaotic [disordered] appearance it presents at first glance, especially in relation to some of the newer . . . parts of the city that surround it, the [traditional] Islamic city is an entirely rational [sensible] structure. Its . . . narrow streets provide vital shade, they keep down winds and dust, and use up little valuable building land.

In fact, there is a clear logic underlying the city's layout, one that is announced in the holy book of Islam, the Koran [Qur'an]. . . . Although there are regional differences, most towns and cities that have developed under the influence of Islam at any time in the last 1,300 years show surprisingly similar features. These apply to hundreds of settlements . . . from southern Spain in the west, to Lahore in Pakistan in the east. Elements of these ideas can be found in cities as far away as Dar es Salaam in East Africa and Davao in the Philippines. . . .

The main guiding principles of Islamic city planning recognize the need to maintain personal privacy, specify responsibilities in maintaining urban systems on which other people rely, such as keeping thoroughfares or wastewater channels clear, and emphasize the inner essence of things rather than their outward appearance. . . .

The major elements of the Islamic city are easily described. At the city's heart lies the Friday mosque, or *Jami,* typically the largest structure in the city. . . . Close to the Jami are the main *suqs* [souks], the covered bazaars or street markets. . . . Within the *suqs,* trades are located in relation to the *Jami.* Closest in are those tradespeople who enjoy the highest prestige [status], such as booksellers and perfumers. Farthest away are those who perform the noxious [unpleasant] and noisy trades, such as coppersmiths, blacksmiths, and cobblers. . . .

Attached to the ramparts [city walls], on which are located several towers and gates, is an immense fortified structure, the *Kasbah.* Usually perched on the highest ground, it was a place of refuge to which the sovereign [ruler] or governor retreated when the main city had fallen to an enemy, or was in the [midst] of a civil war. The *Kasbah* contained not only the palace buildings . . . but also its own small mosques, baths, shops, and even markets.

Everywhere else within the city is filled with cellular courtyard houses of every size and shape, tied together by a tangle of winding lanes, alleys, and cul-de-sacs [dead ends]. Housing is grouped into quarters, or neigh-borhoods, that are defined according to occupation, religious sect, or eth-nic group.

The most important residential unit in the Islamic city, the courtyard house clearly [shows] the application of the various principles of Islamic city planning. Outside walls lining a street are usually left bare and are rarely pierced by windows. If windows are necessary, they are placed high above street level, making it impossible to peer in. Entrances are L-shaped, and doorways opening onto the street rarely face each other, thus prevent-ing any direct views into the house.

In hot climates, courtyards with trees and water fountains provide shade, but they also provide an interior and private focus for life sheltered from the public gaze. But within the courtyard and the house itself the appearance of plainness often gives way to lavish displays of wealth and decoration. A vividness inside parallels the emphasis in the Koran on the richness of the inner self compared to more modest outside appearance.

From "The Islamic City: Order within chaos" (retitled: "The Islamic City") from *The Real World: Understanding the Modern World Through The New Geography* by Philip Boys. Copyright ©1991 by Marshall Editions Developments Limited. Reprinted by permissions of **Houghton Mifflin Company**.

Understanding What You Read After you have finished reading the selection, answer the following questions.

1. How does climate affect the size of streets in Islamic cities?

_____

_____

2. Where can the Kasbah usually be found in an Islamic city? Why?

_____

_____

3. What principles of Islam guided the building of the old Islamic cities? How do their courtyard houses reflect these principles?

_____

_____

Activity

Create an aerial map of a residential section in an Islamic city. Show how the windows and entrances of the houses are located in relation to the street and to other houses.

The Eastern Mediterranean

CULTURE

The Bedouin Way

About ten percent of the people who live in Southwest Asia are Bedouins. Bedouin society is organized into large groups of loosely related family members that can range up to several hundred people in size. The term "bedouin" comes from the Arabic word badawi, *meaning "desert dweller." Today, however, many Bedouins have given up their life as desert nomads in exchange for houses and jobs in cities. The author of this reading describes this trend, but he clearly prefers the old Bedouin ways. Here, he discusses the traditional culture and customs of his people.*

My tribe is called Abuiack. The desert is divided up into tribal areas. In each area we have a limited water supply; the pasture and the right to cultivate the land belong exclusively to the tribe controlling that area. A bedouin tribe is a group claiming common possession over a certain territory. Each tribe knows the boundary of its land. I am the head of my tribe; I was elected by the adult men to oversee their tribal interests.

My women make my tent from goat's hairs woven together. These hairs expand when they're wet, making a watertight roof. In the summer they afford protection from the hot sun and desert sandstorms. The tent is divided by a woven curtain: one half is for the men and one half for the women. It's the natural home of the nomad. A tent is light; we can fold it up and put it on the back of a camel and move on.

Some bedouins have changed from the nomadic life to a settled life, and they prefer to live in buildings. Our life is with the sheep and goats, cultivating the earth: their life is now turning toward industry.

We send our children to school every day to learn. Some of our children will go on to the university, giving up our traditional way of life. Camels used to be our only means of transport, but with the advent of trains and cars the camel has become less useful.

When we entertain, we cook a whole goat or a whole sheep. We make a fire and cook the animal in front of the guests. We, the men, eat the meat and we give the eyes and the brains to the women. We're always making strong black coffee or sweet tea to offer any passerby at whatever time of day or night.

Our tent is our shelter. In Biblical times, Abraham received his guests in his tent. To this day, we have no greater pleasure than offering hospitality. It's part of our desert culture, even if it means sharing our last piece of bread.

My wife must be a Moslem [Muslim] bedouin. My mother will see her first and report back to me—whether she is good looking; whether the economic situation of her family is good; whether she has gold [for the dowry, or marriage gift]—and then I decide if I want to marry her. I see her for the first time on my wedding day.

In my position I can't have a poor woman. . . . Some bedouins still buy their brides with camels. Seven is considered a fair price. I like to marry someone from my family [group], as it strengthens the family unit. If I'm displeased with my wife, I can send her back to her family, but I have to pay for the upkeep of the children.

I am quite happy with two wives; I would like three, but four would be too expensive.

From "Our life is with the sheep and goats" (retitled "The Bedouin Way") from *We Live in Israel* by Gemma Levine. Copyright ©1981 by **Wayland Publishers Ltd**. Reprinted by permission of the publisher.

Understanding What You Read After you have finished reading the selection, answer the following questions.

1. What is the method by which Bedouins own land?

_____

2. In what ways is traditional Bedouin housing appropriate to their lifestyle?

_____

_____

3. Name four ways in which Bedouin culture is changing, according to the author.

_____

_____

4. What evidence is there in this reading that men and women are not equal in Bedouin society?

_____

_____

Activity

Imagine that you are a son or daughter in a Bedouin family. Write a letter to a parent or other family member revealing whether, as an adult, you will continue to live in the traditional Bedouin lifestyle or move to a city. Explain your reasons for your decision.

Name _____ Class _____ Date _____

The Eastern Mediterranean

Visit to a Kibbutz

A kibbutz is a special type of settlement in Israel. The people of a kibbutz own the community as a group, including its land, housing, and factories. They equally share the farming and other work, as well as the community's food and profits. In the 1990s about three percent of Israel's population lived on one of the nation's 270 kibbutzim. Here, an Israeli from Jerusalem describes her visit to a kibbutz.

With a population of about 650 adult members, 400 children, and 150 temporary residents such as volunteers, . . . Makom is one of the largest kibbutzim in Israel. Makom's . . . sources of income come from the production of agricultural machinery and food canning . . . . [and] from the kibbutz's agricultural crops: wheat, cotton, olives, citrus fruit, beef, fish, and honey.

The kibbutz has a . . . school consisting of twelve grades, each class having its own living unit. From the age of six weeks, all kibbutz children are raised in the children's homes and taken care of by a *metapelet* [a job similar to a nanny]. Each afternoon they visit with their parents, then spend the rest of their time in children's company. In addition to studying, participating in social activities, and working, the kibbutz children sleep and take most of their meals together. Parents and children do maintain, however, a very close relationship. . . .

The kibbutz society is a direct democracy. Committees cover all aspects of life, and all the committees (with the exception of the Social Committee) are responsible to the elected secretariat [board of administrators]. The entire adult community may take part in the decision-making process through the assembly, which meets every Saturday night. . . .

From the outside, the apartments of each separate area in the kibbutz look alike; but, within, each room reflects the personalities of its occupants. The apartments of older, long-time kibbutzniks are tiny and extremely modest. . . . The younger members generally live farther out . . . in newer neighborhoods on the hills. Their apartments are spacious and furnished in contemporary [modern] styles; their kitchens are well equipped and adjoin the large living areas. . . .

The children's homes are in the center of the kibbutz, surrounded on all sides by adult homes and, farther out, factories and agricultural buildings. . . . Dogs wander freely though the multicolored fences. The children wear used, sometimes shabby, clothes. In the heat of the summer, many run about barefoot. . . . [But] all give the air [appearance] of being extremely well tended. . . .

The dining room is a huge airy hall. . . . At the entrance, a bulletin board announces various classes, meetings, and trips. People sit in twos and threes, scattered about the room. . . . There is a continuous hum of voices, constant movement. This is an obvious gathering place. . . .

During the week, people are busy working. Nevertheless, numerous people walk unhurriedly on the paths, as if on vacation. They stop, completely at their leisure, to talk with toddlers taken for walks by their *metapelets*. I visit the various "branches": the factories, kitchen, laundry. I take a drive in the fields. . . . I meet several members . . . and wonder at the incongruity [difference] between their personalities, talents, and the kinds of jobs they perform daily. A woman who wrote educational programs for the whole country sits in the laundry room folding shirts, pants, and towels throughout the day. . . . A man who teaches at the kibbutz teachers' college sits, twice a week, on the food line in the factory, sorting olives. . . . Physical work is a value practiced in the kibbutz.

In the evening, lights are turned on along the paths, and the dining hall, at the center of the kibbutz, is brightly illuminated. Parents walk their children back to the children's homes to put them to bed. Most people rest in their rooms, watching TV. Some attend various meetings and study groups.

. . . Tonight, there is a discussion on the future of the assembly meeting [that is held each Saturday], a . . . [practice] that seems to be on the decline. About fifty members attend—the "serious" people of the community and the members of the secretariat. Promptly at 11:00 P.M., a summary is presented by the chairman. There is a policy of closing all meetings at 11:00, to allow for enough sleep before the following day's work.

From Introduction (retitled "Visit to a Kibbutz") from *Kibbutz Makom: Report from an Israeli Kibbutz* by Amia Lieblich. Copyright ©1981 by Amia Lieblich. Reprinted by permission of **Pantheon Books, a division of Random House, Inc**.

Understanding What You Read After you have finished reading the selection, answer the following questions.

1. How are the living arrangements in a kibbutz different from those in a typical American community?

_____

_____

2. How is an Israeli kibbutz governed?

_____

_____

3. What evidence does the reading present to support the statement in the introduction that all the residents of a kibbutz share its workload?

_____

_____

Activity

Using the reading as a guide, make a map of a typical kibbutz.

North Africa

ECONOMICS

Moroccans Confront Their Future

Morocco has both a glorious and a difficult past. It once ruled an empire that stretched from Spain to Libya. However, it also was invaded and colonized by the Romans, Muslims, Portuguese, Spanish, and finally the French. Moroccans are proud of the culture that their checkered history has produced. Yet, at the same time, many are concerned about what the future holds for their small nation.

Today, 40 years after gaining their independence from France, Moroccans are facing an array of challenges perhaps greater than all that have come before. A high birthrate means that half the population is under 20 years of age. That overwhelming reality already exerts pressure on virtually every aspect of society, especially on education (too many students, not enough schools) and on the economy (150,000 young people a year enter a job market that can handle only about 130,000). So many Moroccans emigrate to find work that the money they send home is one of the nation's main sources of hard currency. More and more people abandon the countryside to try their luck in the cities; 30,000 arrive in Casablanca every year. And there remain deep rifts [divisions] between rich and poor, city and countryside. Even within families there are often sharp differences of opinion between generations. . . .

In Morocco the struggle to make a living is ubiquitous [everywhere]. I saw young men in the foggy forest outside Rabat, the capital, tending makeshift stands piled with white truffles [mushrooms], the common local variety. Arranged in neat pyramids, the fungus sold for about three dollars a pound. There were stands strung out along the road for miles, one stand within sight of the next. I never saw a car stop.

There was the ancient man walking slowly down the street in Casablanca carrying a censer [incense burner]. He would enter a shop, a café, or an office and spend a moment gently swinging the censer on its chain to send perfumed clouds into the air. There was no fee; he accepted whatever people wanted to give for this unbidden service.

More common and less beautiful were the shoeshine boys constantly circulating through the cafés, tapping their brushes against small wooden boxes that served as footrests. Then there were the little boys roaming the streets of Fez with mere handfuls of things to sell: small packets of tissues, flashlight batteries, cigarettes. They would pass the cafés and offer these things in a whisper, urgently, watching for police. . . .

Slums—the worst I saw spread northward from the edges of Casablanca, with crude little huts made of corrugated iron, bits of plastic, scraps of wood—are the most vivid example of the poverty many Moroccans continue to endure. . . . Moroccans confront their problems

with particular dignity. Newcomers to the cities endure [bear] the hardships of their new surroundings with the stoicism [acceptance] essential to
farmers and shepherds. . . . Protest and criticism exist but come mainly
from the middle and upper classes; the Moroccan of the countryside simply doesn't complain. . . .

As the only North African country without oil, Morocco has had to
make the most of its other advantages. The ocean off Morocco's Atlantic
coastline is one of the richest fishing grounds in the world. . . . Morocco
also contains the world's largest phosphate deposits, and although the
market was recently depressed, mining remains a major enterprise.

But agriculture has always been Morocco's strength. Morocco's farmers produce everything from wheat and olives to flowers and kiwifruit,
and there is a growing export trade—primarily citrus fruit and tomatoes,
to Europe, Canada, and now the United States. A range of climate and
soil is kind to a variety of crops: in the north, grapes, fruit, olives, and
wheat; to the west, more wheat, oranges, vegetables; in the south, dates.
. . .

As recently as 30 years ago 70 percent of the people lived in the
countryside. Today, rural folk account for slightly less than half the population. Yet except for the Imperial Valley-like farms [large, commercial farms
in California] near Agadir and Fez, most agriculture continues on small
holdings with a minimum of technology.

From "Morocco: North Africa's Timeless Mosaic" (retitled "Moroccans Confront Their
Future) by Erla Zwingle from *National Geographic*, October 1996. Copyright ©1996 by
National Geographic Society. Reprinted by permission of the publisher.

Understanding What You Read
After you have finished reading the selection,
answer the following questions.

1. In what ways have population trends affected Morocco?

_____

_____

2. What strengths does the reading note in Morocco's economy?

_____

_____

_____

Activity

Imagine that you are a Moroccan teenager. Write a journal entry
expressing your views about your country's future. Explain why
you will stay in the country of your birth.

North Africa

GEOGRAPHY

Egypt's Threatened Nile Delta

For centuries the annual flooding of the Nile Delta directed the lives of Egyptians. Today, dams and other man-made changes upstream on the Nile River have altered its natural rhythms. This change has allowed more Egyptians to settle in the delta and make their living there. However, as the reading explains, Egypt has paid a price for this benefit.

An ocean of sand covers Egypt, divided by the dark green vein of the Nile River. The river injects life into the bright green fan at its mouth, while the gray, man-made mass of Cairo eats away at the fan's delicate stem.

The black soil of the Nile Delta has made it the foundation stone of seven millennia of human history. . . . The resulting lifestyle in the Nile River Valley and the delta—growing crops, raising domesticated animals, and fishing—sustained settlements that evolved into the ancient world's first nation-state. Long before the pharaohs built the pyramids, Egypt's glory was the agricultural wealth of its delta. . . .

Today Egypt's battle is to preserve the soil and water that have always given life to the delta. . . . For nearly 30 years the Aswan High Dam, 600 miles south of Cairo, has kept the river from flooding and depositing renewing sediment at its mouth. The delta has instead been inundated [flooded] with catastrophic [consequences]: It is among the world's most intensely cultivated lands, with one of the world's highest uses of fertilizers and highest levels of soil salinity.

Cairo's commercial and residential sprawl has locked priceless soil beneath miles of concrete; the discharge of chemicals into delta lakes threatens the fishing industry and the supply of clean drinking water; and the Mediterranean coast is eroding. If global warming causes the sea level to rise, as some predict, the city of Alexandria and the coastal province of El Beheira will be lost.

"The delta is subsiding," [Cairo University professor Mohammed] Kassas said with a helpless shrug. "It's tilting—the northeastern side is lower, and sinking a half centimeter [about 0.2 inches] a year; the north-western side is sinking three millimeters [about 0.1 inches] a year. . . . Sediments now blocked by the Aswan Dam used to build up the delta but not anymore." . . .

The Ankh, the ancient Egyptian symbol of life, resembles a cross or a key, but it might also be seen as a map of inhabited Egypt. The upright is the Nile, the crosspiece is the east and west—the daily birth and death of the sun—and the loop is the delta. [Most] of Egypt's population lives in the loop of the ankh, on the alluvial [made of silt deposits] land that gave populated Egypt its ancient name Kemet, the "black land," as distinct from Deshret, the bleak "red land" of the desert. The loop meets the crosspiece at Cairo, and it is here, where streets, parking lots, hotels, and apartment buildings have entombed hundreds of square miles of the fertile land, that you can view tons of delta soil in its mummified form: bricks.

"The use of baked mud bricks is worse than urban sprawl," my friend Ibrahim Sadek said, frowning out his downtown Cairo window at new buildings with gray frames and red brick walls. "Those bricks come from the richest soil of the delta. Do you know, peasants were selling off the top yard of their land for brickmaking? And as if that wasn't bad enough, if their neighbors didn't do the same, then all the chemicals leached from the higher land into that lower land, worsening the soil quality." The Egyptian parliament passed a bill to stop the practice, but the new law has not been perfectly enforced. "Think how many people have been affected," Ibrahim said sadly. "Think how many seeds a single brick of earth could hold!"

From "The Imperiled Nile Delta" (retitled "Egypt's Threatened Nile Delta") by Peter Theroux from *National Geographic*, January 1997. Copyright ©1997 by **National Geographic Society**. Reprinted by permission of the publisher.

Understanding What You Read After you have finished reading the selection, answer the following questions.

1. Why has the Aswan Dam increased the use of fertilizer in the Nile Delta?

_____

_____

2. In what two ways has the growth of Cairo affected the delta?

_____

_____

3. Why is the preservation of the Nile Delta so important to Egypt's future?

_____

_____

Activity

Draw an outline map of Egypt on a poster board and position an Ankh on it as described in the reading. Label the Nile River, the Nile delta, and the city of Cairo. Place drawings of things the reading says are threatening the delta on the borders.

West Africa

Enrolling Girls in School

In many parts of the world, including parts of Africa, boys receive more schooling than girls do. In part, this is due to cultural attitudes concerning the roles of males and females in society. However, it is also often due to the fact that poor families cannot afford to educate all their children. This reading reports on a program in the West African country of Benin that is attacking both reasons for denying girls an education.

More and more girls are going to school in Benin's southwestern region of Couffo thanks to a World Food Program (WFP) initiative which distributes "dry rations" to impoverished parents. Known in Pakistan and Morocco as "Food for Learning" and "Food Aid In The Service of Instruction," the project, launched in Benin in November 1998, offers parents a 50-kilogram [110-pound] bag of rice and a 4-liter [about one gallon] can of cooking oil for every girl registered at school.

Many poor parents, who normally would resist sending their daughters to school, are now enrolling four or five of them with the promise of food for each one. Some expressed astonishment at the large amount of food they receive. . . .

In just one school year (1998–1999), the number of girls enrolled in 10 village schools under the WFP project rose considerably, even reversing the previous boy-girl ratio in favor of girls. For example, the number of girls at the public primary school in Dohodji rose from 25 to 107, an increase of 328 percent. WFP's educational campaign was particularly successful in this village. In the neighboring villages of Gnigbandjime and Dekandji II, the number of girls rose from 19 to 72 and from 21 to 55, increases of 279 and 161.9 percent, respectively.

In the 10 pilot schools where the WFP project was launched, inspired by the excellent results achieved in Morocco, the rate of attendance by girls had never before reached the 30 percent mark, or barely one girl for every four boys. Some 92 percent of the 768 girls enrolled in school during the first trimester maintained the attendance required by the project for their families to continue receiving the dry rations benefit.

According to the 1998 WFP annual report, the project supported efforts by Beninois officials to break down certain traditional cultural barriers against the education of girls and their integration into modern society. "For the hungriest and poorest parents, the promise of food assistance is sometimes the only way they'll allow their girls to go to school," said WFP's executive director, Catherine Bertini.

Today, many parents in the 10 villages where the program is underway . . . would allow their daughters to continue school even if the free distribution of rations were to end. . . . An increasing number of mothers now say they "no longer consider the education of their daughters as a waste of time and money, but as a step toward improving the quality of their lives."

. . . [The] WFP will continue to encourage girls' school attendance in the 10 villages in Couffo. . . . Research to choose more pilot schools for the "food aid for the education of girls" program is already underway in Atacora, another of Benin's poorer regions, in the northwest, where the rate of enrollment of girls in school is less than 20 percent.

Bertini hopes that once educating girls becomes a habit, "the old prejudices will crumble, and girls will be able to pursue their education even further. The future for girls, women, their families and communities will continue to glow brighter and brighter."

Adapted from "WFP Hands Out Food to Keep Girls in School" (retitled "Enrolling Girls in School") by Ali Idrissou-Toure from *African News Digest*, November 14, 1999. Copyright ©1999 by **African Media Group, Inc**. Reprinted by permission of the publisher.

Understanding What You Read After you have finished reading the selection, answer the following questions.

1. How are parents in Benin encouraged to send their daughters to school?

_____

_____

2. Why do you think that the program described in the article targets only poor families?

_____

_____

3. What information in this report suggests that a lack of education among Beninois girls is a cultural issue as well as an economic one?

_____

_____

Activity

Design an illustrated poster that the WFP could use in a campaign to advertise its program to the people of Benin.

READING 56 — West Africa

Travels in the Sahara

Few of the world's deserts are less visited than Africa's Sahara, where wars and political unrest have kept outsiders away for decades. In 1997, however, Americans Donovan Webster and George Steinmetz obtained permission from the governments of Niger and Chad to travel in the region. Here Webster describes some of what they found.

The first dead camels turn up on Day 2. They're mounds of pale, chalky bones, scattered atop dishes of . . . apricot-hued fur. Each is the size of a kiddie wading pool, and they rest balanced on low, wind-sculpted pillars of sand. In the . . . Sahara, humidity sometimes hovers in the teens and day-time temperatures can reach 130 degrees Fahrenheit. Consequently, the desert's sandy surface is sterile, and microorganisms can't survive there. Decay comes in the abrasive form of wind-blown grit.

. . . We left Agadez, Niger, driving east in a line of four-wheel-drive vehicles. . . . After a day's drive into the scrublands east of town, we topped a rocky bluff, and beyond it began the Ténéré, a landscape of dune fields and sand plains larger than Germany with a name that means "noth-ing" in the language of the Tuareg.

Here strings of dunes stretch east to west, a hundred feet tall and sev-eral miles long, piled up by the wind. Devoid [empty] of water and com-pletely unsettled, the Ténéré is lonely, hot, and breath-takingly gorgeous in rounded shades of beige.

Most every day we drive about 70 miles across the soft sand, often becoming bogged down and having to dig our way out with hands and shovels. . . . We pause at midday, when the sun heats the desert so thor-oughly its sand grows impassably soft. Then we wait out the inferno for a few hours, hiding beneath a large canvas sheet draped across the roofs of the parked cars—creating the only shade for hundreds of miles. . . .

Having faced down the worst heat and distance of the Ténéré, we sud-denly come upon the town of Bilma, an Eden in the furnace of sand. Here groves of date palms grow and pools of clear water burble from the ground thanks to a . . . break in the desert's deep substrate [base] of rock. One morning, standing at the edge of a pool, I notice an outflowing creek and follow it. Stepping through a wall of brush, I come across irrigation ditches running off the creek into dozens of gardens: corn, cassava, tea, ground-nuts, milo, hot peppers, even some orange, lime, and grapefruit trees.

. . . Heading back to town, I come upon an outpost alone in the desert. Surrounded by cactuses and scrub, it's the local weather station, and the gray-suited man running it is Bilma's weather officer, Nouhou Agah. He may have the least demanding job for a thousand miles. Each day . . . Agah rises, checks the rain gauge, anemometer [an instrument that measures the speed or force of the wind], and barometer, then writes his findings in a ledger, which he sends off to the capital of Niamey once a year. . . He shows me his precipitation ledger, running a finger down its grid of mostly zero rainfall totals. He points out April 29: 1.5 mm of rain. On May 6: Trace. On July 21: 1.1 mm. And—he gets excited—on August 4: 10.5 mm, less than half an inch. "A downpour like we have not seen in most people's lives," he says. . . .

The deserts of Niger and Chad differ, with the topography of each roughly mirroring the spirit of its people. Niger's Sahara is a world of smooth dunes and the friendly . . . Tuareg. Chad is a land of stony, eroded landscapes and the rock-hard Toubou, a seminomadic people whose men wear long daggers lashed to their biceps like advertisements of ferocity. . . .

The Toubou inhabit a desert characterized by rocky spires, volcanic peaks, and screaming gales. So it's fitting that as Steinmetz and I cross into Chad's Sahara, a relentless wind from the northeast, called the harmattan, greets us. This wind whips the desert, turning its air to a gritty scrim [a kind of theater curtain] so dense the sun behind is a pale disk you can stare at directly. It signals an end to the 60- or 80-degree cool of the North African winter. When it leaves, the roasting 120- or 130-degree heat of the Saharan summer will arrive, bringing with it the relief of occasional rain.

From "Journey to the Heart of the Sahara" (retitled "Egypt's Journey to the Heart of the Sahara") by Donovan Webster from *National Geographic,* March 1999. Copyright ©1999 by **National Geographic Society**. Reprinted by permission of the publisher.

Understanding What You Read After you have finished reading the selection, answer the following questions.

1. Why is there water at Bilma when the rest of Niger's Sahara is so dry?

_____

_____

2. What differences does the author observe between the Sahara in Niger and the Sahara in Chad?

_____

_____

Activity

Imagine that you live in Bilma. Write a letter to a pen pal in America telling about yourself and what life is like in your part of Niger.

READING 57 West Africa

Leo Africanus: Description of Timbuktu (1526)

About one thousand years ago, the Ghanaian city of Timbuktu was a major trade center in West Africa. Leo Africanus, a Spanish Muslim, visited the city as a teenager around 1500. Later, he was asked by Pope Leo X to write a geography of Africa based on his travels. This book, The Description of Africa *was published in 1526. For the next several centuries, it provided most of what Europeans knew about the continent. At the time Leo Africanus visited Timbuktu, it was somewhat past its peak. But it was still a thriving Islamic city famous for its commerce and learning.*

The houses of Timbuktu are huts made of clay-covered wattles [sticks] with thatched roofs. In the center of the city is a temple built of stone and mortar, . . . and in addition there is a large palace . . . where the king lives. The shops of the artisans [skilled craftspeople], the merchants, and especially weavers of cotton cloth are very numerous. Fabrics are also imported from Europe to Timbuktu, borne by Berber merchants.

The women of the city maintain the custom of veiling their faces, except for the slaves who sell all the foodstuffs. The inhabitants are very rich, especially the strangers who have settled in the country; so much so that the current king has given two of his daughters in marriage to two brothers, both businessmen, on account of their wealth. There are many wells containing sweet water in Timbuktu; and in addition, when the Niger is in flood canals deliver the water to the city. Grain and animals are abundant [plentiful], so that the consumption of milk and butter is considerable. But salt is in very short supply because it is carried here from Tegaza, some 500 miles from Timbuktu. I happened to be in this city at a time when a load of salt sold for eighty ducats. The king has a rich treasure of coins and gold ingots. One of these ingots weighs 970 pounds.

The royal court is magnificent and very well organized. When the king goes from one city to another with the people of his court, he rides a camel and the horses are led by hand by servants. If fighting becomes necessary, the servants mount the camels and all the soldiers mount on horseback. When someone wishes to speak to the king, he must kneel before him and bow down; but this is only required of those who have never before spoken to the king, or of ambassadors. The king has about 3,000 horsemen and infinity [unlimited number] of foot-soldiers armed with bows . . . which they use to shoot poisoned arrows. This king makes war only upon neighboring enemies and upon those who do not want to pay him tribute. When he has gained a victory, he has all of them—even the children—sold in the market at Timbuktu.

Only small, poor horses are born in this country. The merchants use them for their voyages and the courtiers [gentlemen] to move about the city. But the good horses come from Barbary [northern Africa]. They arrive in a caravan and, ten or twelve days later, they are led to the ruler, who takes as many as he likes and pays appropriately for them.

. . . There are in Timbuktu numerous judges, teachers and priests, all properly appointed by the king. He greatly honors learning. Many hand-written books imported from Barbary are also sold. There is more profit made from this commerce than from all other merchandise.

Instead of coined money, pure gold nuggets are used; and for small purchases, cowrie shells which have been carried from Persia, and of which 400 equal a ducat. Six and two-thirds of their ducats equal one Roman gold ounce.

The people of Timbuktu are of a peaceful nature. They have a custom of almost continuously walking about the city in the evening (except for those that sell gold), between 10 PM and 1 AM, playing musical instruments and dancing. The citizens have at their service many slaves. . . .

The city is very much endangered by fire. At the time when I was there on my second voyage, half the city burned in the space of five hours. But the wind was violent and the inhabitants of the other half of the city began to move their belongings for fear that the other half would burn.

From "Leo Africanus: Description of Timbuktu" from *The Description of Africa (1526)*, translated by Paul Brians from *Reading About the World*, vol. 2, edited by Paul Brians et al. Copyright © by **Paul Brians**. Reprinted by permission of the translator/editor.

Understanding What You Read After you have finished reading the selection, answer the following questions.

1. What evidence does the reading contain that learning and education were important to the people of Timbuktu?

_____

_____

2. What evidence does Africanus provide that the people of Timbuktu enjoyed a high standard of living?

_____

_____

Activity

Search library and other resources for a description of present-day Timbuktu. Write a short report comparing modern Timbuktu to the description provided in this reading.

READING 58

East Africa

Government by Magic Spell

Saida Hagi-Dirie Herzi is a fiction writer from Somalia. In 1991, unrest grew in her homeland after clans in the north finally drove the county's long-time dictator and his followers from power. Civil war erupted in the 1990s, as these clans fought among themselves to control the government. This short story is set in Somalia before the civil war began.

When she was ten, Halima learned that she was possessed by a jinni. The diagnosis came from the religious healer of the village, the Wadaad. . . . With that Halima became famous. The story of her jinni was known from one end of the village to the other within hours after the Wadaad had told her mother. Everyone talked about Halima and her jinni—what it might do and what it might be made to do, for her and for the village. . . .

When Halima was under the spell of her spirits, . . . she experienced a feeling of power, as though she could do things beyond the reach of ordinary human beings. She felt good then. Moreover, whatever she undertook, her spirits seemed to lend a helping hand. Because the fortunes of her family, indeed those of her whole clan, prospered at the time, Halima as well as other people assumed that it was the spirits' doing. In time, Halima came to be regarded as a blessing to her family, an asset to the whole clan. And she gloried in the special status her spirits gave her.

It was because of her special powers that Halima was summoned to the capital. A big part of her clan was there. The most important and powerful positions in the government were held by people of her clan. It had all started with one of their men, who had become very powerful in the government. He had called his relatives and found big government jobs for them. They in turn had called relatives of theirs till the government had virtually been taken over by Halima's people. And that had meant quick riches for everyone concerned. . . anything that had stood in their way had been pushed aside or eliminated. At the time when Halima was summoned, her clan controlled the government and with that the wealth of the country so completely that no one dared to challenge them any more. . . . Still they wanted to secure for themselves the extra protection of Halima's supernatural powers. . . .

Halima did let herself be persuaded to go, but, before she went, she consulted her spirits. They asked her to perform two rituals. One was to prepare 'Tahleel,' a special type of water over which certain rituals were performed. People drank it or bathed in it to benefit from its powers. The second was to perform daily animal sacrifices to Gess Ade, the clan's twin spirit. . . .

In the city . . . Halima wasted no time carrying out the two requests of her spirits. She asked two things from the leaders of her clan. She asked them to bring all the water resources of the city together in one central pool to facilitate [make easier] the performing of the 'Tahleel' and she requested the building of a huge slaughterhouse at the eastern shore. . . .

To centralise the city's water system, two huge water reservoirs were created. . . . This way, all the water consumed in the city came from the same source, and when Halima put her spell of her 'Tahleel' on the two reservoirs, it reached everyone.

One of the effects of the 'Tahleel' was to cure people of curiosity. Those who drank it stopped asking questions. Above all they stopped wondering about the actions of the clan's leading men. They became model subjects doing without question, without objection, what they were told to do. . . .

As things kept going well for the tribe and her, Halima became more and more sure that she was the cause of it all. The clan's leaders too were convinced that they owed their continued success to Halima and her spirits. They heaped honours on her. They consulted her on all important issues and her counsel often proved invaluable. It was Halima, for instance, who thought up the idea of the shortages to keep the common people subdued [quiet]. Shortages of all basic commodities were deliberately created and they kept people busy struggling for bare survival. They did not have the time or energy to spare worrying about the goings-on in the government. The leaders of the clan felt more secure than ever.

From "Government by Magic Spell" by Saida Hagi-Dirie Herzi from *The Heinemann Book of Contemporary African Short Stories*, edited by Chinua Achebe and C. L. Innes. Introduction, Selection and Biographical Notes copyright ©1992 by Chinua Achebe and C. L. Innes. Reprinted by permission of **Heinemann Educational Books, Ltd**.

Understanding What You Read After you have finished reading the selection, answer the following questions.

1. How did members of her clan use Halima to keep themselves in power?

_____

_____

2. Do you think that the author supported the government of Somalia at the time she wrote this story? Explain why or why not.

_____

_____

Activity

Use library and Internet resources to find out what has happened in Somalia since this story was written. Prepare a short report on government in Somalia in the 1990s.

READING 59

East Africa

Along the Great Rift

In this reading the author describes the varied geography of Africa's Great Rift. He compares its geography in Kenya to the conditions it has created farther north in the Horn of Africa.

The road has risen swiftly as we leave Nakuru, a town that sits south of the Equator in Kenya. Now, as we drive beneath cool gray rain clouds, we pass the lush tea plantations of Kenya's colonial past. Abruptly the clouds break, and before our windshield the red earth drops away. A gash 700 meters (2,300 feet) deep and 16 kilometers (ten miles) across—an offshoot of Africa's Great Rift—lies before us. Far to the left, stretching beyond the horizon, I see a glimmering expanse of water—Lake Victoria. . . .

Visitors to Kenya know the rift as the breathtaking escarpments [cliffs] they pass on safari. Few realize it is actually an immense series of cracks in the face of the continent that runs 5,600 kilometers [3,500 miles], from the Red Sea south to Mozambique. Enormous troughs—in places 90 kilometers [56 miles] across and nearly 2 kilometers [1.25 miles] deep—have formed along those cracks.

Here in central Africa the rift has two branches. The eastern bisects [divides] Kenya and skirts both Kilimanjaro and the Senengeti Plain in Tanzania. The western rift cleaves [splits] the heart of Africa, cupping a great chain of lakes. The rifting earth . . . stokes [stirs up] the volcanic fires of the Virunga Mountains, home to the endangered mountain gorilla. Lake Victoria sits atop a plateau between the two branches.

Rifting also generated the highlands of Ethiopia and the Afar desert. It was there I began my journey. How different the shriveling lake known as Assal [in the Afar desert] is from Victoria. As different as the cool Kenya Highlands are from the hellish, brooding landscape we are traversing [crossing] here in Djibouti, a tiny . . . country in the Horn of Africa. Djibouti guards the channel between the Red Sea and the Gulf of Aden.

We leave the capital, Djibouti, at dawn. The humid air is already 37°C (100°F). . . . The land is harsh beyond belief: Even withered thornbushes struggle to survive on black lava ridges. Why am I here, I wonder, as the heat sears [burns] my nostrils. Because, I tell myself, this is where the East African Rift System begins. . . .

Our trip to Lake Assal offers a rare glimpse of earth's crust being formed. We meet Bruce Kinser, a[n] oil driller from East Texas, at a government geothermal project outside Djibouti. Steam roars deafeningly through a well that may one day provide electric power for the country.

"The earth steams here because magma is so close to the surface," he says. "Seawater from the Gulf of Aden leaks down, then boils up through vents." The earth's crust here is thin—perhaps only 25 kilometers [about 16 miles] thick.

In Kinser's truck we bounce down a valley strewn with boulders toward Lake Assal, 156 meters [511 feet] below sea level. As we drive along the tortured black cliffs, Kinser says, pointing to a congealed [hardened] flow of lava, "This land's only ten years old." . . . We pause by a long black fissure [crack]. [In 1978] 800 earthquakes shook this area. Then several square miles of lava oozed forth. . . .

Far below us, nearly smothered in desert haze, lies Lake Assal. . . . We reach the water's edge, and the depression [low place] has become a furnace. My thermometer, good for 50°C (135°F) has gone off its scale. The heat bakes us on all sides, so evenly that I cannot tell where the sun is without looking.

Lake Assal can exist in such fierce heat only because seawater constantly percolates [filters] into the depression. Evaporating rapidly, it leaves salt everywhere. In the clear shallows it drifts like fine snow. Salt cauliflowers knobble [cover like round stones] the shoreline.

For centuries these deposits have drawn the Afar nomads. They pile their camels high with salt, which they then sell to the tribes of the Ethiopian Highlands to the south.

From "Africa's Great Rift," (retitled "Along the Great Rift") by Curt Stager from *National Geographic,* May 1990. Copyright © 1990 by **National Geographic Society**. Reprinted by permission of the publisher.

Understanding What You Read After you have finished reading the selection, answer the following questions.

1. What is the Great Rift and where is it located?

_____

_____

2. How are the location and geography of Lake Victoria and Lake Assal different?

_____

_____

3. Why do you think it is hotter near Lake Assal than at other places in the Afar desert?

_____

_____

Activity

Find out how the width and depth of the Great Rift's troughs compare to the width and depth of Arizona's Grand Canyon. Write a paragraph to report your findings.

READING 60   East Africa

The Kikuyu Meet Europeans

Jomo Kenyatta, the author of this selection, led the movement to free Kenya from British rule after World War II. When Kenya gained its independence in 1963, Kenyatta became the new nation's first president. Here, he describes his people's first contacts with the British in the late 1800s.

The first few Europeans who passed near the Gikuyu [Kikuyu] country were more or less harmless. . . . The Europeans with their caravans kept coming and going the same way from the coast to Lake Victoria and Uganda. In their upwards and downwards journeys they traded with the Gikuyu with little or no conflict. . . . The Gikuyu thought that the Europeans with their caravans did not mean any harm and befriended them. . . .

When the Europeans first came into the Gikuyuland the Gikuyu looked upon them as wanderers (*orori* or *athongo*) who had deserted from their homes and were lonely and in need of friends. The Gikuyu, in their natural generosity and hospitality, welcomed the wanderers and felt pity for them. As such the Europeans were allowed to pitch their tents and to have a temporary right of occupation on the land in the same category as those Gikuyu *mohoi* or *mothami* who were given only cultivation or building rights. The Europeans were treated in this way in the belief that one day they would get tired of wandering and finally return to their own country.

These early Empire builders, knowing what they were after, played on the ignorance and sincere hospitable [generous, friendly] nature of the people. They agreed to the terms of a *mohoi* or *mothami*, and soon started to build small forts or camps, saying that "the object of a station is to form a centre for the purchase of food for caravans proceeding to Uganda," etc. . . .

The Gikuyu gave the Europeans building rights . . . with no idea of the motives which were behind the caravans, for they thought that it was only a matter of trading and nothing else. Unfortunately, they did not realize that these places were used for the preliminary [introductory, beginning] preparations for taking away their land from them. They established friendly relations with the Europeans and supplied them with food for their caravans, taking it for granted that naturally the white wanderers must undoubtedly have their own country, and therefore could not settle for good in a foreign land, that they would feel home-sick and, after selling their goods, would go back to live in their homesteads with parents and relatives. . . .

The early travellers reported that "Kikuyu promised to be the most progressive station between the coast and the lake. The natives were very friendly, and even enlisted as porters to go to the coast, but these good relations received a disastrous check. Owing largely to the [lack] of discipline in the passing caravans, whose men robbed the crops and otherwise made themselves troublesome, the people became [hostile], and . . . murdered several porters." This was the beginning of the suffering and the use of the sticks which produced killing fire. . . . We are told that the Gikuyu were "taught a lesson" . . .

After this event the Gikuyu, with bitterness in their hearts, realised that the strangers they had given hospitality to had planned to plunder [steal] and subjugate [conquer] them by brute force. . . . People were indignant [angered by something unjust] for these acts of ingratitude on the part of the Europeans, and declined to trade with them, thinking that the Europeans and their caravans would get hungry and move away from Gikuyu country; but soon the Gikuyu were made to know that "might is right," . . . and parties [of Europeans] were sent out regularly to take [food] by force! . . .

Soon afterwards the Kenya-Uganda railway . . . was completed. And the Europeans, having their feet firm on the soil, began to claim the absolute right to rule the country and to have the ownership of the lands. . . . The Gikuyu, who are the original owners, now live as "tenants at the will of the Crown." The Gikuyu lost most of their lands through their [good will], for the Gikuyu country was never wholly conquered by force of arms, but the people were put under the ruthless domination of European imperialism [rule] through . . . trickery [and] treaties.

From "The Gikuyu System of Land Tenure" (retitled "The Kikuyu Meet Europeans") from *Facing Mount Kenya: The Tribal Life of the Gikuyu* by Jomo Kenyatta. Copyright ©1938 by Martin Secker & Warburg Ltd. Reprinted by permission of **Secker and Warburg, an imprint of Reed Books**.

Understanding What You Read
After you have finished reading the selection, answer the following questions.

1. Why did the Kikuyu not view the British as a threat at first?

_____

_____

2. How and why did the relationship between the British and the Kikuyu change?

_____

_____

Activity

Prepare a speech to give in a council of Kikuyu leaders. Take the role of a British or a Kikuyu leader. In your speech, explain why the Kikuyu should or should not cooperate with the British traders.

Central Africa

Shopping from Salaula

Charities throughout the United States and Europe dispose of donated cloth-ing they cannot use by selling it to textile recyclers. These recyclers compress this clothing into bales and ship it to countries in Africa to be resold. Second-hand clothing was the sixth largest U.S. export to sub-Saharan Africa in 1997. In this reading, a social scientist examines the impact of such clothing on Zambia.

In Zambia since the mid-1980s, the term *salaula* has referred to second-hand clothing imported from the West. It means, approximately, in the Bemba language, to select from a pile in the manner of rummaging. As such, it graphically captures what takes place in urban and provincial [rural] markets as consumers pick through the piles of imported clothes, selecting garments to satisfy clothing needs and desires. . . .

Zambia's geography of *salaula* retailing contains several distinct segments that are most noticeable in big cities like Lusaka. By the beginning of the 1990s the *salaula* sections of outdoor markets in both urban and rural areas had grown much larger than the food sections. In the mid-1990s *salaula* retailing had spread into urban high-income neigh-bourhoods and downtown offices, and it had spilled out on to the city's main streets. . . . Today, *salaula* is available in most corners of the country, brought out from Lusaka, Chipata, or the Copperbelt by small-scale entre-preneurs or traders' hired hands who travel, for instance to commercial farms and other rural sites offering wage work . . . where they sell their goods to workers on payday, and into the countryside, where they exchange second-hand clothing for agricultural produce, goats, chickens, and fish. . . .

White-collar workers of both sexes from Lusaka's downtown offices often visit *salaula* markets during their lunch hour. But some adult men will tell you that they won't be caught in a *salaula* market. Instead they send their wives to select the right-sized shirts and trousers for them. . . . There is an extensive trade in high-income neighborhoods, as there is in downtown offices, carried on by individuals who notify friends of their purchase of a bale of *salaula* and/or circulate in office buildings, selling clothes to persons who receive a monthly pay cheque [check]. . . .

The scrutiny of *salaula* takes time. Colour co-ordination is keenly attended to. . . . Regardless of income group, most consumers considered 'value for money' a major selection [guideline], discerning [recognizing] 'good value' in terms of both quality and fashion/style. Low-income cus-tomers both in Lusaka and in the province paid attention to garment dura-bility/strength, whereas young urban adults looked for 'the latest.' This is their own term, and it comprises influences from South Africa, Europe, and North America as well as from specific youth cultures. . . . For example, many young adult men who are close to graduating from secondary school are reluctant to wear jeans for fear of being mistaken for street vendors. They have higher job aspirations [goals] for themselves. This contrasts with the search of the young male [street] barbers and vendors . . . for oversize jeans from *salaula* to create the 'big look' they associate with the opportunity and daring of a world away from home. . . .

Consumers are not particularly concerned about the [origin] of the used garments as long as they come from 'the West'. . . . What the West is, above all, is an imagined place, associated with power, wealth, and consumer goods that surpass most local products in quality and style. . . .

While most of the boutiques I saw in Lusaka in 1992 and 1993 exhibited carefully washed and ironed garments, today they display their goods without such intervention [action]. In fact, wrinkles are preferred. This practice, in the words of vendors and customers alike, reduces the fear that such garments are 'third-hand,' which is to say, previously used, and specifically by Zambians. Second-hand clothing displayed with folds and wrinkles straight from the bale is considered to be fresh from the source, and therefore genuine. . . . When shopping for *salaula*, before assessing the 'value for money' aspect, Zambian consumers [examine] first, not the price, but whether the garments are foreign enough and genuinely so.

From "Second-Hand Clothing Encounters in Zambia: Global Discourses, Western Commodities, and Local Histories" (retitled "Shopping from Salaula") from *Africa*, vol. 69, no. 3, 1999. Copyright ©1999 by **International African Institute**. Reprinted by permission of the publisher.

Understanding What You Read After you have finished reading the selection, answer the following questions.

1. Is it accurate to view *salaula* as clothing for poor Africans? Explain.

2. Why do many Zambians prefer second-hand clothing from the West to new items made elsewhere?

3. What example does the writer cite to show how Zambians use clothing to show their place in society?

Activity

Imagine that you are a Zambian teen. Write a journal entry about shopping at a *salaula* market after school.

Central Africa

ECONOMICS

The Lifeline of a Nation

The following two readings are about riverboat traffic on the Congo River in the Democratic Republic of Congo, once known as Zaire. The first describes the writer's trip up the river around 1990. The second reading reports the shutdown of the riverboats in 1993.

Captain Kilundu has sailed the Zaire [Congo] River and its tributaries for 23 years. . . . He sits in his oversize chair at the helm of the *Colonel Ebeya*. . . . "This is not just a boat," he said. "It is a social service. There are no roads here and very few other boats. This boat is the only market, the only pharmacy, the only clinic . . . for hundreds of miles. We bring the town to the people."

The view from the bridge [boat's upper platform] showed a town in itself: The boat was augmented [increased] by the six double-deck barges it pushes, jammed with more than 5,000 people, making [it] one of the largest towns on the 1,077-mile stretch of river between Kinshasa, the capital, and Kisangani. . . .

"This boat is our life," a fisherman named Basese told me as he dumped two small trussed [tied up] crocodiles onto the deck. "Without the boat we have no way to sell what we catch and grow, and no chance to buy the things we need." . . .

I asked Malu [a merchant] how it was possible for the hundreds of merchants to make a living when they all seemed to sell the same things.

"There are very few jobs, so people have to become traders to feed their families. . . . I buy used shirts from the market women in Kinshasa and sell them along the river. . . . When we reach Kisangani, I hope to have none of these shirts [left]. . . . Then, as fast as I can, I buy potatoes and beans, and that is my stock to sell in Kinshasa and again buy shirts." . . .

When we neared Mbandaka, once known as Equator Station, the entire town was waiting for us. "This is a very important place for me," Malu called out as he bundled up his shirts. "If I'm lucky, I can sell as much here as on the whole rest of the trip." . . .

In the midafternoon the boat horn blew, and Malu and the other merchants scrambled back aboard. Fishermen who had paddled downstream to await the boat in town tied on to be towed back up to their homes. Captain Kilundu maneuvered past empty warehouses and rusting, once-grand paddle wheelers lining the shore, and we pulled out into the stream. The next town was 300 miles away.

From "Zaire River: Lifeline for a Nation," by Robert Caputo from *National Geographic,* November 1991. Copyright © 1991 by National Geographic Society. Reprinted by permission of National Geographic Society.

Kisangani, Zaire—For nearly a century . . . riverboats have made the thou-sand-mile voyage upstream between Kinshasa and this port city deep in the immense tropical bush of Central Africa.

But five months ago, the two ancient and dilapidated [worn out] government-owned steamers still working the route, twice a month each way, ceased operating altogether. Port officials said they could no longer afford to buy fuel or spare parts for the journey, which took eight days to two weeks.

There are few roads: the river is the only highway. And the only reli-able means of reaching here now is by plane, whose fare is far beyond the reach of most people in one of the world's poorest countries. . . .

If the riverboat shutdown continues, and many people believe it could last indefinitely given Zaire's devastated [ruined] economy, the region is likely to become increasingly remote and inaccessible [hard to reach]. . . .

"The riverboat was the only link for us to the outside world," said Prof. Boven L. Kumbukama, the chairman of research at the University of Kisangani. "And the future will be much bleaker and desperate without it."

From "A Stillness Falls on the Heart of Africa, As its Main Artery, the River is Cut," (retitled "The Lifeline of a Nation") by Kenneth B. Noble from the *New York Times*, March 18, 1993. Copyright ©1993 by **The New York Times Company**. Reprinted by permission of the pub-lisher.

Understanding What You Read After you have finished reading the selection, answer the following questions.

1. Why does the captain compare his boat to a "town"?

_____

_____

2. How might the lives of the people along the Congo River be affected by the end of riverboat traffic? Explain why.

_____

_____

_____

Activity

Imagine that you are living along the Congo River. Write a letter to government officials in Kinshasa to persuade them that river-boat traffic should be restored.

Central Africa

READING
63

Encounters with Pygmies

Helen Winternitz is an American who visited the Democratic Republic of the Congo when it was known as Zaire. Here, Winternitz describes the Pygmies, a people of the Congo River basin, who helped the travelers when their vehicle was stuck in the mud in the northeastern part of the country.

We climbed out [of the vehicle] into the deep mud. I struggled over to the bank of solid ground at the road's edge and sat down. . . . We were far from anywhere and the forest grew so thickly along the edges of the road that we couldn't even pitch a tent.

. . . A couple of dogs came bounding out of the forest a few yards from where I sat. The dogs, dun-colored and sharp-eared, were unusually small and close behind the dogs, a band of Pygmies came stepping out of the greenery, two men, two women, and three children. True to their reputation, they were diminutive [small]; the taller of the men reached a little more than four feet. They all had the same . . . features—triangularly wide noses, prominent cheeks, and large, dark eyes accustomed to the gentle, shielded light of the deep forest—and they were full of smiles despite their shyness. The men of this little band waded out into the mud to help. . . .

The men had laid their hunting tools on the bank—nets, which they carry bunched over their shoulders and use to trap animals, and tiny bows, which measure only about two feet and launch poison-tipped arrows at game as large as elephant. The women were carrying deep storage baskets on their backs slung by straps slung from their foreheads. . . .

The Pygmies are thought to be descendants of the original inhabitants of the central African forest. They may have settled in the Congo Basin . . . tens of thousands of years before Europeans came to the African continent. Unlike the villagers who cling to the road and battle the vegetation, the Pygmies do not war against the forest. They gather its fruits, hunt its game, fish its rivers, feast on dark wild honey, and roam to its most secret corners. They move through the forest, not against it. . . .

With the Pygmies' help and plenty of digging, pushing, and swearing, we got the Land Rover forward onto solid ground. . . . almost instantly, the entire band . . . disappeared into the forest. . . .

After our first encounter with the band of Pygmies and their hunting dogs, we [began] seeing groups of them all along the road, but never for very long. Before you could take a second look, much less raise a camera to take a photograph, they would be gone, melted into the shadows and the leaves, stepping onto a path invisible to the non-Pygmy, retreating into their green sanctuary [safe place].

As a people, the Pygmies are extraordinarily gentle, disinterested in the warfare, ancient and modern, that has episodically [periodically] swept through central Africa. Starting about the time of [Christ], Bantu tribes migrated in massive numbers into the Congo Basin where the Pygmies had settled thousands of years earlier. They came planting corn and herding cattle, these tribes with their warrior traditions and iron weapons, but the Pygmies did not try to fight the newcomers. Instead, they moved deeper into the forest. Somewhere between 150,000 and 300,000 Pygmies remain scattered through the Congo's watershed. Concentrated in the Ituri [in northeastern Democratic Republic of the Congo] are the BaMbuti, who are the most isolated and traditional of their kind. As hunters and gatherers, they have never acquired some of the simplest of technologies, like the use of matches or flintstones to light fires. Each new fire must be lit from another in a chain of dependency from some original fire, whose site has been long forgotten by the wandering Pygmies and whose flame may be the oldest continuous one in the world. When they move their settlements about the forest, a periodic chore to find fresh hunting grounds, they carry burning coals wrapped in thick green leaves.

Because the villager's fear the deep forest and are ignorant of many of its secrets, they depend on the Pygmies to bring them game and honey in exchange for vegetables and other farm produce. Over the years, the villagers have come to consider the Pygmies as inferiors who are duty-bound to labor in their service, which the Pygmies will do until they choose to return to their secluded settlements in the forest's . . . shadows.

Excerpt (retitled "Encounters with Pygmies") from *East Along the Equator: A Journey Up the Congo and Into Zaire* by Helen Winternitz. Copyright ©1987 by Helen Winternitz. Reprinted by permission of **The Atlantic Monthly Press, an imprint of Grove/Atlantic Inc.**

Understanding What You Read After you have finished reading the selection, answer the following questions.

1. How do other Central Africans depend on the Pygmies?

_____

_____

_____

2. In what ways do the Pygmies differ from the other peoples who live in the Congo Basin?

_____

_____

_____

Activity

Research the native tribes of Papua New Guinea. Write a paragraph that compares them with the Pygmies.

READING 64 — Southern Africa

Namibia's Skeleton Coast

The Atlantic coast of Namibia is a largely unsettled region that is so dry and forbidding that is appropriately known as the Skeleton Coast. However, two Australian filmmakers spent eight years living there in order to film, photograph, and learn about this region of southwest Africa. The following reading reports some of their findings.

All we could see at first was a boiling cloud of dust, storming across the desert like some frightful dervish [demon] run amok. Then we realized that there was an elephant ahead of the dust cloud. The elephant was trying to charge us. . . .

Elephants in the desert? In northwest Namibia, an area known as the Kaokoveld, such apparitions [appearances] are not mirages. Neither are the giraffes that haunt the barren plains and black rhinoceroses that ascend steep, rocky slopes. Foraging for seasonal grasses, mountain zebras and antelope keep a wary eye out for lions, whose far-reaching tracks extend all the way to the seashore, where they hunt . . . seals and other marine mammals.

Here, too, much more diminutive [small] creatures, ingeniously [cleverly] adapted, live among, and even within, the seemingly sterile [lifeless] dunes. Some of the mounds . . . even roar when an avalanche of sand slowly cascades down their steep slopes.

In all, the Namib Desert stretches 1,300 miles along Africa's southwest coast. We have seen and marveled at the survival techniques of creatures great and small while filming the . . . northern Namib, which covers some 19,000 square miles. Imagine an area of sand and rock nearly as big as Lake Michigan. . . .

The Namib has existed for perhaps 55 million years; it is one of the world's oldest and driest deserts. Rainfall . . . averages a little more than half an inch a year, What sustains this ecosystem is a series of rivers—rivers that are nearly always dry. In the distant past they carved their way . . . from the interior highlands westward to the Skeleton Coast. Today, only if enough rain falls in the highlands do some rivers occasionally flow. This is by no means an annual event, and when it does happen, the rivers' largesse [gift] usually trickles into the sand well short of the coast.

But water remains trapped under the sand, turning the dry riverbeds into what scientists studying this country often call "linear oases." Following these life-giving channels, wildlife seeks out permanent springs—elephants can tap new sources by digging with their trunks—and feeds on the . . . vegetation sustained by subterranean [underground] water sources. . . .

Just offshore flows another natural source of abundance, a permanent force without which life on the Skeleton Coast would be impossible. The Benguela Current sweeps northward along the coast, bringing waters from Antarctica. Prevailing winds create a constant upswelling of cold bottom waters that sustain great pastures of marine life. The Benguela also brings a vital source of water to the desert: fog.

When warm air farther out to sea sweeps in across the cold Benguela, fog forms. This fog drifts onshore most of the year. In the dead of the desert night, on leaves, rocks, grass, even on the bodies of living things, that fog condenses. Thus, lives that might not be able to wait for thunder to roll over Etosha [a large salt basin in northern Namibia] and for dry riverbeds to heave with a lifetime flood—those . . . lives have another chance.

Nearly everything depends on fog and dew, from plants to massive animals. . . . Giraffes . . . frequent the lower Haonib, where fog condenses on the leaves of the acacia trees they feed on, helping fulfill their water needs.

When a searing hot spell strikes . . . the fog disappears. After the heat subsides, on the first evening of the fog's return, the desert is a busy place. On one such night we were camped in the dunes near the Haonib, a hundred yards from a colony of dune ants. . . . Ants of this species are normally . . . in their holes by night. But many from this colony were outside digging furiously. Later we found them still outside and all nearly motionless. Fog had condensed on the ants themselves, and they were drinking the droplets from one another's bodies—one of the desert's unique rites of survival.

From "Africa's Skeleton Coast," (retitled "Namibia's Skeleton Coast") by Des and Jen Bartlett from *National Geographic*, January 1992. Copyright ©1992 by **National Geographic Society**. Reprinted by permission of the publisher.

Understanding What You Read After you have finished reading the selection, answer the following questions.

1. How do the desert's dry riverbeds sustain wildlife? Why do elephants have an advantage in finding water?

_____

_____

2. Describe the Benguela current and its role in the Namib.

_____

_____

Activity

Imagine you have made a movie about life in the Namib. Create a movie poster that symbolizes the region's harsh environment.

Southern Africa

GOVERNMENT

Experiencing Apartheid in South Africa

Lettie Khuzwayo was a nurse at a health clinic in Alexandria, a township for black South Africans on the edge of the city of Johannesburg. In this interview, conducted before apartheid ended in South Africa, she describes life in her township under the system of apartheid.

We used to have freehold [land ownership] rights here. When they wanted to get rid of that, they decided to do it by getting rid of the husbands! The police used to wait at the corners early in the morning, take their pass [documents that all Blacks were required to carry, which stated where they could work and live], and "stamp them out." Then you had to leave Alex [Alexandria] and go to Meadowlands. So they used to stamp every man out and tell them, "You go to Meadowlands next day." Then they try to abolish your house and you're moved, just like that. But certainly in all the time I've been here they couldn't abolish us all . . . what they've done now is to buy all the land, so the little right to stay now depends on our passbook, just like everybody.

My husband was born here and his father had a property. We're fighting now because it's been sold to the administration [government] without our permission. In other words, they took it over at a very low price that we hadn't agreed. We love this place. We both work here, the shops are close, our friends are near. We've got Pick and Pay [a grocery store] just round the corner—in Meadowlands and Diepkloof people have to go miles to the cheaper shops.

There were freehold rights here for more than a hundred years, . . . but this government is afraid of that, it gives us the power to stay. . . . We'd like to take over the township ourselves and have our own municipality [town]: the running of the place, the financing, the decisions. The roads aren't made, the gutters are filthy, there's only bucket sewerage. We'd like to have proper toilets and electricity . . . at the moment it's paraffin lamp and candles, which is very expensive; and not easy when the children are at home alone. When we are away, most of the time I worry in the evening: we often get children with quite severe burns at the clinic.

Its quite different, going out to work with children at home. When they were small they had to wait outside the house after school till I got home. There was one that used to be at school at eight, and knocks off at twelve: from twelve o'clock till I got home at four he just roams around. . . .

We no longer find the police in the streets, with lorries [trucks] packed with people whose houses are going to be knocked down and abolished . . . . . . Because the clinic is just outside the township, on the Joh'burg [Johannesburg] side, women used to come and sit here at five o'clock in the morning in those days, so that if the police came they could say they weren't in the township. Imagine, every morning they came! They would run across the street to the clinic and the police would just look at them . . . when you ask them why, they'd say, "Now we're not in a proclaimed [off limits] area, the police cannot catch us."

We don't see so much of the police now . . . at the time there was a yard with many illegal people staying: you'd find them too outside at five in the morning, making fires with paper to keep themselves warm; they were afraid to be in their shelters in the yard in case the police came. Outside they had the chance to run! What's happened over the years is that the administration board has bought properties and come in and knocked down some of them. We did fight as a community, as well as by ourselves.

From "Urban Life" (retitled "Experiencing Apartheid in South Africa") by Lettie Khuzwayo from *We Make Freedom: Women in South Africa* by Beata Lipman. Copyright ©1984 by Beata Lipman. Reprinted by permission of **Routledge**.

Understanding What You Read After you have finished reading the selection, answer the following questions.

1. According to Khuzwayo, what two methods did the government use during apartheid to force residents out of certain townships?

_____

_____

2. What clue does the interview give that education for black South Africans was limited under apartheid?

_____

_____

3. What do you think created the "yard" that Khuzwayo refers to in Alexandria township, and why were people living on it in temporary shelters? Why does she call these people "illegal"?

_____

_____

Activity

Pressure from the United States and other nations helped end apartheid in the early 1990s. Write a letter as an American to the president of South Africa, persuading him that apartheid is wrong and should be abolished.

Southern Africa

The Moors of Mozambique

In the early 1500s, Portuguese adventurer Duarte Barbosa traveled the east coast of Africa and reported on the people and places he visited there. These peoples included both Arabs who had lived along the coast for centuries and the Swahili, an African people who adopted many Arab customs. Here, Barbosa describes the Swahili of Sofala, a coastal village in present-day Mozambique. He also traveled to Kilwa, an island in present-day Tanzania near its border with Mozambique. Note that Barbosa refers to the Arabs and the Africans of this region as "Moors." This was the European term of the time for anyone, regardless of race, who was a Muslim—that is, a follower of the religion of Islam.

The manner of their traffic was this: they came [to Sofala] in small vessels named *zambucos* from the kingdoms of Kilwa, Mombasa [an island off the coast of present-day Kenya], and Malindi [on the coast of southeast Kenya], bringing many cotton cloths, some spotted and others white and blue, also some of silk, and many small beads, gray, red, and yellow, which things came to said kingdoms from the great kingdom of Cambay [in Northwest India] in other greater ships. And these wares the said Moors who come from Malindi and Mombasa [purchased from merchants who brought the goods there] paid for in gold at such a price that these merchants departed well pleased. . . .

The Moors of Sofala kept these wares and sold them afterwards to the heathen of the Kingdom of Benametapa, who came thither [toward that place] laden [loaded down] with gold which they gave in exchange for the said cloths. . . . These Moors collect also great store [supplies] of ivory which they find hard by [near] Sofala, and this also they sell in the [Indian] Kingdom of Cambay. . . . These Moors are black, and some of them tawny [tan or golden in color]; some of them speak Arabic, but the more part use the language of the country. They clothe themselves from the waist down with cotton and silk cloths, and other cloths they wear over their shoulders like capes, and turbans on their heads. Some of them wear small caps dyed . . . in chequers [multicolored squares] and other woolen clothes in many tints, also camlets [fabric made from camel hair] and other silks.

Their food is millet [a type of grain], rice, flesh [meat] and fish. . . . In the country near Sofala are many wild elephants, . . . lions, deer and many other wild beasts. It is a land of plains and hills with many streams of sweet water.

In this same Sofala . . . they make great store of cotton and weave it, and from it they make much white cloth, and as they know not how to dye it, or have not the needful dyes, they take the Cambay cloths, blue or otherwise colored, and unravel them and make them up again, so that it becomes a new thing. With this thread and their own white they make much colored cloth, and from it they gain much gold. . . .

Journeying from Sofala forty leagues [between about 100 to 175 miles] more or less towards Mozambique there is a very great river which they call Cuama [the present-day Zambezi River], which leads into the inner country more than a hundred and seventy leagues. . . . By this river comes much gold from Benametapa. . . .

Going [north] along the coast . . . there is an island hard by the mainland which is called Kilwa, in which is a Moorish town with many fair houses of stone and mortar, with many windows after our [European] fashion, very well arranged in streets. . . . Of the Moors [of Kilwa] there are some fair and some black, they are finely clad in many rich garments of gold and silk and cotton, and the women as well; also with much gold and silver in chains and bracelets, which they wear on their legs and arms, and many jewelled earrings in their ears. These Moors speak Arabic and follow the creed [teachings] of the Alcoran [the Koran, the holy book of Islam]. . . .

This town was taken by force from its king by the Portuguese, as, moved by arrogance, he refused to obey the King [of Portugal] our Lord. There they took many prisoners and the king fled from the island, and His Highness [the king of Portugal] ordered that a fort be built there, and kept it [the island] under his rule and governance.

Excerpt (retitled "The Moors of Mozambique") from *The Book of Duarte Barbosa*, translated by Mansel Longworth Dames. Copyright ©1918 by **Hakluyt Society**. Reprinted by permission of the publisher.

Understanding What You Read After you have finished reading the selection, answer the following questions.

1. What items did the Swahili of the coast sell to the non-Muslim peoples in East Africa's interior? What did they receive in exchange?

   _____

   _____

2. Where did the Arab and Swahili traders get the goods that they brought to Sofala? What did they use to pay for these goods?

   _____

   _____

Activity

Using Barbosa's descriptions as a guide, create a drawing of a Swahili resident of Kilwa or Sofala. You may wish to research the traditional costumes of the Swahili to add color to your drawing.

China, Mongolia, and Taiwan

READING 67

How Dragon Pond Got Its Name

Dragons appear frequently in Chinese folktales. Early Chinese believed that dragons lived in the water and the sky. Dances involving humans dressed in dragon costumes remain an important part of traditional Chinese culture today. So may some of the beliefs about dragons. According to the story-teller, the following event happened "several decades ago" near Dashiqiao, a town in Liaoning province in far northeast China.

It was summer and the peasants were working in the fields. Furious, dark clouds suddenly covered the sky, like wild horses running on the plain. The wind blew very hard, and branches swung from side to side. The peasants hurried home to shut their doors tightly.

It was so inky black that nothing could be seen. People looked out their windows in surprise. It rained heavily. Thunder sounded as if it would deafen their ears; lightning flashed as though it would blind them. To the peasants' surprise, they saw something enormous fall down to the ground from the heavens as the lightning flashed, then they heard a loud thud as it landed. It rained hard for another hour, then gradually the sky began to clear. Eventually the rain stopped. A beautiful rainbow appeared, and the sun came out from behind the clouds. Everything looked fresh, and men, women, and children went outdoors again.

The peasants were very surprised to find a big new pond near the road with a very large animal lying in it. It had long, thick hair on either side of its mouth and a head like a horse's, but much bigger. It also had a pair of huge antlers. Its body was more than one hundred meters (nearly 100 yards) long, covered with thousands of fishlike scales, each more than one meter in diameter. The creature had four large talons shaped like a rooster's, as well as a long tail.

An old man recognized the creature as a dragon who was in charge of rain. There are many kinds of dragons, and they all have different jobs. Some are in charge of fire, some of rain, some of wind, some of sand, and so on. They are all ruled by the Emperor of Heaven and live in the seas, rivers, lakes, and even wells. At times they fly above the clouds, or even change form into people or other animals. Of course, dragons have magnificent palaces in the water. In ancient times, emperors of China regarded themselves as descendants of dragons. This was a sign of absolute power. Many temples were built to honor the dragon, and when it was dry people would pray to dragons for rain.

This dragon was dying. The people realized that he must have committed a serious crime against the Emperor of Heaven and had been punished by being hurled down to earth by the Emperor's troops. That is to say, the Emperor had taken back the dragon's supernatural powers. The people pitied the dragon from the bottom of their hearts. They felt that they must help him get back to heaven. Wasting no time, they knit a big mat of dried reeds and covered the dragon with it to prevent the sun from burning him. Then they went back to the village. Two men were left to take care of the dragon. One of the old men told the villagers to make preparations to send the dragon off, so they beat drums, blew horns, burned spices, and prayed to the Emperor of Heaven to allow the dragon to go back.

The villagers did this for nearly three days. On the third day a thick fog filled the village. As the day passed, the fog became thicker and thicker, so thick that people could not see each other. When the fog finally disappeared, several villagers ran to see the dragon but found that it had vanished. All of the townspeople gathered around the pond in astonishment. The new pond remained but the dragon was gone. It was a real miracle, and the people cheered.

As the years went by, the villagers found that the pond was never dry, even when the rains did not come. Moreover, the pond was rich in fish, shrimp, and crab. To memorialize this strange event, the villagers of Dashiqiao call this place Dragon Pond.

From "Dragon Pond" (retitled "How Dragon Pond Got Its Name") from *Chinese Folktales* by Howard Giskin. Copyright ©1997 by **NTC/Contemporary Publishing Group**. Reprinted by permission of the publisher.

Understanding What You Read After you have finished reading the selection, answer the following questions.

1. According to this folktale, how do dragons influence everyday life?

_____

2. Why did the dragon fall to earth? How did the villagers help it?

_____

3. How does the story suggest that the dragon rewarded the villagers for their help?

_____

_____

Activity

Draw a color picture of the Dashiqiao dragon, using the description in this folktale as a guide. Color your dragon in traditional Chinese colors.

China, Mongolia, and Taiwan

GEOGRAPHY

China's Coming Great Flood

China is currently home to one of the world's most ambitious construction projects. When it is completed in 2009, the Three Gorges Dam will control the waters of the Chang (Yangtze), the world's third longest river. The dam will provide enormous benefits for China. But it will bring great changes as well. Here, a visitor assesses what the effects of the new dam will be.

The great dam is slowly rising, a thousand miles up the Yangtze from the sea. . . . Yangtze waters irrigate China's "land of fish and rice," the great central valley where close to half the nation's food is grown. . . . Yet at the same time the river has brought China misery. Devastating floods have repeatedly inundated [covered] thousands of square miles and claimed more than 300,000 lives in [the 1900s] alone.

To most Chinese the river is known as Chang Jiang—the Long River. On maps it traces the sinuous line of a dragon. Its . . . tail curls out of the ice of the Tibetan Plateau and tumbles to China's largest city, Chongqing. Its torso [middle] twines through the fabled Three Gorges; . . . its neck winds across the flatlands to the river's mouth near Shanghai.

Beijing's plan to harness this dragon . . . is daunting [awesome]. The dam will stand 607 feet high and more than a mile wide. It will create a reservoir 370 miles long, with a system of locks designed to bring prosperity through maritime commerce to China's interior. There are taller dams and there are wider dams, but none has this might: . . . 26 turbines of perhaps 400 tons each, the largest ever built, will generate 18,200 megawatts of electricity, equivalent to the output of 18 nuclear power plants.

. . . No fewer than 1.9 million people will be forced from ancestral homes and farms and relocated elsewhere. . . . To assay [analyze] the dam and its impact on the region, I embarked on a . . . 400-mile [journey] down the middle Yangtze, covering the stretch where the new reservoir will be. . . . I heard many expressions of enthusiasm and pride. . . . But I also heard voices of anger and foreboding [fear]. All along the way I saw new construction on a scale that boggled the imagination—new cities, bridges, and highways being thrown up along the river's mountain flanks. It is all predicated [based] on the success of the dam. . . .

Chongqing, my first stop, was on a building binge. . . . On the river-front . . . the deepwater port will be expanded to handle vessels ten times larger than those now navigating the river. [This will] increase commercial traffic in coal, tung oil, silk, and an array of agricultural products that southwest China would like to ship to markets on the coast and the world beyond.

But the Chang Jiang is one of the most sediment-filled rivers in the world. . . . Opponents of the dam contend [argue] that a still-water reservoir will cause even more sediment to be deposited, obstructing the passage of deep-draft vessels. . . .

Wanxian, at the midpoint between Chongqing and the dam, stands so high above the river that porters with red-curtained sedan chairs [line] up at the landing to haul tourists up its 183 steps. But its elevation will not save the city. . . .In the center of the city stands a red-and white sign indicating the level to which the waters will rise. All below it—two-thirds of the city proper, embracing 8.5 square miles and 900 factories—will be drowned. A quarter million people will be uprooted and moved to an unknown location. Wanxian will be the reservoir's costliest victim.

The good news is that a new Wanxian will rise above the reservoir. . . . An airport capable of handling jumbo jets will be built . . . on the south side of the river. Tying the airport to the city, one of the world's longest single-arch bridges, now under construction, will span the Chang Jiang.

At the bridge site I met Zhang Mingtai, general manager of . . . the region's largest industrial complex. We stood at the edge of a precipice [cliff] above the river, and Zhang swept a hand across the vista—the doomed city, the Chang Jiang running red with iron-rich soil, the immense valley reaching back into distant mountains. "This is central China," Zhang said over the wind. "The resources here are unknown to outsiders. We're enormously rich in coal, salt, and natural gas. . . . When the dam is built, the opportunities here will be limitless."

"Without the dam?" I asked.

"Without the dam," he said brusquely [sternly], "we'll have nothing."

From "China's Three Gorges: Before the Flood" (retitled "China's Coming Great Flood") by Arthur Zich from *National Geographic*, September 1997. Copyright ©1997 by **National Geographic Society**. Reprinted by permission of the publisher.

Understanding What You Read After you have finished reading the selection, answer the following questions.

1. Name three reasons that China is building a dam on the Yangtze River?

_____

_____

2. Why do opponents of the dam think it will hurt trade on the river?

_____

_____

Activity

Imagine that you are one of residents of Wanxian who will be flooded out of your ancestral home by the Three Gorges Dam. Write a journal entry expressing your feelings about the project.

READING 69

China, Mongolia, and Taiwan

Democracy Comes to Taiwan

For more than 40 years, the anti-communist Chinese who escaped from mainland China in 1949 controlled the island of Taiwan and the Taiwanese people. Today, however, Taiwan has become one of Asia's most stable democracies. A longtime observer of Taiwan and a specialist in Asian affairs explains how this change came about.

"You're a garbage heap!" cried the legislator. "You're the fattest cockroach feeding on the garbage!" his political opponent [foe] shouted. It was but one moment in a session of the Li-fa Yuan, the highest lawmaking body of Taiwan, characterized by shouting and bloody brawls that have sent at least three parliamentarians [members of the legislature] to the hospital. . . .

Only a few years ago such an exchange in the . . . halls of the Taiwan congress would have been unthinkable. Now it symbolizes a sea change in the government and politics of Taiwan—the first prosperous, stable democracy in the history of the Chinese people. . . .

But Taiwan could hardly have traveled a more tortuous [winding] road to reach its success. In 1949 China fell to the communists. The battered army of Nationalist Generalissimo Chiang Kai-shek fled to China's offshore possessions with two million refugees. . . . Chiang's followers maintained that they would once again rule one China under the Nationalist flag. They made Taipei, Taiwan's largest city, their capital-in-exile until they could regroup and recapture the mainland. Their chances for achieving reunification seemed to wane [get smaller] with each passing year, but their policy toward the communists remained resolutely [firmly] based on no contact, no negotiation, and no compromise—the "three noes."

Nationalist legislators, who had been elected on the mainland as representatives of all China in 1947, kept those positions in Taiwan for more than 40 years. In effect the Nationalist Party and the Taiwan government were one and the same, and their legitimacy [authority] rested on the principle of one China. On that point they would brook [allow] no argument. And so, in practice, they added a fourth "no": no political dissent by native Taiwanese. Wielding [using] the authority of martial law, the Nationalists restricted free speech, press, and assembly; prohibited opposition parties; and punished dissenters with jail, torture, even death. They sought to cultivate a sense of "Chineseness" and suppress the islanders' separate identity as Taiwanese, even banning Taiwanese history in the schools and the Taiwanese dialect [language] from public life. . . .

"In grade school we were fined a dollar for every Taiwanese word they caught us using," recalls Fan Yun, a 24-year-old Taiwanese. . . . "We don't want to live under a mainland regime," Fan said. "The old leaders here were outsiders. To them, Taiwan was a hotel. They reckoned they were going back to the mainland, so they spent huge sums on the armed forces and next to nothing on roads, rails, and harbors. . . ."

In 1978, Chiang Ching-kuo, the eldest son of Chiang Kai-shek and long-time head of the secret police, succeeded to the presidency. . . . I wondered where this man, known to many by the initials CCK, might lead Taiwan. I was as surprised as anyone when, in July 1987, he ended martial law. . . . In January 1988 CCK died. But his hand-picked successor, President Lee Teng-hui, the first chief of state born in Taiwan, kept the movement alive. Last December [1992] the citizens of Taiwan elected a whole new legislature, finally replacing the old members who had been elected in 1947. Democracy had arrived. . . .

What made this peaceful transition possible? Prosperity. Since 1951 the island's annual economic growth has averaged almost 9 percent. This year [1993] per capita income will approach $10,000, bringing Taiwan into line with the other members of Asia's industrial elite.

From "Taiwan: The Other China Changes Course," (retitled "Democracy Comes to Taiwan") by Arthur Zich from *National Geographic,* November 1993. Copyright ©1993 by **National Geographic Society**. Reprinted by permission of the publisher.

Understanding What You Read After you have finished reading the selection, answer the following questions.

1. What complaints did the Taiwanese have about Chinese rule on Taiwan?

_____

_____

2. What event in 1992 finally brought democratic government to Taiwan?

_____

3. How did economic conditions in Taiwan affect the movement for democracy?

_____

_____

Activity

Suppose that you are a Taiwanese newspaper editor living on Taiwan in December 1992. Write an editorial explaining why your readers should vote for Taiwanese rather than Chinese candidates to the national legislature in the upcoming election.

READING 70

Japan and the Koreas

The Talisman

This short story by Japanese writer Masao Yamakawa is actually a story within a story. The story's main character tells his own story to the reader. That character is a middle-class office worker named Sekiguchi Jirō. Through Sekiguchi's story, the writer is expressing his own views about Japan's urban culture and society.

It was late one night. . . . There were no more buses, and I took a taxi and got off at the main gate [of my apartment complex]. . . . There was a man in front of me. I had the feeling that I was looking at myself from behind. He had on the same felt hat, and he had the same package in his left hand. . . . It was a foggy night, and I wondered if I might be seeing my own shadow.

But it was no shadow. He walked on, the image of me, I thought—and he went into Wing E, where I lived. He went up the stairs I always go up. . . . He came to the third floor and knocked on the door to the right.

It was my apartment. And then I was even more startled. The door opened and he was taken in, like any tired husband home from work.

I climbed the stairs quietly. . . . I put my ear to the door. . . . He was not he. He was I myself.

. . . I'm not crazy. But I thought I was. I could hear her [his wife] saying "Jirō, Jirō," and laughing and telling me what my sister had said when she had come calling that day. And I could hear my own tired voice in between. She was off in the kitchen getting something to eat, and "I" seemed to be reading the newspaper. I did not know what to think. There was another "I," that was clear. And who, then, was this I, standing foolishly in the hall? Which was "I" and which was I. Where should I go? . . . I opened the door only because I could think of nothing else to do with the I that was myself.

"Who's there?" she said.

"I," I finally answered.

It was quite a scene. My wife came out screaming. She looked at the other "I," and screamed again, and threw herself on me. Her lips were moving and she began to cry. The other "I" came out. His face was white. His name was Kurose Jirō. . . .

Kurose was all apologies. When he handed me his name card I saw what the mistake had been. I lived in E-305, he in D-305. He had come into the wrong wing and gone up to my apartment.

My sister is named Kuniko. He was a civil engineer and he had a cousin named Kuniko. His [first] name was Jirō, so is mine. He lived alone with his wife. The coincidence was complete.

"I did think she seemed a little young. I've been married four years after all," he said as he left. He said it as if he meant to flatter, but I was not up to being pleased. It weighed on my mind, the fact that until I opened the door, neither of them had noticed the mistake.

"But I went off to the kitchen, and he sprawled out with the newspaper the way you always do. It didn't even occur to me that it wouldn't be you."

I reprimanded [criticized] her, and she looked timidly [nervously] around the room. "Not just the room. They must be exactly like us themselves. You saw how he thought I was his wife. It scares me."

I was about to speak, but I did not. To mistake a person or a room—that made no difference. It happened all the time. What bothered me was that Kurose had mistaken our life for his own. . . . I began to wonder whether . . . we were like all those toy soldiers lined up on a department-store counter. Like standardized puppets. . . .

Kurose became for me the representative of all those numberless white-collar workers, all the apartment-house husbands, the toy soldiers, exactly like myself. The representative of all those numberless people who were "I." . . . I resented him. He was not I. I was not one of them, those office workers so much like myself. I was *I*, I was most definitely not he. But where was the difference? Where was there positive evidence to establish the difference?

From "The Talisman" by Masao Yamakawa from *Life*, September 11, 1964, pp. 94-97. Copyright ©1964 by **Time Life Syndication**. Reprinted by permission of the publisher.

Understanding What You Read After you have finished reading the selection, answer the following questions.

1. Identify five coincidences that allow the incident that occurs in this story to take place.

_____

_____

2. What point is the author making when he has Sekiguchi observe that "Kurose had mistaken our life for his own"?

_____

_____

Activity

Imagine that you are Sekiguchi Jirō. Compose a poem, or song lyric to express your view of your everyday life.

Japan and the Koreas

North Korea on the Edge

Journalist Hilary Mackenzie was the first foreign journalist allowed into North Korea in the late 1990s. She went to report on a famine in that closed and secretive nation. Here, she describes what she saw.

They stand still in lines, hands by their sides, faces expressionless. Some with swollen bellies, some with ribs poking through their T-shirts looking like a birdcage. Some, like Hwang Yun Young, with rickets, a disease caused by lack of vitamins. Hwang stands in the front of the Sinsong kindergarten in the capital city of Pyongyang, in a pretty pink lace dress, her hair neatly pulled back in a ponytail, her feet badly swollen. . . .

I would have guessed that Hwang and her classmates are 3-year-olds. But the teacher says they are 6-year-olds. Stunting [slowed growth], caused by long-term malnutrition, means 80 percent of the school's children do not meet the standard height and weight for their age. Doomed to go through life as "nutritional dwarfs," many are also permanently mentally and emotionally damaged from malnutrition. . . .

This is the face of North Korea today, one of the last communist nations in the world. . . . North Korea [is] one of the world's most repressive [controlling] and isolated nations. Kim Il Sung, who ruled the nation for 50 years, espoused [upheld] a philosophy of complete political and economic independence from the world. For years, foreigners were barred from entering the country and North Korea's people had virtually no contact with the outside world. Since his death in 1996, his son, Kim Jong-Il, has steered the same course.

But North Korea's economy began to falter in 1991 with the collapse of the Soviet Union, its major trading partner, and as a result of failed agricultural policies. When it was hit with three years of successive crop failures, brought on by floods and drought, famine set in. . . . At least three quarters of the nation's 23 million people are hungry. Deaths have been widespread, possibly numbering in the millions. . . .

The tragedy has been complicated by politics. Many nations haven't wanted to help North Korea because of its hostility to foreign countries, its Communist system, or both. Western nations feared that food aid would be used to feed only North Korea's army. And for a long time, the North Korean government, which portrays the country as a happy, socialist paradise, tried to hide the problem from the world. . . .

Pak Yong Sun, the school principal, sits beneath a poster of Kim Il Sung. It shows him giving directions to healthy, chubby children, attentive and bursting with energy. . . . "The children here can't concentrate," she says. "They don't pay attention. Some just lie on their desks." . . .

At lunch, the school serves a paltry 8.75 ounces of bread, noodles, and porridge made from corn given by the World Food Program to all children under age six. Korean radishes, cucumbers, and cabbage are added during the short vegetable season. The rest of the year, roots, tree bark, and leaves are mixed in.

Driving to Yomju, I see child "worker-brigades" marching into the fields to weed. . . . Red revolutionary flags stake the fields where the workers toil. "They spur people on," my translator says. Martial [military] music blares from the loudspeaker van further exhorting [urging on] the workers, knee-deep and bent double in the . . . mud under a hot sun.

"We have to sing that our country is best in the world," a female voice crackles over the loudspeaker to the worker-brigades. "And we are making every endeavor [effort] to overcome all the difficulties before us." By the roadside, emaciated [extremely thin] men and women lie slumped over bundles of goods. "It is because they are desperately hungry," the Yomju country chairman explains. "They are exhausted.". . . Factories and mines have been closed because the state cannot feed the workers. Nurseries and kindergartens are entirely dependent upon the international community for all food.

Even the Communist party faithful, who usually receive larger rations, have been touched by the famine. "My own daughter ate one meal a day," before the arrival of food aid, the county chairman says, his loyalty symbolized by a Kim Il Sung badge. "She was very sleepy and listless."

From "Stubbornly Starving: Widespread Famine in North Korea" (retitled "North Korea on the Edge") by Hilary Mackenzie from *Scholastic Update*, September 21, 1998, vol. 131, no. 2. Copyright ©1998 by **Scholastic Inc**. Reprinted by permission of the publisher.

Understanding What You Read After you have finished reading the selection, answer the following questions.

1. What factors inside North Korea caused a food shortage in the 1990s?

_____

2. Why did it take so long for other countries to help North Korea?

_____

_____

3. How did the famine affect North Korea's industries? How did it affect the North Korean people?

_____

_____

Activity

Use library and other resources to learn about the food situation in North Korea today. Summarize your findings in a short report.

Southeast Asia

CULTURE

Life in Rural Thailand

In this reading, a rural Thai couple who live about 40 miles north of Bangkok on the Chao Phraya River, tell about their country and their lives.

We meet Jaran Pomwat at the sawmill where he works. We see that there are hundreds of sawmills next to each other on the banks of the river.

"Nearly half of Thailand's 500,000 square kilometers (198,000 square miles) is covered with forest, mostly of hardwoods like teak," Jaran Pomwat tells us. The timber comes from the north and is transported by river, or road to the sawmills. Outside the sawmills there are thousands of tree trunks piled up together. It is an impressive sight.

"In the old days," Jaran says, "elephants used to help with the forestry. Nowadays, it is mostly done by machines. Sometimes, on particularly difficult ground, elephants are still used to move the tree trunks."

Jaran takes us into the mill and shows us where he works. He uses a circular saw to cut the trunks up into planks. "There are about 200 people working here, and there are as many women as there are men . . . ," he says.

Some of the timber produced here is sold abroad. "Thailand exported much more teak in the past than it does nowadays. In this country other types of trees are used more often than teak. Redwood costs only half as much and is popular for building and furniture-making," he explains.

We leave the mill and drive the short distance to the Pomwats' home. We walk along a path between tall grasses and trees. . . . The Pomwats' house is built in the side of the broad Chao Phraya, the River of Kings. Four small rivers which rise in the hills in the north of Thailand, merge to form the Chao Phraya. It is Thailand's most important river.

The Pomwats' house is built on stilts because of the danger of flooding, and is made of wood from the local sawmills. Beneath the house there is space enough for keeping hens and ducks. There are several similar houses nearby, with ladders leading up into them. We take our shoes off at the bottom of the ladder and climb up after Jaran. Taking your shoes off before entering a house, or temple, is a Thai custom.

Pensri, Jaran's wife, greets us warmly, holding Pontip, their three-year-old daughter. Prasit and Tornygoo, Pensri's parents, greet us too. They live in the house as well. We all sit down on the floor in the main room and talk. The house is small . . . . Through the open windows we have a view down the river, where we can see the family's boat tied up at the water's edge. . . .

We are sitting together on the floor in the main room when Pensri brings in the supper. . . . We are about to eat the family's favorite dish, Pat Preeowahn. This is made with fresh shrimp, pineapple, and garlic. . . . "We usually serve it with rice," Pensri tells us. . . . Jaran goes and fetches us water from a large jar, in the corner of the room. It is rainwater that has been collected, and is the family's only source of drinking water.

We all talk together over the meal. . . . We ask Pensri what she wants for Pontip. "She shall have a good education and then marry a man who can provide for her. I don't mind whether she makes good use of her education or whether looks after a home and family, as I have, she says.

It is getting late. We tell Jaran that we must leave. He shows us to the door and shines a flashlight onto our shoes at the bottom of the ladder. We thank the family for the delicious meal, and for spending their time with us. Then we climb down the ladder, collect our shoes and wave our good-byes to the Pomwat family.

From "Working in a sawmill" and "Meeting the Pomwat family" (retitled "Life in Rural Thailand") from *A Family in Thailand* by Peter Otto Jacobsen and Preben Sejer Kristensen from *Families Around the World* series. Copyright ©1985 by Peter Otto Jacobsen and Preben Sejer Kristensen. Copyright ©1985 by **Wayland Publishers Ltd**. Reprinted by permission of the publisher.

Understanding What You Read After you have finished reading the selection, answer the following questions.

1. What resource does Jaran Pomwat reveal is important in Thailand's economy?

_____

2. Why do you think many sawmills are located on the Chao Phraya?

_____

3. From where do Pomwats get their drinking water? Why would they not use the other source of water available to them?

_____

_____

4. What clues does the reading give about the roles of women in Thai society?

_____

_____

5. What do you think is happening to the rainforest in Thailand? Explain.

_____

_____

Activity

Make a drawing the Pomwats' house and its surroundings.

Southeast Asia

The Chicken Industry Lays an Egg

In the early 1990s foreign investors attempted to start a poultry industry in Indonesia. This reading describes how foreigners' poor understanding of the country contributed to the industry's failure and the loss of millions of dollars in investments.

It looked like one of those ideas that couldn't miss. In the early 1990s the sprawling nation of Indonesia, with its 200 million hungry citizens, was in the midst of an economic boom. It wouldn't be long before they would be adding meat protein to their diets. And since pork is forbidden to the majority Muslims and beef to the minority Hindus, the logical choice was chicken. . . . Encouraged by international financial institutions like the World Bank and by chicken retailers such as KEG and McDonalds . . . local entrepreneurs began forming chicken companies.

Quickly, foreign investors began pecking at the hen-house door. Poultry optimists projected Indonesians would soon be eating 60 chickens a year each, or 12 billion chickens, up from an average of one chicken per year when the boom began.

Almost overnight chickens were roosting everywhere. . . . But making a killing in chickens was not to be. As it turned out, it was the investors who got plucked. . . . Analysts say the foreign investors were victims of ignorance and naiveté [innocence]. Not only did they grossly overestimate the Indonesian population's interest in eating chicken, but they backed a highly fragile, fledgling [new] and corrupt business structure that was, among other problems, totally dependent on imported chicken feed. When the [Asian] financial crisis [of the late 1990s] more than doubled the cost of those imports, disaster was inevitable [certain]. . . .

Trouble began when it became clear that there was no reliable transportation network to bring the chickens to market. But the crucial weak point was chicken feed, consisting mostly of soybean meal and corn. Indonesia grows some corn, but not for animal feed. And it produces soybeans—a local version of tofu [a soybean product] . . . is a staple [basic food]. But soybean meal for chicken feed had to be imported because Indonesia does not have milling [processing] capacity . . . for animal feed. To make such mills viable [economically practical], investors would need a market for soybean oil—a byproduct [of producing chicken feed]. But soybean oil isn't price competitive in Indonesia, which is the world's second-largest producer of palm oil. A chicken grower could substitute fish meal, which is available locally, but the result is a fishy tasting chicken. . . .

Already wobbly, the business suffered mightily after the [Asian financial crisis of 1997]. . . . By the end of 1997, chicken feed had more than doubled in price. Chicken processors had little choice but to pass those costs on to consumers, and so by January 1998 the price of chicken in local markets had also more than doubled, thus drastically reducing demand.

That set off a spiral of bankruptcies among small farmers. . . . By early 1998 the industry was in chaos. In February many major chicken producers . . . stopped operating. Local executives of McDonald's, which has 51 restaurants in Indonesia, declared an emergency; they could find no chicken to make their McNuggets. . . .

The collapse is now complete, and lots of investors are left with, yes, egg on their faces. . . .Meanwhile, in Indonesia the rebuilding process is not going well. Throughout the main island of Java, hungry mobs have . . . raided the remaining chicken farms, making off with all the birds they can carry and destroying equipment.

From "Beggar's Chicken" (retitled "The Chicken Industry Lays an Egg") by Christine Hill from *Institutional Investor*, May 1999. Copyright ©1999 by **Institutional Investor**. Reprinted by permission of the publisher.

Understanding What You Read After you have finished reading the selection, answer the following questions.

1. Why did people in the early 1990s think chicken farming could succeed in Indonesia?

_____

_____

2. How did Indonesia's transportation system affect the industry?

_____

3. Why was feeding the chickens a big problem? What solution was found?

_____

_____

4. How did the Asian financial crisis of the late 1990s cause the industry's collapse?

_____

_____

Activity

Make a list of things you would want to find out about another country before you would invest in a chicken farm there.

Southeast Asia

Escaping from Vietnam

Vo Thi Tam was one of the Vietnamese "boat people." She fled South Vietnam after communist North Vietnam took over that country in the mid-1970s. Here, she explains why she and her family decided to leave, and she describes the first part of her dangerous escape.

They [the Communists] gave us tools and a little food, and that was it. We just had to dig up the land and cultivate it. And the land was very bad.

It was impossible for us to live there, so we got together with some other families and bought a big fishing boat, about thirty-five feet long. Altogether, there were thirty-seven of us that were to leave—seven men, eight women, and the rest children. . . .

After we bought the boat we had to hide it, and this is how: We just anchored it in a harbor in the Mekong Delta. Its very crowded there and very many people make their living aboard the boats by going fishing, you know. So we had to make ourselves like them. We took turns living and sleeping on the boat. We would maneuver [move] the boat around the harbor, as if we were fishing or selling stuff, you know, so the Communist authorities could not suspect anything.

Besides the big boat, we had to buy a smaller boat in order to carry supplies . . . . little by little, on the little boat to the big boat. To do this we sold jewelry and radios and other things that we had left from the old days.

On the day we left we took the big boat out very early in the morning—all the women and children were in that boat and some of the men. My husband and the one other man remained in the small boat, and they were to rendezvous [meet] with us outside the harbor. Because if the harbor officials see too many people aboard, they might think there was something suspicious. I think they were suspicious anyway. . . .

Anyway, the big boat passed through the harbor and went ahead to the rendezvous point where we were to meet my husband and the other man in the small boat. But there was no one there. We waited for two hours. . . . After a while we could see a Vietnamese navy boat approaching, and there was a discussion on board our boat and the end of it was that the people on our boat decided to leave without my husband and the other man.

When we reached the high seas, we discovered, unfortunately, that the water container was leaking and only a little bit of water was left. So we had to ration the water from then on. . . . After seven days we ran out of water, so all we had to drink was the sea water, plus lemon juice. . . .

During this time we had seen several boats on the sea and had waved to them to help us, but they never stopped. But [one] morning . . . we could see another ship coming and we were very happy, thinking maybe it was people coming to save us. When the two boats were close together, the people came on board from there—it happened to be a Thai boat— and they said all of us had to go on [their] boat. . . . They pried up the planks of our boat, trying to see if there was any gold or jewelry hidden there. And when they had taken everything, they put us back on our boat and pushed us away.

They had taken all our maps and compasses, so we didn't even know which way to go. And because they had pried up the planks of our boat to look for jewelry, the water started getting in. We were very weak by then. But we had no pump, so we had to use empty cans to bail the water out, over and over again.

That same day we were boarded again by two other boats, and these, too, were pirates. They came aboard with hammers and knives and everything. But we could only beg them for mercy and try to explain by sign language that we'd been robbed before and we had nothing left. So those boats let us go and pointed the way to Malaysia for us.

That night at about 9:00 P.M. we arrived on the shore, and we were so happy to finally land somewhere that we knelt down on the beach and prayed, you know, to thank God.

From "How We Came Here: Immigration to America" (retitled "Escaping from Vietnam") from *Emerging Voices: Readings in the American Experience*, 2nd ed., by Janet Madden and Sara M. Blake. Copyright ©1990, 1993 by **Holt, Rinehart and Winston**. Reprinted by permission of the publisher.

Understanding What You Read After you have finished reading the selection, answer the following questions.

1. Why did Vo Thi Tam want to leave Vietnam? What did she have to sacrifice to accomplish this?

2. Why was it necessary to purchase two boats?

3. What events made the refugees' voyage more difficult? What act of mercy allowed their escape to finally succeed?

Activity

Compose a poem that tells the story of Vietnam's "boat people."

India

READING 75

GEOGRAPHY

Bombay: City of Hope

Bombay, on the west coast of the Deccan, is not India's largest city. That status belongs to Calcutta, on India's east coast. However, Bombay is by far India's most prosperous city. Its average production per person is three times that of Delhi, India's second most prosperous city. Bombay alone pays one third of all the taxes collected in India. Here, a non-Indian resident of the subcontinent describes this amazing city.

For the 13 million residents of India's commercial capital. . . . making money is Bombay's karma [destiny]. . . . When the English received what is now Bombay from the Portuguese in 1661 . . . no one in England gave the place much thought. . . . The king was happy enough to lease Bombay to the East India Company—a group of London-based merchants. . . . .

In 1669 Gerald Aungier became an East India Company president, and Bombay, then populated mostly by local fishermen, fell under his control. Visiting his new dominion, Aungier saw that this string of seven small islands . . . was situated [located] next to the largest deepwater harbor on India's west coast. Aungier promptly set about developing the harbor. . . . By the time of his death eight years later, Bombay's native population had increased sixfold to 60,000. . . .

Now Bombay has no more room to grow. Though the seven islands Aungier visited have long since been joined by land reclamation, the result is not quite two-thirds the size of New York City. This has not stopped people from moving in, however. Their greatest motive: jobs. Of an estimated 300 newcomers arriving each day, only a small percentage fail to find work. . . . While employment may not be a major problem in Bombay, housing is. Roughly half of all Bombayites live in city slums. . . .

Nothing ever goes to waste in Bombay. I was reminded of this the day I went to Dharavi, generally regarded as Asia's largest slum, where an estimated 600,000 people live wedged within less than one square mile. I soon discovered that it is very easy to get lost in Dharavi, with its maze of alleys often passable only by turning yourself sideways. Squeezing past clusters of . . . children and stray dogs, I peered into improbably small houses where families of 12 or more lodged. Most of these structures were divided into two stories by rough platforms, with no more than five feet of headroom either on the ground floor or in the loft, and with no furniture to speak of, lest it preempt [take] the floor needed for sleeping.

Although most people in Dharavi do not have indoor plumbing, they do have jobs, and sometimes three or four. . . . I saw all sorts of shops and businesses aggressively competing for the . . . cash of the area's residents. Beyond the shops, . . . tanneries churned out leather to be made into fashionable garments for export to Europe, the United States, and Asia.

At the end of the road I came upon a glittering tower of neatly stacked aluminum cans. . . . Beyond them I saw lofty stacks of collapsed cardboard boxes, mountains of plastic bags, pyramids of steel barrels. I had arrived at the site of one of Dharavi's principal industries—recycling.

A young man appeared suddenly beside the tower of cans and eyed me suspiciously. "What do you want?" he asked. I said I wondered how he happened to have so many cans. "I found them," he said. "And now I'm going to sell them." . . . The man went on to tell me that selling other people's old cans was a great business. "I used to be a truck driver in [the rural state of] Gujarat," he said, "but I gave that up nine years ago to try my luck in the Bombay garbage trade." Now 30, he is confident that he made a wise career move. "After all," he explained, "trash is this city's only inexhaustible resource."

I asked how much he made selling cans. "Twice as much as I made as a truck driver—15,000 rupees a month, and sometimes even more." Fifteen thousand rupees is about $480 U.S. A pretty good salary—especially since a college professor's average pay is only 8,000 rupees a month. I raised a skeptical [unbelieving] eyebrow. He shrugged. "That's nothing. There are people out here making 60,000 a month doing the same thing."

From "Bombay: India's Capital of Hope" (retitled "Bombay: City of Hope") by John McCarry from *National Geographic,* March 1995. Copyright ©1995 by **National Geographic Society.** Reprinted by permission of the publisher.

Understanding What You Read After you have finished reading the selection, answer the following questions.

1. Why do hundreds of people move to Bombay every day?

_____

2. Why does Bombay have such a serious shortage of adequate housing? How has this shortage affected the lives of Bombay's citizens?

_____

_____

3. Why would the recycling business be a good occupation in Bombay?

_____

_____

Activity

Imagine that you have come to Bombay from a rural village to look for work. Write a letter to a family member or friend back home reporting on your experiences in the city.

READING 76 **India**

A Village Comes Into Its Own

Anees Jung is an Indian writer whose books explore her country's people and culture. Here she reports on life in Chapoli, a small village in the Western Ghats about 250 miles south of Bombay. Jung finds that after generations of isolation, decline, and neglect, the villagers finally have a reason to hope for a better life.

The village is 60 kilometres [30 miles] form Belgaum, a town that is growing with industry and has an airfield. It seems far as we travel up a bad tar road, circled by clouds of red dust that gets into our hair, fogs our vision, gradually settling down as town yields to jungle, deep, green and still primeval. In this wilderness of less than 100 houses live invisibly a thousand people. There is little land on their forest slopes where paddy [rice fields] can turn green. Wheat is a luxury here, where flour is crushed from a wood-like root and made into bread.

The forests that once treasured a thousand perfumed flowers where bees droned and made honey have begun to recede. Walking around this desolate hamlet we realize that its isolation from the world is more than physical. Strangers inspire fear and suspicion. Women move away from open doors and take shelter behind frail walls. Children stare without wonder and prefer not to follow us around.

One lone old man remains sitting in the morning sun as if its magic warmth will drive away his cold and fever. He has no access to medicine. The nearest health centre is eight kilometers [about five miles] away, in the township of Jamboti, where a bus stops, linking this wilderness to the world beyond. In the government inventory, though, Chapoli has already earned its way into the "civilised" world for it has, as does every village in the state, electricity, a bore well [drilled well] and a school.

Chapoli's school house is . . . . one bare room with a mud floor and a grass roof. It is empty except for a wobbly wooden chair that has collapsed from disuse. It nevertheless suggests authority, that of a school-teacher. In this case as in many across the land, the teacher is an absentee functionary [government employee] of the education department who trudges down from the next village, when convenient, to register his presence.

. . . [Recently, however,] the school has acquired a vague sense of importance. A new teacher has been appointed. Children have begun to trickle in. There will soon be a blackboard in the school house. . . . "Where nothing has happened there is only hope," says one old man who claims to be a freedom fighter. Efforts, seemingly small, have begun to spell hope, even change.

It all began when a team of young enthusiastic men from the nearby plant of Indian Aluminum ["Indal"] in Belgaum decided to adopt Chapoli as one of the 10 villages in the company's rural development scheme.

"When we first came here no one came out to meet us. Not even the children," says Patil, Indal's public relations man. . . .

"In their minds a company meant jobs. We told them that we had come not to give them jobs but [to] help them in keeping themselves employed. When we approached the village headman and asked him to arrange a meeting, only 22 people . . . turned up. . . . All were very poor. Few of them had land. They were farm labourers who during off season migrated to seek work in Goa [a nearby state on India's west coast]. They were keen to go back to bee-keeping, an ancient vocation [occupation] in these parts. Earlier they would walk into the forest and bring back honey-combs to extract honey. We decided to give them bee hives that they could safely keep in their yards with women of the house looking after them. We selected ten persons from the poorest families in ten villages for intensive training in bee-keeping. We will arrange to have the honey processed and marketed. . . ."

As an ancient art is being revived, the economic base of the village is beginning to change, albeit slowly. "Very little has changed here in my 80 years of life," says the old freedom fighter. . . .

From " A village comes into its own" from *The Song of India* by Anees Jung. Copyright ©1990 by Anees Jung. Reprinted by permission of **Himalayan Books**.

Understanding What You Read After you have finished reading the selection, answer the following questions.

1. On what activity was the economy of Chapoli traditionally based? Why did the village's economy go into decline?

_____

_____

2. In what ways is Chapoli isolated? How have the villagers been affected?

_____

_____

3. Why do the villagers have reason to hope their lives will get better?

_____

_____

Activity

Imagine that you are a resident of Chapoli. Write a letter to persuade the government to help your village.

READING 77

The Indian Perimeter

Getting Married in Pakistan

Arranged marriages are common in many parts of the world. Although the practice is staring to weaken, it continues in Pakistan and the rest of South Asia. Ramla Warek Ali was 16 years old and had just completed her schooling when she was told that she would be the bride of Urfi Jafri, a young businessman in Karachi. Here, at 17 and shortly after her wedding day, she describes the highly traditional ceremonies and what she expects of life as Urfi's wife.

When my mother first told me I was to be married I thought she was joking. But then I realized that she was serious and I cried because I knew I would be leaving my home. Marriages in Pakistan are different from those in the West, where couples make their own decisions. Here it is always a surprise and there is no time to plan for the future.

The first time I saw Urfi was after our parents had discussed our marriage and arranged our first meeting. Three months later our families announced our engagement and we started going out together, but always with one of my sisters as a chaperone.

When Urfi's mother first saw me she thought I would make a good wife for her son: mothers in my country have a duty to look for a bride for their sons.

The wedding ceremonies lasted over two weeks. First I stayed inside the house, seeing only my family, and during this time I wore special mustard-colored clothes. . . .

The next ceremony was *Mehndi* [a reddish-brown dye made from the leaves of the henna plant is applied with a small stick], when my family visited Urfi's house while I stayed home, and Urfi's family came to my house the following day, while he stayed home. The day they came to my house they touched my hand symbolically, with *Mehndi*. Later my palms were decorated with it. It took a long time to apply and many hours to dry, so my family had to feed me! *Mehndi* fades in a few days, but the decorations are all part of the wedding. During this ceremony I wore yellow clothes. For the wedding ceremony I wore a white dress, *Gharara*.

Next came *Nikah*, when the priest asked me, through a relative, if I would marry Urfi, and he was asked the same question. The contract was written and the amount of dowry [a money or property marriage gift] agreed upon. The amount varies, but it is usually between 25,000 and 100,000 rupees [$1,750–$7,000].

After the *Nikah* ceremony Urfi took me back to my parents' house and then followed a week of pre-marriage ceremonies. These ended in *Rukhsati* [departure], when Urfi came in a decorated car and sat in a special place. I was then taken to him. After *Rukhsati*, Urfi's family gave a *Valima* [reception] for all our guests.

I shall now follow the ways of Urfi's family. Traditionally, I'm just his property, but times are changing. Although the two of us had no say in the first place, we are in love. I was brought up to believe that men must be obeyed, but I shall also try to help and guide my husband.

I have to get used to my new life with Urfi's family. At first I will be treated like a queen, but after a week or two I will be helping the women with the chores. That's a wife's job.

From "Urfi's mother thought I would make a good wife" (retitled "Getting Married in Pakistan") from *We Live in Pakistan* by Mohamed Amin from *Living Here* series. Copyright ©1984 by **Wayland Publishers Ltd**. Reprinted by permission of the publisher.

Understanding What You Read After you have finished reading the selection, answer the following questions.

1. What is the *Mehndi* ceremony?

_____

_____

2. Name three ways in which traditional marriage in Pakistan differs from most marriages in the United States.

_____

_____

3. In what three ways are weddings in Pakistan like weddings in the United States?

_____

_____

4. What hints does Ramla provide that she does not accept the traditional role of a wife in Pakistan? What parts does she seem to have accepted?

_____

_____

Activity

Imagine that you are a young person in Pakistan who has just been told that you will soon be married to someone who has been chosen for you. Write a journal entry that expresses your feelings about this development.

READING 78 — The Indian Perimeter

The Water of Life

The nation of Bangladesh sits just a few feet above sea level on one of the world's greatest river deltas. The flooding of these rivers and violent cyclones from the Bay of Bengal have resulted in some of the greatest natural disasters on Earth in recent decades. Here, however, the author focuses on the benefits that water provides for the people of Bangladesh.

Water completely defines Bangladesh. Every year floods sweep across much of the land. Catastrophic tropical cyclones bring storm surges as well as murderous winds. Yet the power of the water to destroy is almost equally matched by its power to create.

I began to understand this on a *char,* a sort of pancake of land, in the middle of the Jamuna River. Chars change shape continually as the rivers move silt—two billion tons a year—into the Bay of Bengal. During flood season most chars rise only a foot or so above the water. Almost always they disappear within a decade.

Yet many people have no choice but to live on these temporary islands: Bangladesh is among the most densely populated countries in the world, with 2,000 people per square mile (a density comparable to putting half the population of the United States into the state of Wisconsin). . . . Many people told me that despite the risk, they prefer chars to the squalid [dirty and wretched], crowded city slums.

Manushmara char was only 2,000 feet long and 70 feet wide, yet 475 families lived there. . . . On another char, near the confluence [junction] of five rivers, a man named Abdul Aziz took me to the water's edge. Great cracks ran from the bank back toward a small settlement. Chunks of land crumbled into the water. . . . Before a char is engulfed [swallowed up by the river], its residents must look for another. . . .

Land is the real hunger in Bangladesh. Eighty percent of Bangladesh's population is rural. Sixty percent is landless. Just 10 percent of rural house-holds possess more than 50 percent of the arable [farmable] land. . . .

Many sections of land are like saucers, with riverbanks forming their rims. Silt raises the riverbeds, not only creating chars but also causing the rivers to spill over their banks, sometimes carving out a new course. The resulting floodplains make Bangladesh one of the most fertile nations in the world. Everywhere among the . . . rivers are bountiful fields. Bangladeshis call their land *sonar Bangla,* or golden Bengal, for the gold of ripening paddies.

In many places peasant farmers grow three rice crops a year, thanks to a combination of hard work, river-brought fertility, and high-yield rice introduced by international aid agencies. . . . When the rivers swell with monsoon rains and snowmelt from the mountains of India and Nepal, much of the land goes underwater. Villagers wait for the water to subside [fall back], then plant again. . . .

The rivers form a vast transportation network for the entire country. Huge rafts float bamboo and jute. Other watercraft carry rice, wheat, wood for fuel, coal for waterside brickmaking kilns (ovens). And, of course, people travel in boats of all kinds. The waterways offer better connections than Bangladesh's limited road system. And so I was traveling . . . up the Meghna River to Chhatak just below India. . . . Roads and rice fields were underwater. Here and there clusters of small huts huddled on tiny patches of higher ground. Every so often a tree or a telephone pole jutted out of the water.

The monsoon rains had come, and even the river . . . was underwater. It had . . . become a freshwater sea as far as you could see. . . . All day I had been traveling across flooded rice fields, and in my mind that added up to catastrophe, disaster. But to Rajendra [a local fisherman] the flood meant good things: the chance to use his boat to visit neighboring villages, rather than walking all day; an abundance of fish; and sediment left behind that makes the land bountiful [highly productive] and gives him the chance to grow his own rice. "Such water," he said, "what the Lord has given us."

From "Bangladesh: When the Water Comes," (retitled "The Water of Life") by Charles E. Cobb, Jr. from *National Geographic*, June 1993. Copyright ©1993 by **National Geographic Society**. Reprinted by permission of the publisher.

Understanding What You Read After you have finished reading the selection, answer the following questions.

1. What is a *char?* What function do they serve for landless Bangladeshis?

_____

_____

2. What causes the rivers of Bangladesh to flood? How does flooding benefit farmers and shape their lives? In what other ways do the rivers benefit Bangladeshis?

_____

_____

Activity

Water also can bring tragedy to Bangladesh. Research library and other resources to find and photocopy headlines and photographs from magazines and newspapers. Then make a collage that illustrates the results of cyclones and other floods in Bangladesh.

READING 79 Australia and New Zealand

Australia's Uncertain Future

One popular image of Australia is of a country of wide open spaces and great opportunity— not unlike the American West of a century ago. Australia does share some of the Old West's characteristics—vast lands for raising crops and livestock, a wealth of mineral resources, and rapid population growth. However, this reading suggests that, without major changes, Australia's best times may be in the past, rather than in its future.

Imagine a country on the Pacific Rim, 10 times the size of Texas, rich in mineral resources, well endowed with farmlands, . . . and populated by about 18 million mostly well-educated people who have enjoyed stable government since the beginning of [the twentieth] century. Surely such a country would be a leading economic tiger in the region. . . .

The answer is—no. Australia today is what some locals . . . call an NDC, a Newly Declining Country; a seller of raw materials, not finished ones; a purveyor [supplier] of livestock, meat, and wheat on undependable world markets; . . . an economy with an uncertain future. . . .

Australia continues to rank as a high-income economy. . . . In the late 1990s, Australians on average earned far more than Thais, Malaysians, Chinese, or Koreans. . . . Australian cities, where more than 85 percent of all Australians live, are not encircled by crowded shantytowns. . . . Life is orderly and unhurried. . . . Standards of public transportation, city schools, and health care provision are high. Spacious parks, pleasing waterfronts, and plentiful sunshine make Australia's urban life more acceptable than almost anywhere else in the world. . . . But Australia's privileges are being eroded away, and standards of living are in danger of serious decline. The country's cultural geography evolved as that of a European outpost, prosperous and secure in its isolation. Now Australia must reinvent itself as . . . a Pacific partner in a transformed [changed] regional economic geography.

Distance has been an ally as well as an enemy to Australia. Its remoteness helped save [it] when Japan's empire expanded over the western Pacific [during World War II]. From the very beginning, however, goods imported from Britain (and later from the United States) were expensive, largely because of transport costs. This encouraged local entrepreneurs to set up their own industries in and near the developing cities. . . .

When the prices of foreign goods became lower because transportation was more efficient and therefore cheaper, local businesses demanded protection. . . . This was done by [the colonial governments] enacting high tariffs [taxes] against imported goods. The local products now could continue to be made inefficiently because their market was guaranteed. . . . How could Australia [afford this]? . . . The colonies could export valuable minerals whose earnings [supported] those inefficient, uncompetitive local industries. By the time [of independence], the income from [agriculture] contributed as well. So the miners and the farmers paid for those imports Australians could not reproduce themselves, plus the products made in the cities. No wonder the cities grew: here were secure manufacturing jobs. . . . Australians once [had] the highest per capita GNP in the world, [but] this was achieved in the mines and on the farms, not in the cities.

. . . The good times had to come to an end. The prices of farm products fluctuated [changed frequently], and international market competition increased. The cost of mining ores and minerals . . . and [exporting] them also rose. . . . Unemployment crept upward. [Yet] in 1995, only 18 percent . . . of Australian exports were the kind of high-tech goods that have made East Asia's economic tigers so successful. That was double the 1985 figure, but still far below what the country needs to produce. . . .

Australian manufacturing . . . remains [focused on] local domestic markets. Do not expect to find Australian [manufactures] challenging the Pacific Rim's economic tigers for a place on world markets. . . . [But] Australia's shops are full of goods from Japan, South Korea, Taiwan, and Hong Kong. [This is because] despite its long-term protectionist practices, Australia still does not produce many goods that could be manufactured at home. Overall, the economy continues to display symptoms of a . . . still-developing . . . country.

From "The Australian Realm: Chapter 11 and Australia: Dilemmas Downunder" (retitled "Australia's Uncertain Future") from *Geography: Realms, Regions, and Concepts* by Peter O. Muller and H. J. de Blij. Copyright ©1977 by **John Wiley & Sons Inc**. Reprinted by permission of the publisher.

Understanding What You Read After you have finished reading the selection, answer the following questions.

1. What places does the reading suggest are the "economic tigers" of Asia?

_____

_____

2. Why are Australia's industries inefficient and uncompetitive? How have these industries been able to survive ?

_____

_____

3. Why is Australia's economy not as well off as it was in the early 1900s?

_____

_____

_____

Activity

Imagine that you are campaigning for election to Australia's parliament. Prepare a five-minute campaign speech outlining your concerns for your country's future and suggesting changes to make it brighter.

READING 80 | **Australia and New Zealand**

The Maori People of New Zealand

Maori warden Peter Waldron is a descendent of the original settlers of New Zealand. In this reading he explains his role of warden and tells about the culture of his people. He also touches on the challenge of living as a Maori in New Zealand's society.

The Maori warden movement evolved from [grew out of] a desire to promote law and order within the Maori community in a way that was acceptable to their culture. It was also part of a repeated effort by Maoris to control their own destiny. Our Maori society has traditionally been a communal one, with authority being exercised by the tribal elders. Offenders were dealt with by people who knew and cared for them, and were respected by them. Maori wardens are not policemen. The only power they have is the respect, called *Mana*, that their community has for them. It is a voluntary job, but it is considered a great honor to be elected as a warden. We work within our community to promote law and order by treating the causes of disorder, rather than by disciplining offenders.

There are 290,000 Maoris in New Zealand. Over the years most have settled in the cities. The Maori word for the white man is Pakeha. Our furniture and houses are of *Pakeha* design, but the Maori values are retained within our homes. We place great importance on family ties, including those with our ancestors who have passed on. We are much closer to the earth and nature than our *Pakeha* counterparts. Different families have traditionally held special skills, as orators [story tellers], healers, or planters. These skills are handed down through generations, and held with great pride by the families.

The place where Maoris feel their culture the strongest is on a *Marae*. Each community has its own *Marae*—an area of land containing a meeting house. A *Marae* is a sacred place; there are many traditions to be observed by locals and visitors, but there is a strong sense of belonging for all Maoris. Some *Maraes* are simple buildings, others richly decorated with carvings. The traditions are more important than the surroundings. *Maraes* are used for meetings, weddings, and all social occasions, but priority is always given to a *Tangi*.

We believe that when one of our people dies, their spirit rests in the body for three days before making the journey to their spiritual homeland. During this time the person lies in rest at the *Marae,* and is kept company by loved ones. It's a time for grieving, but it's also a time to express many other emotions, to tell stories, and to come to terms with the loss. A *Tangi* is a very moving experience; it brings out our feelings as Maoris, and as a community of caring people; it is our way of saying goodbye to a loved one, within our own traditions and culture. . . .

We all live and work in a *Pakeha* world. The old Maori lifestyle was doomed by the onslaught of *Pakeha* technology, but Maoris are becoming more and more aware of the spiritual values of their culture. They see that these values can be transplanted into a *Pakeha* environment. There is a regeneration [rebirth] of Maoridom, which is being seen in a more positive light by both Maori and *Pakeha*. I see our culture as playing an increasingly important role in New Zealand society in future years.

From "A tangi is a very moving experience" (retitled "The Maori People of New Zealand") from *We Live in New Zealand* by John Ball from *Living Here* series. Copyright ©1982 by **Wayland Publishers Ltd**. Reprinted by permission of the publisher.

Understanding What You Read After you have finished reading the selection, answer the following questions.

1. Who are the Maori? What values and attitudes are important in Maori culture?

_____

_____

2. How are Maori wardens like police officers? How do they differ from police officers?

_____

_____

3. What is a *Marae* and what function does it serve?

_____

_____

4. Why do the Maoris feel that their culture is threatened? How do *Maraes* and the warden movement help the Maoris to keep their culture strong?

_____

_____

Activity

Design a bumper sticker to increase public awareness of Maori culture in New Zealand. Include an image and a "catchy" slogan on your bumper sticker.

READING 81

The Pacific Islands and Antarctica

Returning to the Rain Forest

The daughter of American missionaries, Edie Bakker grew up in Wagu, Papua New Guinea, a remote village deep in the Hunstein rain forest. Eleven years after leaving Papua New Guinea, a threat to the people of the village brought Bakker back to her childhood home.

The Sepik River meanders [wanders] through the vast wetlands of north-western Papua New Guinea. . . . We watched from our motorized dugout [canoe] for a chink [small opening] in the towering grasses that marks a seasonally flooded channel—a *baret*—leading to the Bahinemo village of Wagu. . . .

As we beached on the rough, pebbled shore of Wagu village, people rushed toward us hugging, clinging, laughing and crying. . . . There is no Bahinemo word for "hello," and only an extended absence requires a greeting: "You're here," they said. "I'm here," I replied.

What brought me back to Wagu was a crisis—the Hunstein is on the verge of being logged. Some of the world's last major rain forests are in Papua New Guinea. . . . and the thought of such destruction in the Hunstein was intolerable.

The Papua New Guinea government has left land-use questions with local owners. But I worried that foreign logging companies would not tell the Bahinemos the truth about what logging would do to their forest, still crucial to their livelihood and culture. And did the isolated Bahinemos understand what their treasure means to the world? . . .

A woman named Moyali Yalfei, about 45 years old and the widow of the head of the largest landholding clan, told me she thought she *had* to agree to logging. "The [government] forestry department said they wanted it, so I'll have to give it to them, won't I?"

It's not naive [ignorant] of her to think that. A Bahinemo thinks of wealth in terms of personal alliances, not profits. While Westerners base business decisions around profit and expect to cultivate [make] some friends in the process, Bahinemos aim for friendships and hope to earn some money in the process. Some 15 clans control various-size holdings in the Hunstein, and it is an honor to give permission for other people to use your land.

Compounding [adding to] the confusion of Moyali and other Bahinemos is the overwhelming modern need for cash. As it is, the Bahinemos must struggle for years to obtain an outboard motor, clothes, cassette players, ... and if they want to send their children away to high school, they must save hundreds of dollars for tuition and board. "Trees are our only real source of income," Moyali said. . . .

With fresh ideas and the best of intentions, . . . conservation groups such as Greenpeace, Friends of the Sepik, and the East Sepik Council of Women have been trying to help the Bahinemos find alternatives to mass logging that will bring the development so desperately desired. They also want local owners to be paid more for their lumber. "Currently, they'll make $40 for an average tree, which would sell for $2,750 on the international market," said American conservationist Glen Barry. "That's ridiculous. . . ."

As an alternative to clear-cutting [cutting down every tree in an area] they [also] are promoting portable sawmills. Local people can then selectively harvest trees and rotate the mills through the forest to allow regrowth. There is no need to cut a wide road and no damage from heavy machinery. . . . Moyali, for one, has not been impressed: "It looks like the forest is still being ruined, only less money for us." Logging companies—who promise to "replant every tree"—would give her clan a larger . . . payment for clearing the land "only one time." . . .

The stability of the rain forest makes it difficult for the Bahinemos to envision the consequences of logging. Their physical world has not taught them to think in terms of cause and effect. If the Hunstein is destroyed, Bahinemo culture will die also. Not just their outer culture—what they eat, what they wear—but . . . their inner culture. Who they are as a people, how they approach life, will lose its sustaining environment.

From "Return to Hunstein Forest," (retitled "Returning to the Rain Forest") by Edie Bakker from *National Geographic*, February 1994. Copyright ©1994 by **National Geographic Society**. Reprinted by permission of the publisher.

Understanding What You Read After you have finished reading the selection, answer the following questions.

1. Why did the author return to Papua New Guinea?

_____

2. Why did the Bahinemo decide to allow logging in their forest?

_____

_____

3. Explain why you think the author agrees or disagrees with the decision.

_____

_____

Activity

Prepare a speech to make at a Bahinemo tribal council. Take the role of a Bahinemo, a government official, a conservationist, or a logging company representative and recommend what the Bahinemo should do about logging the Hunstein forest.

Name _____ Class _____ Date _____

The Pacific Islands and Antarctica

GEOGRAPHY

Hunting Meteorites in Antarctica

The meteorites that strike Earth from space are the oldest things on the planet. Despite the bitter cold, Antarctica is the ideal place to look for them. This reading explains why.

Ralph Harvey can ride a Ski-doo as well as anyone, and he looks pretty good in antlers—just the guy to search Antarctica for pieces of other worlds. Ralph Harvey holds a shooting star in his mitten. It's a meteorite, a piece of outer space some 4.5 billion years old. This rock has seen the infancy of the solar system. . . . You cannot help feeling a sense of awe. You might feel other things as well, if only you weren't numb from riding around on a Ski-doo in a -40 degree windchill for the past three hours.

Meteorite hunting is not for wimps. The best places to look are also the coldest and windiest. You need very old ice, and you need wind, lots of it, strong and unrelenting. Antarctica fits the bill. This year, the Antarctic Search for Meteorites (ANSMET) has set up camp out beyond the Transantarctic Mountains, smack dab nowhere on something called the East Antarctic Ice Sheet. It's not that more meteorites fall in polar regions. (Earth gets an evenly distributed smattering—about one meteorite falls to the ground every two days.) It's that they . . . are easier to spot. . . .

Here is what happens: Meteorites that fall on Antarctica are buried beneath snow that is in turn buried under more snow until the pressure of the weight turns it to ice. This ice, with its chocolate-chip load of meteorites, makes its way slowly, on the order of about ten feet a year, downhill toward the fringes of the continent, where it eventually calves [breaks] off into the sea. Unless a mountain range gets in its way. In which case the ice collides with the mountains and, like water against a cliff, surges upward. . . . Enter the wind. A cold, dense . . . wind rolls down from the top of the gently sloping plateau. It clears the snow off the ice and powers . . . airborne ice crystals that scour away at the surface ice, wearing it down so that the meteorites trapped within are gradually exposed. One by one, a hundred millennia's worth of meteorites appear at the surface.

One by one, Harvey and his colleagues find them. . . . This season's tally is 374, including the 15 found so far this afternoon. Meteorite hunting is a one-of-a-kind pursuit, combining the systematic precision of a crime-scene search for evidence with the giddy anticipation of an Easter-egg hunt. The six team members ride on snowmobiles 50 feet apart, moving slowly forward in a line while scanning the ice around them. When they reach the perimeter of the area they're searching, they turn around, line up on the next strip of ice, and go back the other way.

While it is wind that allows them to do what they do, it is also wind that gets in their way. When the gusts top 20 miles an hour, blowing snow obscures the ice, and not even expedition-weight thermal underwear and

Copyright © by Holt, Rinehart and Winston. All rights reserved.

The Pacific Islands and Antarctica • Readings 163

Darth Vader-style face shields (actually motocross masks) can keep out the chill. . . . ANSMET's other nemesis [source of harm] is the crevasse. Mountain ranges have an unkind tendency to rend [tear] deep, deadly cracks in ice sheets, the sort of cracks that swallow up entire snowmobiles. . . .

This year's ice field sits far enough back from the mountains to be free of crevasses. The ice is pale blue and its surface rises and dips in shallow swells, giving it the appearance of a vast frozen sea. Most of the snow is blown away. . . . There are days when sky and clouds so closely mirror ice and snow that the horizon is anyone's guess.

It is an otherworldly place, so much so that the occasional meteorites sitting on the ice seem in comparison familiar-looking sights. With their blackened fusion crust—burn scars from the hot air compressed in front of them as they plummet [fall] through our atmosphere—they look less like space rocks than charcoal briquettes. It's as though someone emptied a Weber [grill] from 30,000 feet. . . . Meteorites are easy to spot, as there's absolutely nothing else on the ice, save the occasional scrap of snowmobile tread. This was not always the case. "Few years back we had a guy who loved prunes and spit out the pits," says Harvey. "Gave us no end of trouble for years and years."

From "Meteorite Hunters," (retitled "Hunting Meteorites in Antarctica") by Mary Roach from *Discover Magazine*, May 1997. Copyright ©1997 by **Discover Magazine**. Reprinted by permission of the publisher.

Understanding What You Read
After you have finished reading the selection, answer the following questions.

1. Why is Antarctica such a good place to hunt for meteorites?

_____

_____

2. How do meteorite hunters go about their work?

_____

_____

3. Describe the process by which meteorites turn up in Antarctica.

_____

_____

Activity
Imagine that you are an ANSMET worker. Write a letter home describing your living and working conditions in Antarctica.

Answer Key

Reading 1

1. He was a Greek scholar, scientist, theater critic, and librarian who lived in Alexandria, Egypt. He used the angles of shadows to calculate Earth's circumference.
2. Ptolemy introduced the ideas of longitude and latitude and scale.
3. Marshall Islanders tied sticks together to show wind and wave patterns; prehistoric Europeans drew maps on cave walls, the Inca made relief maps of stone and clay; the Shoshone drew wavy lines on the ground to depict a river and piled mounds of sand to show mountains.
4. Scale is the idea that distances on a map are expressed in proportion to the real distances. If a map has no scale, its user will not known how far away places are, the true location of places, or their actual location in relation to other places.

Reading 2

1. Images in regular color film are often affected by atmospheric haze.
2. SLAR records radar images instead of light images as a camera does. Unlike a camera, it can be used when the area is cloudy, hazy, or in the dark.
3. Answers will vary, but students should recognize that such imagery provides a "macro" view of the data that would be harder to record or comprehend by moving across the region on the ground.

Reading 3

1. There was no known geologic evidence of a past subduction quake, and they assumed the Juan de Fuca plate was sliding smoothly beneath the continent. Then a scientist found evidence of a tsunami in Washington State.
2. A story of a tsunami existed in local Native American lore.
3. Because they are at sea level they would be vulnerable to quake-related tsunamis.

Reading 4

1. The Coriolis Force is the effect of Earth's rotation on all moving things; it is named for the Frenchman who first analyzed it.
2. It pushes moving objects to the right of their intended direction.
3. They would make a large circle because Earth's rotation would continually push them to either the left or the right of their intended path, depending on whether they were in the Northern or the Southern Hemisphere
4. Answers will vary but should suggest that Earth's rotational forces make people in the Southern Hemisphere feel more natural and comfortable on the left, despite human rules to the contrary.

Reading 5

1. It puts large amount of methane, carbon dioxide, and other compounds into the air. Plants reduce the carbon dioxide by using it in photosynthesis.
2. Erosion occurs as soil is blown away; ecosystems shrink, causing some species to die; rainfall distribution may change because of reduced evaporation from plants.
3. It could melt frozen water in glaciers and polar ice caps, which would cause sea levels to rise. This could be serious for humankind since half the world's people live within 30 miles of a coast.

Reading 6

1. Environmental changes would have included an earthquake/explosion; a shockwave of debris killing plants and animals; a fireball and widespread wildfires that would raise global temperatures killing more plants and animals; a dust cloud reducing sunlight causing temperatures to drop, again killing plants and animals; then a gradual recovery and return to normal conditions.
2. Living underground, they were protected from the fires, heat, and cold. Being small,

they did not need to find as much to eat as larger animals.

Reading 7

1. Some crops have been improved by cross-breeding with wild forest species. One in four Western medicines are based on rain forest plants.
2. Accept any four of the following: loss of plant life; loss of animal life; soil deterioration; soil erosion; harm to indigenous peoples; less rainfall at the regional level; build-up of greenhouse gases at the planetary level.
3. Accept any three of the following: rising world-wide concern for the rain forests and their peoples; governments and businesses being pressured to help the rain forests; the spread of the Chipko movement; establishment of national parks; establishment of reforestation projects; idea of debt relief for countries that protect their rain forests.

Reading 8

1. They had tunneled beneath the border and were mining coal that was in German territory.
2. Answers will vary, but students should recognize that what's within Germany's borders beneath the ground is just as much a part of that country as what's on the surface, and that when the miners took the coal they took part of Germany.
3. Iraq accused Kuwait of stealing Iraqi oil reserves and invaded Kuwait, which led to the war.
4. Answers will vary, but students should realize that air pollution from industry in one country can be blown across the border into its neighbor.

Reading 9

1. Technological developments in farming have raised food production to unprecedented levels.

2. Answers will vary, but should show an understanding that enough food is now produced to feed the world's population, but that it is not always available in the places where it is most needed—making hunger a matter of location instead of population.
3. Two possibilities that could cause food shortages are outbreaks of plant diseases that slow food production and continued population growth so that total population again exceeds food production capacity

Reading 10

1. It is the permanent or temporary movement of people from one place to another because they want or need to move.
2. Six basic reasons for migration are religion, war, political upheaval, economic opportunity, environmental disasters, and enslavement.
3. Answers will vary but should show recognition that as groups move from one place to another they bring their culture with them and, as they intermingle with the existing people of the new place, influence the culture and society that is already there.
4. Answers will vary, but students should understand that by testing blood, researchers can look for genetic similarities in people from different places that show they have a common origin.

Reading 11

1. a mix of wastes and the leavings of industry, such as raw sewage, spilled oil, polychlorinated biphenyls (PCBs); a successful battle with General Electric over the discharge of PCBs, followed by increased watchfulness over water quality
2. At first the problem was one of economic decline related to loss of industries and river traffic. Now the problem is one of controlling economic growth and development.
3. Answers will vary, but students should note that this focus on what is best for the

region or community at large can restrict the options that the landholder has regarding what to do with his or her property.

Reading 12

1. flat, expansive, hot, and semiarid with a ranching economy
2. That they drive 80 miles across the ranch to reach the ranch house, and that Bick did not think 90 miles was far for his family to come, suggests that Texans perceive "reasonable" distances as greater than do people who live in smaller states.

Reading 13

1. There are no schools for them to attend on the islands where they live.
2. junior high students; that school is located on Mayne Island, which is closer than Salt Spring Islands, location of the high school.
3. Some students are not able to participate in extracurricular activities because of the boat schedule and the amount of time required for the commute.
4. boarding on the school island during the school week

Reading 14

1. Answers will vary but should recognize that it was part of the infusion of southern Canada's culture into Inuit society. Along with television and other practical benefits came social and political ideas, one of which was self-determination.
2. They had to give up all aboriginal claims to any other lands. Answers about significance will vary, but students should note that not only will the Inuit govern the territory themselves, but it comprises about a fifth of Canada's landmass.

Reading 15

1. political stability, land reform, development of distribution of oil wealth, paved roads, schools, economic reforms, NAFTA

2. by rigging elections, buying loyalty with local improvement projects, and suppressing freedom of speech and the press
3. The government's slow and inefficient response after a 1985 earthquake caused Mexicans to lose faith in its ability to take care of them.

Reading 16

1. Cars and factories emit pollutants into the air, which are then trapped in the city by the mountains that surround it.
2. Dried fecal matter from the city's million stray dogs is blown into the air to mix with other suspended particles and chemical pollutants.
3. Elimination of leaded gasoline, and various motor vehicle laws have reduced some pollutant levels. Reforestation has reduced air-borne soil particles, but more work is needed in this area, along with better enforcement of existing dog and motor vehicle laws and conversion to natural gas.

Reading 17

1. by the colors and patterns of the clothing they wear
2. Spanish Guatemalans live in the cities, are Roman Catholic, and follow the latest fashion and entertainment trends. The Maya live in highland villages, retain their own gods, speak their own languages, wear traditional clothing, and follow centuries-old customs.
3. He will likely walk. That he is draining the blood from the sheep to make it lighter suggests this. His walk could range up to 12 miles.
4. Christian saints guide them in family life and the Mayan gods guide them in farming and other work.

Reading 18

1. Its activity has caused the south part of Montserrat to be evacuated, concentrating the population on the sparsely populated

north side of the island. About a third of the people have left the island altogether.

2. Answers will vary but should include loss of homes, farms, jobs, businesses and recreational opportunities; disruption of government services; and psychological trauma.

Reading 19

1. The Pacific lowlands is a heavily settled area of farms and fertile soil. The Mosquito Coast is swampy, rainy, more thinly populated, and has a fishing economy.

2. Answers will vary but should point out that few of the nation's schools and businesses are in eastern Nicaragua. Ethnic differences also play a part. Students should recognize that the lack of roads across the country contributes to their isolation and lack of knowledge about the Mosquito coast, a condition that generally contributes to prejudice.

Reading 20

1. The mother and three of the seven children work as pickers on a nearby coffee plantation. The father works as a bricklayer and painter. The mother earns about $2.40 a day, and the father about $72 per month. The children earn less than their mother.

2. They live near the coffee plantation in a mountainous area of the country. The house is made of bricks, wood planks, and branches and has a leaky roof. There are only three rooms and the family sleeps together in one of them.

3. Children go to school until they are 13, but usually have to start working part-time when they are 10, to earn money to help their families.

Reading 21

1. They act aggressively and physically challenge and threaten visitors.

2. their reputation and off-putting behavior, their location in a remote rain forest, and

government policies that keep other people out of the area

Reading 22

1. Because land, food, and water are available there without cost; a person can pick out a spot, build a small house and clear a little land to farm.

2. They cultivate potatoes and manioc on small plots of land and fish in the river for other food.

3. Found in the Amazon Basin are: half the world's freshwater fish—2,500 to 3,000 species; more species of plants and animals than anywhere else; and during the rainy season, one-fifth of all fresh water on Earth.

Reading 23

1. geography: It is landlocked and surrounded by larger, more populous neighbors; history: The isolation imposed by its dictators

2. Men without land: The war left Paraguay financially ruined. To raise money it sold its surplus land to foreigners. Then there wasn't enough land available later, when Paraguay's population grew. Land without men: Ninety percent of Paraguay's adult male population died in the war. It remains one of the world's most sparsely populated countries.

3. Under the dictatorship the government would not help landless people obtain land. The new government is forcing large landholders to sell their land so that the farmers can own some of it.

Reading 24

1. houses and streets, sidewalk cafes, elegant shops

2. because of the European architecture, the large numbers of European immigrants, and the dominance of European culture over Indian or other traditional Latin American cultures

Reading 25

1. the name (meaning "country people") for the native people of Bolivia; Quechua and Aymara Indians

2. Valles: region of hills and fertile valleys southeast of Sucre that is Bolivia's main agricultural region; Oriente: vast eastern lowlands that contain new farmlands and oil and natural gas deposits

3. Following reforms in 1952 the *compesinos* got the right to vote and some of their land back that the Spanish had seized long ago. Frequent changes in government have undone many of these reforms, however, and they struggle to keep their rights and improve their standard of living.

Reading 26

1. All the country's wealth goes into the pockets of its president, El Benefactor, who shares little of it with the people; a dictatorship

2. He wants to convince the world that he is not a crude barbarian peasant.

3. Answers will vary but should recognize the irony in naming such a harsh dictator "the helper." Students should suggest that Allende's opinion of such people is a strongly unfavorable one, since she portrays her character as ill-mannered, greedy, corrupt, self-serving, paranoid, and totally unloved by the people he rules.

Reading 27

1. cattle and sheep ranching

2. hardy grass that is resistant to the cold; good grass allows the sheep to produce high-quality wool, which would bring a higher price than wool of an inferior quality

3. any four of the following: the ranching economy (division of the region into ranches); the size of the ranches (over 12,000 acres); only two workers on the ranch; the long trip to Santiago; the need to move to town so his children can attend high school

Reading 28

1. to share their home with their parents for as long as they live

2. As a godparent or wedding sponsor, a *koumbaros* is a spiritual member of the family, while a patron is an outsider who represents and serves the family in return for its loyalty and support.

3. *Patrida* does this by fostering a kinship with non-relatives who are from the same home region. *Philoxenia* strengthens community by extending hospitality and help to people in need.

Reading 29

1. The location kept Rome far enough from the coast to avoid surprise attack by sea and exposure to the corrupting influences of other cultures. At the same time, its location allowed Rome to easily ship its unneeded goods abroad and to bring needed goods from the interior.

2. Surrounded by land, no enemy could attack it without first being heard enroute, marching or crashing through the forest. Its location on steep hills required a difficult, uphill attack by the enemy.

Reading 30

1. In some provinces farms are *minifundios*, or small landholdings. In other province most of the land is owned by a small minority of farmers in large estates called *latifundios*.

2. In the provinces with *minifundios*, residents are poor because their farms are too small to grow enough to make a profit. In provinces with *latifundios*, most residents are poor because they don't own any land and must work on the *latifundios* as farm laborers.

3. The traditional method was to divide the land into small farms called *masoverias* and rent them to tenant farmers in return for a third of their crop. Low crop prices have nearly ended this system because it is no longer profitable for the tenants.

Reading 31

1. Many Italian, Spanish, and Portuguese came to France to help it rebuild after each of the wars. Many of these workers stayed.

2. Algeria and Vietnam both are former French colonies. When the French empire collapsed, many people from these places sought refuge in France. Some may not feel patriotic because of France's colonial history in their countries. Others may be put off by the nativist sentiments of some of the French people.

Reading 32

1. that East Berliners would be able to travel to West Berlin without permission or restrictions; answers will vary, but students should recognize the euphoria and that large numbers of people crossed the border that night and the next day.

2. She points out that the wall kept East Berliners from realizing how good life was in West Berlin and from learning about all the things available there that they were having to do without.

Reading 33

1. new roads, jobs at the resorts, profits from businesses that sell goods and services to the skiers

2. Roads, ski runs, and resorts have thinned forests, which has promoted erosion and destabilized mountainsides, bringing more mudslides, floods, and avalanches.

3. Because there are fewer cows to eat the grass, it grows longer, which lessens its ability to hold the snow in the winter. This increases the risk of avalanches.

Reading 34

1. In the daytime life went on pretty much as normal. At night German planes would drop bombs, causing many deaths, heavy damage, and fires in the city.

2. Answers will vary but might include not going out onto the streets, sleeping in subways or other underground shelters, movies and most entertainment closing early, and very little dining out.

Reading 35

1. commercial fishing, maritime commerce, manufacturing

2. the references to factories and docks, to ragged children, and to shabby streets where the fishermen's families lived

3. Answers will vary, but students should realize that Ireland was owned by England at the time, that cricket is an English sport, and that England was a predominantly Protestant country. Students should realize that Ireland is predominantly Roman Catholic.

Reading 36

1. across the Finnish-Scandinavian arctic region and along the mountains on both sides of the Swedish-Norwegian border

2. They have established permanent villages in the breeding areas. Villages are administrative and economic units as well as a geographic grazing areas. Reindeer have become less important because making profits is difficult, especially since the Chernobyl accident contaminated the reindeer meat.

3. Answers will vary but might include sending their children to school, settling in villages, using aircraft, motor vehicles, and snowmobiles in herding, and turning to tourism and sale of traditional crafts as a livelihood.

Reading 37

1. Estonians are a Finno-Ugric, Scandinavian people, closely related to the Finns. Latvians and Lithuanians are Indo-European peoples.

2. Answers will vary, but students should recognize that Estonia has been conquered and dominated by the Germans, Swedes, and Russians, all of whom have left

cultural influences and people behind. Russian migration policies when Estonia was part of the Soviet Union are a major factor. One of four residents was born somewhere else. This history would likely make ethnic Estonians extremely nationalistic and protective of their culture.

3. Ethnic Estonians tend to live in the rural areas while the ethnic minorities dominate Estonia's cities. Estonian individualism and love of solitude probably contribute to this pattern of settlement.

Reading 38

1. Both have this designation because they were accomplished without violence.

2. to the ethnic unrest that plagued parts of the former Yugoslavia—such as Croatia, Bosnia, and Serbia—in the 1990s

3. Answers will vary, but most students should point to the common history and cultural heritage of Czechs and Slovaks—also pointed out by political leaders in the reading—to suggest that the two nations will probably enjoy good relations. Some students may point to the underlying hostility and jealousy between Czechs and Slovaks that is evident in the in the reading's quotes and come to another conclusion.

Reading 39

1. wool, milk, and cheese

2. To have grass for their sheep they must spend most of their time in summer and winter pastures, and in traveling back and forth between these locations.

3. In mid-May the women—and the children after school is out—leave the village and go to the summer sheepfold to help with the milking and cheese making.

Reading 40

1. Responses might mention the attempted coup, the comments on the bus about Gorbachev, the strikes, and the difficulties people are experiencing.

2. Answers will vary but should suggest that Ilya did not previously conceive of the full range of freedoms—and their implications—beyond freedom or speech.

3. Answers will vary but should be supported by evidence and reasoned arguments.

Reading 41

1. Life has become more difficult for most Muscovites in many ways. Many have to work harder by taking second and third jobs in order to survive. More people are homeless than before.

2. Answers will vary, but students should realize that the picture the author paints of Moscow is of a city of the indulgent rich and the struggling poor, where everything is based on how much money one has.

Reading 42

1. The town's main industries formerly produced military goods for the government. Now, because there is no longer such production, over half their workers are laid off. Even people who have jobs may not be paid regularly or may not be paid enough to keep up with the rising prices of things they need.

2. Answers will vary, but students should realize that communism provided security for Russians in the form of a job and basic minimal living assistance. Now that safety net is gone. However, the author suggests that attitudes in Russia are such that Russians will likely never wish to return to their former system.

Reading 43

1. His greatest joy was working the farm and being with its animals. Most unsettling was the memory of and hearing the voice of his dead sweetheart.

2. Answers will vary but should reflect the Hutsuls' attachment to agriculture, nature, and the land; the simplicity of their life; and their belief in the occult.

Reading 44

1. Many Caucasians in Russia and in the nations of the Caucasus are Muslims. Moscow worries that they may have loyalties to toward Turkey or Iran, the two major powers in the area, which could pose a potential threat to the security of Russia's southern border.

2. Answers will vary but should focus on the region's tremendous ethnic diversity, which has resulted in territorial disputes and nascent nationalism.

3. The collapse of the USSR destabilized the region. For the decades that the Caucasus was part of the Soviet Union, the ironfisted Communist rule kept ethnic grievances under control. Once Soviet power was no longer there to keep them in check, these grievances erupted into the open.

Reading 45

1. It is the Uzbek word for district or neighborhood. It is the center of and defines an Uzbek's identity, daily activities, and lifelong relationships.

2. It is a strained one. Neither wants to live with the other. This is due to the Russians' feelings of superiority toward the Uzbeks and the fact that they once were at the top of society as Uzbekistan's occupiers.

3. their emphasis on gardens, fruit trees, and outdoor activities; some even keep sheep or a cow in their gardens.

4. Answers will vary but should show recognition that the provincialism inherent in the defining importance of the *mahalla* could weaken unity and nationalism.

Reading 46

1. All children are seen as the gift of God, but boys are especially desired. The birth of sons is publicly celebrated; the birth of a daughter is not. Both sexes are sent to school at about age eight. The sons of poor parents are sent into the service of a rich man, but girls are kept at home.

2. They bow when given an order and keep a respectful distance from adults at meals. They call the old men of the village Bâbâ, or grandfather.

Reading 47

1. They are nomadic herders of sheep, camels, and goats.

2. The camels provide the Āl Murrah with milk, which is the basic food in their diet.

3. Sand hills called *goz* provide desert grasses and bushes for grazing, as do the areas behind 'ergs, or sand dunes.

4. The bush remains edible as a source of food for camels for up to four years after a rain. The moisture it retains would also help the camels survive.

Reading 48

1. They have better access to higher education; they seem to want more equal treatment and more personal freedom in public. Young people are important because they comprise two-thirds of Iran's population, making them a powerful political force.

2. Benefits include paved roads, water, and electricity in most rural areas and a greater sense of national unity; journalists and artists object to government censorship, while workers and businessmen are upset about the government's poor handling of the economy.

Reading 49

1. Each street contains shops that sell the same type of merchandise or do the same type of business.

2. They have filled the wide walkways of a modern concrete shopping facility with stalls to create the maze of a typical souk.

3. Answers will vary but should focus on the maze-like nature of a souk, the twists and turns, and the lack of street names and other identifiable geographic markers.

Reading 50

1. The climate is warm. Streets are narrow to provide shade and keep down dust

2. It is usually on the city's highest ground because it was a place of refuge for city leaders and was placed where it could be more easily defended.

3. Courtyard houses are guided by the principles of privacy, individual responsibility for public systems, and the importance of the inner essence over outward appearance; to protect privacy, houses had no or only highly placed outside windows and doorways did not face each other or the street. Life centered on the inside courtyard. Outside walls were bare, but inside, houses were lavishly decorate, reflecting the Qur'an's emphasis on the inner self.

Reading 51

1. Land is held by the tribe rather than by individuals. Each tribe has its own territory.

2. Tents, which are easily moved, are appropriate for their nomadic lifestyle. The tents are made of goat hair, which is readily available because the Bedouins raise goats.

3. Bedouins are living in buildings instead of tents; they are working in industry instead of farming and herding; they are using cars and trains for transport instead of camels; they are getting college educations.

4. Answers will vary but might include that only the men eat the meat of slaughtered goats and sheep. In addition, men select their wife, may have multiple wives, and can send a wife away if they are not happy with her. There is no evidence that women enjoy reciprocal rights in these areas.

Reading 52

1. Children do not live with their parents, but as a group.

2. The kibbutz is governed by direct democracy; there is a meeting of the entire community every Saturday night. Committees oversee all activities and the community

elects a secretariat to handle the day-to-day operations.

3. An educator works in the laundry; a teacher processes olives in the food factory twice a week.

Reading 53

1. not enough schools; more people entering the job market than there are jobs for them; many people have to struggle to earn a living; many people emigrate to find work

2. A strong agricultural sector produces a variety of crops, including some for export. Rich fishing grounds exist off the coast. The world's largest phosphate deposits make mining an important industry.

Reading 54

1. Damming the Nile has stopped its soil-enriching silt from being deposited there. Farmers have to use fertilizer instead to enrich the soil.

2. As the city grows, its concrete and buildings cover former farmland. Also delta farmers are digging up and selling their soil to be made into bricks for building materials.

3. It is Egypt's main agricultural area. If the delta is lost, Egypt may not be able to produce enough food for its people and its farm economy might suffer.

Reading 55

1. The World Food Program (WFP) is offering 110 pounds of rice and about a gallon of cooking oil for each daughter that a family sends to school.

2. Answers will vary, but students should suggest that the offer of free food would be less compelling to families that were not poor and/or that the problem might be greater among poor Beninois.

3. The reading mentions the attempts of Beninois officials to break down the "cultural barriers" to educating girls and notes

that some Beninois mothers now no longer consider educating their daughters to be a "waste of time and money."

Reading 56

1. There is a break in the rock that lies beneath the desert, which allows underground water to reach the surface.
2. The Niger Sahara is mostly sand dunes, while the Sahara in Chad is characterized by rocky spires and volcanic peaks.

Reading 57

1. The author says that Timbuktu had teachers, that the king honored learning, and the sale of books was the most profitable type of trade.
2. Answers will vary but should note, in addition to the references to books and learning and to the skilled trades already mentioned, the descriptions of the people's wealth, housing, and to their food and water resources. The amount of leisure time the people enjoyed is also indicative of a high standard of living.

Reading 58

1. She put a spell on the drinking water to make people not cause trouble and obey the clan leaders who controlled the government.
2. Answers will vary but should recognize that the story is a criticism of Somalia's government and its effect on the Somali people.

Reading 59

1. a series of cracks in the Earth's crust running from the Red Sea south to Mozambique
2. Lake Victoria is a cool freshwater lake located between the rift's two branches on a plateau in Kenya. Lake Assal is a hot, salty lake located right on the rift, below sea level in the desert of Djibouti.

3. Answers will vary but students should note that Earth's crust is very thin there and that magma is close, which produces heat from the ground in addition to the sun, which heats the rest of the desert.

Reading 60

1. They seemed to be traders who were only passing through Kikuyu territory. The Kikuyu viewed them as wanderers who would someday return home.
2. After an incident resulted in British retaliation against the Kikuyu, they refused further trade. The British then began to seize food from the Kikuyu and soon claimed ownership of their land.

Reading 61

1. No, because this clothing is sold to, and sought after by, Zambians of all income levels, from poor farmers to white-collar workers and residents of upper-income neighborhoods.
2. They believe it is more fashionable and of higher quality than other clothing. It also symbolizes the power, wealth, and opportunity that the West represents to many Zambians.
3. She states that Zambian high school students won't wear jeans because they do not want to be mistaken for street vendors.

Reading 62

1. because his boat provides services typically available in a town, such as a clinic, a pharmacy, and a market, as well as a population of 5,000 aboard
2. Many people's access to the goods and services the boats provided would be greatly reduced as would their ability to travel from place to place. There would also be less opportunity to sell their own goods. This is because there are few roads and the river is the region's main "highway."

Reading 63

1. They provide the villagers with honey and game in return for the villagers' vegetables and other farm produce.
2. Unlike other peoples of the region, who live in villages, practice agriculture, have a warrior tradition, and fear the deep forest, the Pygmies are peaceful hunters and gatherers who have a relatively primitive lifestyle and are most comfortable in the jungle.

Reading 64

1. Water is trapped in the sand and comes to the surface in springs that animals seek out. Elephants use their trunks to poke holes in the sand and make springs.
2. It is a cold ocean current that sweeps up from Antarctica to the Namibian coast, where warm air blows over it and creates fog. This fog comes ashore and condenses at night on leaves, rocks, grass, and even living things, providing moisture that the desert animals drink to survive.

Reading 65

1. The police would transfer husbands to live somewhere else and then would demolish their house, which would force the rest of the family to leave. The government would also buy the residents' land and demolish their house.
2. She says that one of her children only went to school four hours a day, from 8 a.m. to noon.
3. Answers will vary, but students should recognize that the "yard" was vacant land on which the houses had been demolished. The people who lived in the yard were probably the owners of demolished houses, who were no longer authorized to live in the township and were supposed to leave.

Reading 66

1. cotton and silk cloths and small colored beads; they received gold

2. from the Kingdom of Cambay in northwest India; they paid in gold and in ivory gathered from around Sofala
3. Their king refused to give allegiance to—or obey—the king of Portugal.

Reading 67

1. They control the elements, such as wind, rain, and fire.
2. It committed some offense against the Emperor of Heaven, who revoked its powers and expelled it from heaven. The villagers covered the dragon with a reed mat to keep the sun from burning it, and prayed to the Emperor of Heaven to take it back.
3. It made sure that the pond where it was found never dried up and remained rich in fish, shrimp, and crabs.

Reading 68

1. The dam is being built to control flooding on the Yangtze River (Chang Jiang); to provide electricity; and to promote the region's trade with the coast and the world.
2. They argue that because the Yangtze is full of sediment, damming it will cause sediment to build up, which will block the passage of trade vessels.

Reading 69

1. Martial law existed; basic freedoms were restricted; opposition parties were banned; and dissenters were severely punished. The Nationalists also suppressed the islanders' culture and banned Taiwanese history in the schools and the Taiwanese language from public life. Because the Chinese thought they would someday return to China, they did not spend much money to improve Taiwan.
2. Taiwan elected a new legislature, finally replacing the old members who had been elected in 1947.
3. High levels of prosperity allowed reform to occur without violence.

Reading 70

1. Accept any five of the following: Both Sekiguchi and Kurose were office workers; both had the first name of Jirō; both looked, dressed and acted alike; the wives of both looked alike; both lived in identical-looking apartments in identical locations in their building; both had relatives named Kuniko.

2. Answers will vary, but students should recognize that the author is criticizing the conformity and uniformity of his country's urban culture.

Reading 71

1. Factors causing the food shortage included the government's failed agricultural policies and three straight years of crop failures brought on by floods and droughts.

2. North Korea tried to hide the problem from the world. Once they found out, countries hesitated to aid North Korea because of its communists system, its hostility to others, and fear that food aid would go to its army.

3. Factories and mines closed because the government couldn't feed workers and they became too weak to work. Other effects on people were malnutrition and fatigue and, among children, poor concentration, stunted growth, and permanent mental and emotional damage.

Reading 72

1. Wood is an important resource for Thai use and export, especially teak and redwood.

2. The river would be a major source of transportation for getting logs to the mill and shipping wood products to market.

3. They get their drinking water from rainwater that they collect; they would not drink river water because it would be less pure and doing so would likely make them sick.

4. Some women work in the economy and others are homemakers; both are acceptable roles for women in Thai society.

5. Answers will vary, but students should realize that the importance of Thailand's timber industry likely means its rain forest is shrinking.

Reading 73

1. The nation's prosperity at the time allowed people to afford more meat in their diet. Because of the country's numbers of Muslims and Hindus, investors though that this meat would be chicken.

2. It was hurt by the fact that there was no reliable way to get the chickens to market.

3. Answers will vary, but students should recognize that Indonesia does not grow enough corn or soybeans, or have the processing capacity, to manufacture food for both humans and chickens. Also, the soybean oil byproduct of making chicken feed was not marketable in a country where palm oil dominated the market. So the industry imported its feed.

4. Answers will vary but should show recognition of the following points: It caused the price of imported feed to double. When producers raised prices to cover these increased costs, consumers stopped buying chicken. With no market for their product, the producers went bankrupt.

Reading 74

1. Bad land and the communists made life difficult. She had to sell many of her possessions and ultimately lost her husband.

2. A small boat was needed to ferry supplies for the planned escape to the big boat little by little, so the authorities would not become suspicious.

3. They ran out of fresh water, were robbed of everything by pirates, and their boat began to leak; another group of pirates, seeing they had no maps or anything left to steal, told them how to get to Malaysia.

Reading 75

1. People move to Bombay because the jobs are there.

2. Bombay is a relatively small area to hold all the people who live there and who continue to arrive. The shortage of housing has caused crowded slums to develop.

3. Answers will vary, but students should recognize that a city as large as Bombay would produce a lot of recyclable trash.

Reading 76

1. Chapoli's economy was traditionally based on keeping bees in the forest and gathering the honey they produced. The forest has receded causing honey collection to go down.

2. It's deep in the forest on a bad road; it had no dependable permanent schoolteacher; and health care and the bus line are five miles away. Because of their isolation, the villagers have become withdrawn and suspicious of outsiders.

3. A company in nearby Belgaum has decided to help the town by reestablishing the traditional bee-keeping economy, training the villagers as bee-keepers, and helping them to get the honey processed and sold.

Reading 77

1. The *Mehndi* ceremony is one in which the bride's and groom's parents exchange visits, and the bride's hand are painted with a dye from the henna plant

2. Pakistani marriages differ in that the marriages are arranged; a dowry is paid; and the marriage ceremonies take more than two weeks.

3. Pakistani marriages are similar to U.S. marriages in that the bride wears white, the couple goes away after the ceremony; and there is a reception after the wedding.

4. Answers will vary but should note that she observes that times are changing and emphasizes her intention to help and guide her husband over her expected role

of obedience. She seems to have accepted living with her husband's family and doing household chores that are considered a "woman's job."

Reading 78

1. A char is a temporary piece of land in a river that is created by a buildup of silt. Landless Bangladeshi prefer char to the city slums and live on them until the land is washed back into the river.

2. Monsoon rains and snowmelt in the mountains of India and Nepal cause the flooding. It makes the soil rich and allows for three rice crops a year. Flooding controls when the farmers can plant their crops. Rivers also transport people and products since Bangladesh does not have many good roads.

Reading 79

1. The economic tigers of Asia are Japan, South Korea, Taiwan, and Hong Kong.

2. The Australian industries are inefficient because they are uncompetitive. They are uncompetitive because they are protected by high taxes on imported goods. Students should recognize that the money made from mining and agricultural exports enabled people to buy these industries' products anyway.

3. Answers will vary, but students should recognize that the mining and agricultural exports that helped Australia to prosper in the past are no longer as competitive on world markets, and that Australian manufacturing is not geared up to fill the economic void left by their decline.

Reading 80

1. The Maori are the native people of New Zealand. Family, tradition, and community are important in the Maori culture.

2. Wardens are similar to police officers in that they keep law and order in the community. They differ from police officers in that they have no power beyond the

respect the position has among the Maoris. They keep law and order by treating causes of disorder rather than by disciplining offenders.

3. A *Marae* is a sacred piece of land containing a building where Maori weddings, funerals, meetings, and other social occasions are held.

4. Answers will vary but should note that the number of Maoris is small and that most live in cities, where white (*Pakeha*) culture predominates. Although Maori values are retained inside their homes, a Marae gives them a place to meet, carry out their traditions, and maintain the sense of community that is important to their culture. The warden movement also protects their culture by dealing with law and order problems in Maori ways instead of depending on white social and legal systems.

Reading 81

1. The author returned to the village because the surrounding forest where she grew up was about to be logged and she did not want the villagers to be taken advantage of.

2. They needed cash to buy things and they believed that their trees were their only good source of income.

3. The author appears to disagree. She reports that the Bahinemo are not getting paid what their trees are worth and she worries about how the loss of their forest will affect their culture.

Reading 82

1. Antarctica is a good place to hunt for meteorites because the surface is flat, clean, and nearly white, making the blackened meteorites easy to spot.

2. They ride back and forth across an area on snowmobiles, in a search pattern that is similar to mowing a lawn.

3. The meteorites fall into the snow. More snow then compresses the snow around them to ice. The ice moves until it meets mountains, where it is pushed up. Ice crystals in the wind then erode the ice around the meteorites until they finally pop to the surface again.

First Facts™

Manners

Manners on the Playground

by Terri DeGezelle

Consultant:
Madonna Murphy, PhD, Professor of Education
University of St. Francis, Joliet, Illinois
Author, *Character Education in America's Blue Ribbon Schools*

Capstone
press
Mankato, Minnesota

First Facts is published by Capstone Press
151 Good Counsel Drive, P.O. Box 669, Mankato, Minnesota 56002
www.capstonepress.com

Library of Congress Cataloging-in-Publication Data
DeGezelle, Terri, 1955–
      Manners on the playground / by Terri DeGezelle.
      p. cm.—(First facts. Manners)
      Includes bibliographical references and index.
      Contents: Fun on the playground—Being kind—Showing respect—Being patient—Sharing—
Having courage—Playing fair—Good manners—Amazing but true!—Hands on: play a game
of tig.
      ISBN 0-7368-2647-5 (hardcover)
      1. Etiquette for children and teenagers. 2. Play—Juvenile literature. [1. Etiquette. 2. Behavior.]
I. Title. II. Series.
BJ1631.D44 2005
395.5'3—dc22   2003023389

Editorial Credits
Christine Peterson, editor; Juliette Peters, designer; Wanda Winch, photo researcher;
      Eric Kudalis, product planning editor

Photo Credits
BananaStock, Ltd./Picture Quest, cover (foreground)
Capstone Press/Gem Photo Studio/Tim Nehotte, 4–5, 6–7, 8, 9, 10–11, 12–13, 14, 15, 16, 17, 18–19
Corbis/Richard Gross, cover (background)
Craig Lovell, 20

1 2 3 4 5 6 09 08 07 06 05 04

Table of Contents

Fun on the Playground 4

Being Kind 7

Showing Respect 8

Being Patient 11

Sharing 12

Having Courage 14

Playing Fair 16

Good Manners 18

Amazing but True! 20
Hands On: Play a Game of *Tig* 21
Glossary 22
Read More 23
Internet Sites 23
Index 24

Fun on the Playground

Manners help everyone have fun on the playground. People with good manners are **polite** to others. They are **kind** and treat people with **respect**. People enjoy the playground more when they use good manners.

Fun Fact!
In 1885, the first U.S. playground opened in Boston, Massachusetts.

4

Being Kind

Kind people show others they care. They make new friends. Kind kids can **invite** someone who is alone to play. Being kind helps everyone have fun. Games are more fun when everyone gets to play.

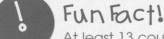

Fun Fact!

At least 13 countries are part of the World Kindness Movement. This group wants people in all countries to be kind to others.

Showing Respect

People show respect when they listen
to others. They care about the ideas and
feelings of others. Kids show respect by
listening to a friend's idea for a game.

8

Kids can also show respect for their surroundings. They take care of the playground. Kids put **litter** in the trash can. They keep the playground clean.

Being Patient

Playgrounds can be busy places. Boys and girls may have to wait their turn to play. They are **patient** as they wait in line for the monkey bars. Patient kids wait for a friend to get all the way across the bars. Then, they begin their turn.

Sharing

People have fun when they share playground equipment. Boys and girls share by taking turns on the swings. They say "please" and "thank you" when they ask for a turn on the swings.

Having Courage

Some kids are afraid to go down a tall slide. Other kids may **tease** them. It takes **courage** to stick up for someone who is being teased.

14

After being teased, some kids still go down the slide. Their friends can help them be brave. It takes courage to let go and race down the slide.

Playing Fair

Good sports play fair during kickball games. They make sure everyone gets to play. Players follow the rules so everyone has fun.

Good sports cheer for both teams.
Players shake hands after the game.
Good sports have fun playing even
if they lose the game.

Good Manners

Kids can practice good manners on the playground. They can be kind and invite new friends to play. Kids can wait patiently in line. They can be good sports. Good manners help everyone have fun on the playground.

! Fun Fact!
In the early 1900s, most U.S. playgrounds had a small slide, sandbox, swings, and a climber.

New York City's Central Park has many statues and playgrounds for people to visit. At the park, kids can climb on 13 hippopotamus statues. Statues of Alice in Wonderland and Balto are also popular. People can also splash in water sprays, go fishing, or play in a tree house.

Hands On: Play a Game of *Tig*

Kids around the world love to play the game of tag. Kids have many different ways to play tag. In England, kids call the game *tig*, instead of tag. Have fun playing *tig* with friends.

What You Need

a group of friends
a playground or large open area

What You Do

1. Choose one player to be "it."
2. The remaining players scatter and run around the playground or open area.
3. The player who is "it" chases the others and tries to gently tag them.
4. When the player who is "it" tags another player, they join hands. They run together to try to tag someone else.
5. The game continues until all the players are holding hands.

Glossary

courage (KUR–ij)—bravery or fearlessness

invite (in–VITE)—to ask someone to do something or go somewhere

kind (KINDE)—friendly and helpful

litter (LIT-ur)—pieces of paper or other garbage that are scattered around carelessly

manners (MAN-urss)—polite behavior

patient (PAY–shuhnt)—able to wait quietly without getting angry or upset

polite (puh-LITE)—having good manners; polite people are kind and respectful.

respect (ri-SPEKT)—belief in the quality and worth of others, yourself, and your surroundings

tease (TEEZ)—to make fun of someone

Read More

Amos, Janine. *Taking Turns.* Courteous Kids. Milwaukee: Gareth Stevens, 2002.

Nelson, Robin. *Being Fair.* First Step Nonfiction. Minneapolis: Lerner, 2003.

Raatma, Lucia. *Politeness.* Character Education. Mankato, Minn.: Bridgestone Books, 2002.

Internet Sites

FactHound offers a safe, fun way to find Internet sites related to this book. All of the sites on FactHound have been researched by our staff.

Here's how:
1. Visit *www.facthound.com*
2. Type in this special code **0736826475** for age-appropriate sites. Or enter a search word related to this book for a more general search.
3. Click on the **Fetch It** button.

FactHound will fetch the best sites for you!

Index

afraid, 14

brave, 15

Central Park, 20
courage, 14–15

feelings, 8
friends, 7, 8, 15, 18

games, 7, 8, 16–17
good sports, 16–17, 18

invite, 7, 18

kickball, 16
kind, 4, 7, 18

line, 11, 18
litter, 9

monkey bars, 11

patient, 11, 18
playing fair, 16–17
please, 12
polite, 4

respect, 4, 8–9
rules, 16

shaking hands, 17
sharing, 12
slide, 14–15, 18
swings, 12, 18

taking turns, 11, 12
teams, 17
teasing, 14–15
thank you, 12

World Kindness Movement, 7